ISBN 978-1-330-87967-2
PIBN 10116271

English
Français
Deutsche
Italiano
Español
Português

www.forgottenbooks.com

Mythology Photography **Fiction**
Fishing Christianity **Art** Cooking
Essays Buddhism Freemasonry
Medicine **Biology** Music **Ancient**
Egypt Evolution Carpentry Physics
Dance Geology **Mathematics** Fitness
Shakespeare **Folklore** Yoga Marketing
Confidence Immortality Biographies
Poetry **Psychology** Witchcraft
Electronics Chemistry History **Law**
Accounting **Philosophy** Anthropology
Alchemy Drama Quantum Mechanics
Atheism Sexual Health **Ancient History**
Entrepreneurship Languages Sport
Paleontology Needlework Islam
Metaphysics Investment Archaeology
Parenting Statistics Criminology
Motivational

AMERICAN
LAW AND PROCEDURE

VOLUMES I TO XII PREPARED UNDER THE
EDITORIAL SUPERVISION OF

JAMES PARKER HALL, A.B., LL.B.

Dean of Law School · University of Chicago

AND

VOLUMES XIII AND XIV BY

JAMES DeWITT ANDREWS, LL.D.

FORMERLY OF THE LAW FACULTY
NORTHWESTERN UNIVERSITY

Author of "Andrews' American Law," Editor "Andrews'
Stephens' Pleading," "Cooley's Blackstone,"
"Wilson's Works," etc.

A Systematic, Non-Technical Treatment of American
Law and Procedure, Written by Professors and
Teachers in Law Schools, and by Legal
Writers of Recognized Ability.

PUBLISHED BY
LA SALLE EXTENSION UNIVERSITY
CHICAGO

AMERICAN LAW AND PROCEDURE

VOLUME V.

PREPARED UNDER THE EDITORIAL SUPERVISION OF

JAMES PARKER HALL, A. B., LL. B.

Dean of the University of Chicago Law School

HISTORY OF
REAL PROPERTY LAW

BY

JOHN ROMAIN ROOD

LL. B. (University of Michigan)
Professor of Law, University of Michigan

TRANSFER OF TITLE TO REAL
ESTATE

BY

ALBERT MARTIN KALES

A. B. (Harvard University), LL. B. (Harvard University)
Professor of Law, Northwestern University

MORTGAGES

BY

JAMES WIGGINS SIMONTON

A. B. (Indiana University), J. D. (University of Chicago)
Chicago Bar

MINING LAW

BY

GEORGE PURCELL COSTIGAN, Jr.

A. B., A. M. (Harvard University), LL. B. (Harvard University)
Professor of Law, Northwestern University

IRRIGATION LAW

BY

ROSCOE POUND

A. B., A. M., Ph. D. (University of Nebraska), LL. M. (Northwestern University)
Story Professor of Law, Harvard University

CONTENTS

HISTORY OF REAL PROPERTY LAW.

TRANSFER OF TITLE TO REAL ESTATE.

PART I.

TRANSFER OF TITLE WITH CONSENT OF OWNER.

CHAPTER I.

Form of Conveyance and Description of Property.

CHAPTER IV.

Extralateral Rights Under Act of 1872.

NOTE.

Coal, Timber, and Stone Land Entries and Patents.

IRRIGATION LAW.

CHAPTER I.

Systems of Water Law.

SECTION 1.

Common Law Doctrine.

SECTION 2.

Roman and Civil Law Doctrines.

HISTORY OF REAL PROPERTY LAW

BY

JOHN ROMAIN ROOD,

LL. B. (University of Michigan)

———

Professor of Law, University of Michigan.

———

§ 1. Value of history of land law. The excuse for the existence of the present article cannot be better explained than in the language of that incomparable commentator, Sir William Blackstone. He says: "In the course of our observations in this and many other parts of the present book, we may have occasion to search pretty highly into the antiquities of our English jurisprudence; yet surely no industrious student will imagine his time misemployed when he is led to consider that the obsolete doctrines of our laws are frequently the foundation upon which what remains is erected; and that it is impracticable to comprehend many of the rules of the modern law in a scholarlike, scientific manner, without having recourse to the ancient. Nor will these researches be altogether void of rational entertainment as well as use; as in viewing the majestic ruins of Rome or Athens, of Balbec or Palmyra, it administers both pleasure and instruction to compare them with the draughts of the same edifices in their pristine proportion and splendor'' (1).

Section 1. History of Tenures.

§ 2. **Saxon period.** The growth of the common law dates from the days of the Saxons before the Norman Conquest (1066), and any later point of beginning the narrative must be arbitrarily chosen and will require an explanation of earlier events to avoid being misleading. In the Saxon period we find England still composed of many petty kingdoms and clans, each protecting itself by force and cunning against the threatened encroachments and invasions of its neighbors. The individual, unsupported by alliance with a clan, could scarcely defend any possession in such rigorous times. Land titles were largely involved in police administration. Every man was lord, vassal, or outlaw, the lordless man was a vagabond. Any landholder who lost his lord by accident, would, as a measure of self protection, bind himself to

---

(1)   2 Bl. Com., 44.

some lord of the neighborhood, pledging fidelity and service for protection. By such an alliance the liberties of the man and his rights concerning the land were of necessity restricted in no small degree. Still the relation was then more one of lord and man than lord and tenant. Since there was little commerce, travel, or communication between different parts of the island, the customs which grew up here and there differed widely. As more of the island was in each succeeding generation brought under one rule, the tendency was undoubtedly toward greater uniformity. But even at the time of the Norman Conquest land descended to the oldest son in a few places and only a few; to the youngest according to the custom called borough English in other places; but for the most part descended to all the sons equally. The daughters were generally excluded entirely if there were sons. There is no reason to suppose that there was much buying and selling of land among the Saxons. Local customs, surviving the Conquest in many places, of getting from the village consent to the transfer suggest that perhaps this, as well as the consent of the presumptive heirs, was generally essential to a valid sale. It has been said by a great historian that the extant specimens of Anglo-Saxon wills of land, from which it has been inferred that lands were freely devisable among the Saxons, were instances only of devises of great folk holding by special charter, and that there is no reason for thinking that the ordinary free landholders could dispose of their lands by will, or were in the habit of making wills for any purpose (2). But, on the other hand, it is believed that the same logic which enables the naturalist to know the water-fowl by its web feet, enables us safely to infer such a custom, in places at least, from the fact that the ancient custom of London and other places permitted devises of all lands within the city long before they were authorized by statute; and it is easier to assume that these customs were survivals of ancient Saxon usage than that they grew up by special privilege against the rules of the Norman tenures.

§ 3. **Saxon procedure in disputes over land.** In Saxon times the common law and special custom were ascertained and adjudged in disputes concerning land and all property and rights, primarily in the local folk courts, which were open-air meetings of the freemen of the clan, who decided each case without the aid of the professional lawyer, for there was then no such class. The suitors were the court; there were no judges in the modern sense of persons learned in the law specially appointed to preside. One who had diligently sought justice in the local courts and failed might seek it at the hands of the king's council of wise men; and resort might be had to this council in the first instance where land granted by the king was in question, and perhaps in some other instances. The final judgment was not put into effect by an officer of the court on process, as at the present time; but the successful party was left to gather the fruits of the judgment himself; of which we see the last survival in the custom of permitting the landlord

---

(2) Maitland, Domesday Book and Beyond, 106.

in later times to take the tenant's goods by "distress" to enforce the payment of rent; and such distress might be taken without any resort to court in advance to ascertain the right, merely on claimant's own opinion of his right, as well as after his right had been adjudged.

§ 4. **Early Norman period.** While unmistakable evidences of feudal tenures exist in the Saxon records, it remained for the military genius of the Norman conquerors under William and his successors to establish as the national policy of England that system of society and government invented by the northern Teutonic tribes, and used with such decisive effect by them in their invasion of the provinces of the decaying and disintegrating Roman empire, and in establishing themselves in their newly acquired territory. This social order, called the feudal system, in which political rights depended on land tenure, varied in different times and places, but was brought to perfection and its highest refinement by the Franks and Normans; and this was the system to which William and his followers were accustomed on the continent before they came to England. By this system the chief of the invading host parceled out the conquered territory among his followers as their share of the spoils and as a reward or fee for services rendered; but to provide for the future maintenance and protection of the new acquisition, each feuditory agreed to render certain services for his fee in the future, to follow his lord in his wars, attend his court in peace, and defend him against all assailants; and in return for this service he received from his lord the pledge of protection. The

vassal in like manner parceled out the lands among his
followers, under the like conditions except that they
agreed to defend him against all but the king.

§ 5. Feudal system as a basis of military defense.
"This introduction, however, of the feudal tenures into
England by William does not seem to have been effected
immediately after the conquest, nor by the mere arbitrary
will and power of the conqueror; but to have been gradually established by the Norman barons and others in
such forfeited lands as they received from the gift of
the conqueror, and afterwards universally consented to
by the great council of the nation, long after his title
was established.   Indeed, from the prodigious slaughter
of the English nobility at the battle of Hastings, and the
fruitless insurrections of those followers who survived,
such numerous forfeitures had accrued, that he was able
to reward his Norman followers with very large and extensive possessions; which gave a handle to the monkish
historians and such as have implicitly followed them,
to represent him as having by right of the sword seized
on all the lands of England and dealt them out again to
his own favorites; a supposition grounded upon a mistaken sense of the word 'conquest,' which in its feudal
acceptation signified no more than acquisition.   And this
has led many hasty writers into a strange historical mistake, and one which, upon the slightest examination, will
be found to be most untrue.   However, certain it is that
the Normans now began to gain very large possessions
in England; and their regard for the feudal law under

which they had long lived, together with the king's recom-
mendations of this policy to the English as the best way
to put themselves on a military footing and thereby to
prevent any further attempts from the continent, were
probably the reasons that prevailed to effect its establishment here by law. And, though the time of this
great revolution in our landed property cannot be ascertained with exactness, yet there are some circumstances
that may lead us to a probable conjecture concerning it.
For we learn from the Saxon chronicle, that in the nineteenth year of William's reign an invasion was appre-
hended from Denmark; and, the military constitution of
the Saxons being then laid aside and no other introduced
in its stead, the kingdom was wholly defenseless; which
occasioned the king to bring over a large army of Normans and Bretons, who were quartered upon every landholder, and greatly oppressed the people. This apparent
weakness, together with the grievances occasioned by a
foreign force, might co-operate with the king's remon-
strances, and the better incline the nobility to listen to
his proposals for putting them in a posture of defense.
For, as soon as the danger was over, the king held a
great council to inquire into the state of the nation; the
immediate consequence of which was the compiling of
the great survey called domesday-book, which was finished the next year. And in the latter end of that very
year the king was attended by all his nobility at Sarum;
where all the principal landholders submitted their lands
to the yoke of military tenure, became the king's vassals, and did homage and fealty to his person. This

may possibly have been the era of formally introducing the feudal tenures by law'' (3).

§ 6. **Feudal system extended to other objects by legal fictions.** "In consequence of this change, it became a fundamental maxim and necessary principle (though in reality a mere fiction) of our English tenures, 'that the king is the universal lord and original proprietor of all the lands in his kingdom: and that no man doth or can possess any part of it, but what has mediately or immediately been derived as a gift from him, to be held upon feudal services.' For this being the real case in pure, original, proper feuds, other nations who adopted this system were obliged to act upon the same supposition, as a substruction and foundation of their new polity, though the fact was indeed far otherwise. And indeed, by thus consenting to the introduction of feudal tenures, our English ancestors probably meant no more than to put the kingdom in a state of defense by establishing a military system; and to oblige themselves (in respect of their lands) to maintain the king's title and territories, with equal vigor and fealty, *as if* they had received their lands from his bounty upon these express conditions, as pure, proper, beneficiary feudatories. But whatever their meaning was, the Norman interpreters, skilled in all the niceties of the feudal terms, gave a very different construction to this proceeding; and thereupon took a handle to introduce not only the rigorous doctrines which prevailed in the duchy of Normandy, but also such fruits and dependencies, such hardships and

---

(3)   2 Bl. Com., 48-50.

services, as were never known to other nations; as if the English had, in fact as well as theory, owed. everything they had to the bounty of their sovereign lord. Our ancestors, therefore, who were by no means beneficiaries, but had barely consented to this fiction of tenure from the crown as the basis of a military discipline, with reason looked upon these deductions as grievous impositions, and arbitrary conclusions from principles, which as to them, had no foundation in truth. However, this king and his son William Rufus kept up with a high hand all the rigors of the feudal doctrines: but their successor, Henry I, found it expedient, when he set up his pretensions to the crown, to promise a restitution of the laws of King Edward the Confessor, or ancient Saxon system; and accordingly, in the first year of his reign, granted a charter whereby he gave up the greater grievances; but still reserved the fiction of feudal tenure, for the same military purposes which engaged his father to introduce it. But this charter was gradually broken through, and the former grievances were revived and aggravated by himself and succeeding princes, till in the reign of King John they became so intolerable that they occasioned his barons or principal feudatories to rise up in arms against him; which at length produced the famous Great Charter of Runnymede, which, with some alterations, was confirmed by his son Henry III'' (4).

§ 7. **Original incidents of military feuds.** The principal properties of original pure feuds were that they were gratuitous in theory at least; were conferred by the

---

(4) 2 Bl. Com., 51-52.

ceremony of livery and corporal investiture in the presence of the other vassals, that memory might be had of the fact, nature, and subject of the gift; were held under a personal pledge of homage, fealty, and protection, formally declared at the time of the donation, which prevented any later transfer of either the lord's seigniory or the tenant's estate to another without the mutual consent of both lord and vassal; bound the lord to protect the vassal in his possession, and if ousted to restore the lost property or give other of equal value; bound the vassal to follow and fight for his lord in war, and attend his court in peace. These original feuds were purely military; but lost their simplicity and became corrupted, when by degrees the tenants came to sublet parts of their holdings to others in imitation of their own tenure, but reserving a rent in agricultural service, produce, cattle, or money, instead of military service; and on the other hand, came to commute with their lords in like manner, making payments of money or goods as a substitute for the required military service. Feuds began to be bought and sold, and came to be classed as proper and improper. "But," says Sir William Blackstone, "as soon as the feudal system came to be considered in the light of a civil establishment, rather than as a military plan, the ingenuity of the same ages, which perplexed all theology with the subtility of scholastic disquisitions and bewildered philosophy in the mazes of metaphysical jargon, began also to exert its influence on this copious and fruitful subject; in pursuance of which the most refined and oppressive consequences were drawn from what origin-

ally was a plan of simplicity and liberty, equally beneficial to both lord and tenant, and prudently calculated
for their mutual protection and defense'' (5).

§ 8. **Incidents of knight service tenure.** The development of these oppressions will appear by a review of
the chief incidents of knight service tenure, in addition
to those above mentioned, namely: aids, reliefs, primer
seizins, wardship, marriage, fines for alienation, and
escheat. The three ancient aids required of the feuditory
to his lord were: To ransom the lord when captured; to
bear the expense of knighting the lord's eldest son,
which could not be required till he was of sufficient age
to bear arms, fifteen years; and to furnish the marriage
portion for the lord's eldest daughter on her marriage.
From these taxes no rank or profession was exempt,
even the monasteries being required to contribute to the
aid of their founder. Originally these aids were mere
gratuities by the tenant to his lord when in distress; but
in time came to be a tax demandable and not to be
avoided; and besides these aids the lords came in time
to demand also that the tenant should pay the lord's debts
to his over lord, till the Magna Charta of King John declared that none but the three ancient aids should be
demanded, which was confirmed by statute in 25 Edw.
I (1297). This charter also provided that only reasonable
aids should be demanded by inferior lords, and that aids
taken by the king should be settled by Parliament; and
by the statute of Westmin. I, 3 Edw. I, c. 36, the amount
of the aids payable to inferior lords was fixed at 20 shill-

(5) 2 Bl. Com., 58.

ings for each knight's fee, which was an amount of land estimated to have a yearly value of 20 pounds.

A relief was a fine imposed by the feudal lord as a composition with the heir of his deceased vassal for recognizing and admitting him as successor, which custom dates back to the time when fees were for life only or less. We are told that the English regarded these as the greatest grievance of military tenures, because they were based on an assumption of original gratuitous donation, which was not the fact with the English. William the Conqueror fixed the amount of the relief at 100 shillings for each knight's fee, which, though not observed by his immediate successor, was re-established by Henry I. What has been said applies to the tenure of mesne lords; tenants in capite (who hold directly of the king) were required to pay a greater relief, called primer seizin, which was one whole year's profits of the land regardless of the value.

These reliefs and primer seizins were payable only in case the heir were of age at the death of the ancestor. But if he were under age, 21 years if male, and 16 years and unmarried if female, the lord was entitled by the later feudal law to take the property into his possession as guardian in chivalry, and appropriate the whole profits of it during the minority of the ward as a reasonable recompense for the services which the minor by reason of his age was incapable of performing. But when the heir became of age he was bound to pay the further tax of half a year's value of the land for suing livery or ousterlemain; and also, if a tenant in capite of a knight's fee, he was then further compellable to take upon him the order of knighthood or pay a fine to the king, an expedient resorted to by Queen Elizabeth and other sovereigns as a means of raising money. The lord had the right also to tender to his ward if unmarried a suitable match, and appropriate to himself whatever anyone would pay him for the same, and if the ward refused the offer the lord could recover the value from the ward's property. Marriage without the lord's assent amounted to a forfeiture of double the value which anyone would pay the lord for the alliance. In feuds as a military institution females could in no wise succeed to the inheritance because of their inability to perform the military service; and when they were admitted to the inheritance there was some reason in permitting the lord to have something to say as to who should be his tenant to perform the service for her as her husband would, though there never was any excuse for the sale of the marriage other than as a means of revenue for the lords. The right to offer a spouse to the male heir seems never to have been demanded till the charter of Henry III provided that heirs should be married without disparagement; from which failure to designate the sex of the heir, the lords took the liberty to demand right of marriage of heirs male or female.

The excuse of demanding fines for alienation came from the original confidential relation between lord and vassal, wherefore the vassal could not put another in his stead without the consent of the overlord, who took occasion to charge for such consent what the contracting parties would be willing to pay for it; but in England these fines seem to have been taken only of tenants in capite.   Another consequence of tenure was escheat; which was a reversion of the land to the over-lord upon the extinction of the blood of the tenant by his death without heirs of his blood, or by the civil corruption of his blood by conviction and attainder for treason or felony.

From the time of Henry II the custom was general for the king to demand escuage or shield money instead of the personal service contemplated by the original institution of feuds; so that this also became from that time another species of tax to which the feudal tenant was subject, first at the mere caprice of the king, but by the terms of the Magna Charta only on consent of Parliament; and by this degeneration of personal military service into a mere system of taxation, all the advantages of the feudal constitution were destroyed and nothing but the hardships remained.

§ 9. **Hardships of** feudal tenure. It seems indeed strange that a people of the spirit of the English should so long have endured oppressions so complicated and extensive; and the explanation in part no doubt lies in the fact that avenues of escape were found through entails and conveyances to uses. But when these avenues were effectually closed by the passage of the celebrated statute of uses, 27 Hen. VIII, c. 10, and other statutes, and the establishment of the court of wards and liveries by the statute of 32 Hen. VIII, c. 46, by which the greedy sovereign then reigning designed to make more swift and

certain the collection of the tax, the burden became un-
bearable. A striking picture of the condition of the tenant in chivalry at this time is given in Blackstone's Com-
mentaries, as follows: "The heir on the death of his
ancestor, if of full age, was plundered of his first emol-
uments arising from his inheritance by way of relief
and primer seizin; and, if under age, of the whole of his
estate during infancy. And then, as Sir Thomas Smith
very feelingly complains, 'when he came to his own, after
he was out of wardship, his woods decayed, houses fallen
down, stock wasted and gone, lands let forth and plowed
to be barren,' to reduce him still farther, he was yet to
pay half a year's profits as a fine for suing out his livery; and also the price or value of his marriage if he refused such wife as his lord and guardian had bartered
for and imposed upon him; or twice that value if he married another woman. Add to this the untimely and expensive honor of knighthood, to make his poverty more
completely splendid. And when by these deductions his
fortune was so shattered and ruined that perhaps he was
obliged to sell his patrimony, he had not even that poor
privilege allowed him without paying an exorbitant fine
for a license of alienation" (6).

§ 10. **Abolition of military tenures.** Finally, when
the crisis came in the breach between Charles I and his
people, the court of wards and liveries was suspended by
resolution of the House of Commons, Feb. 24, 1645; after
which no feudal revenues were collected during the whole
commonwealth; and at the restoration of Charles II.

---

(6) 2 Bl. Com., 76.

1660, by statute 12 Car. II, c. 24, the court of wards was formally abolished, and aids, wardships, liveries, primer seizins, ousterlemains, values, tenures by knight service and escuage, and forfeitures of marriage, by reason of any tenure of the king or others, were totally taken away; and all sorts of tenures held of the king or others were turned into free and common socage, save only tenures in frankalmoign, copyholds, and the honorary services (without the slavish part) of grand serjeanty.

§ **11.** **Modern English tenures.** By the abolition of knight service tenure the prominence of tenures in the law was very much reduced; but the reader must not assume that tenures were thereby abolished. On the contrary all tenures were reduced to a few sorts, simple, burdenless, and well known in the law of England from the time of the Norman Conquest, in fact the socage tenures are apparently the old Saxon tenures; and they are of three principal sorts: Petit serjeanty, a tenure of the king by payment to him annually of some small implement of war, as bow, arrow, or the like; burgage, a tenure of land in any ancient borough by a certain rent, and peculiar in that lands held by such tenures usually descended to the youngest son to exclusion of the older; and gavelkind, the tenure in Kent, most clearly of Saxon origin, held by rent certain, devisable by will at the common law before the statute of wills, descendable to all the sons together and not to the eldest, and not liable to forfeiture by escheat for felony. To these must be added the tenure in ancient demesne, which is none other than tenure by certain rent of lands originally held of the crown direct by the king's villeins; and tenure by copy of the manor court roll, called copyhold tenure, a tenure meanly descended but of an ancient house, being the holdings of the villeins of the ancient manors, now enfranchised by long neglect and the law's presumption in favor of liberty. For a villein might be freed by express deed of manumission, or impliedly by being sued or contracted with by his lord, and none would be presumed a villein without strict proof. Now the quality which puts all these tenures in a class is the certainty of the rent due from the tenants, in which their tenure differed materially from the military tenures, in which the tenants were called to serve as needed. It will be instructive now to compare these socage tenures with the military tenures before mentioned by enumerating their properties, viz: They were both held of a superior lord; both subject to a rent, or feudal return, these certain, those uncertain; both held by a mutual bond of fealty; both subject till the statute 12 Car. II, c. 24, to payment of aids to the over-lord; both subject till that statute to the payment of reliefs, but very different in kind, being 5 pounds (one-fifth of the supposed annual value) for a knight's fee, but for socage land a year's rent according to the tenure, be it more or less; both subject to escheat, except that gavelkind lands did not escheat for felony; both apparently subject when held in capite to fines for alienation, till such fines were entirely abolished by the statute above mentioned; and both subject to primer seizins till these were abolished by said statute; but wardship in socage was to the next of kin of the heir who could not inherit of him, and he was called to account for the mean profits when the heir was of age; and the guardian in socage was also accountable to the ward for the value of any marriage contracted by him for the ward, whether he received anything for the marriage or not.

§ 12. **American tenures.** By the royal charters, the lands of the colonies of Connecticut, Massachusetts, Rhode Island, and Virginia were granted to their proprietary lords to be held of the king by tenure of free and common socage as of the manor of East Greenwich, in the county of Kent, and not in capite. The lands in Maryland were likewise granted to Lord Baltimore to be held by free and common socage of the king as of the castle of Windsor in the county of Berks. The other royal colonial charters were much the same. By the American Revolution the feudal services, if not before suspended, were abolished or enured to the states. In the western and central states there never existed any practical tenures in fact; and by statutes in these and the eastern states, where tenures existed before the Revolution, it has quite generally been declared that all tenures are abolished, and all titles are absolute; but the terms of the feudal language are still used to designate the conveyance, owners, interest, etc.

SECTION 2. HISTORY OF RESTRAINTS ON ALIENATION.

§ 13. **Struggle for perpetuities.** A prominent trait of human nature is the desire to exercise control over persons and things, and to impress the will of the individual upon all persons present and to come; and this trait is manifested in the struggles of land owners during the last thousand years or more in the history of the English law of real property to create indestructible, inalienable estates in land in perpetuity, and in the determination of the courts during the greater part of that period to prevent the creation of such perpetuities, as manifestly injurious to the public in general and dangerous to society. It is also a curious fact, that, while the whole course of the history of the law of real property is strewn with the wrecks of schemes devised to consummate this desire by the best legal talent of each generation, without a single enduring success, the series of efforts has served to develop perhaps more fundamental and important doctrines of the law than any other purpose that can be named. In the following subsections an attempt will be made to trace the course of this struggle from the beginning of the common law to the present time, noting as we pass the great fundamental doctrines of the law of real property developed in the course of the conflict.

§ 14. Relation between lord and tenant. As originally constituted feuds were inalienable, if for no other reason, because of the fact that the original donation was made and to be held by the tenant in consideration of personal services to be by him performed for the lord continually during the whole period of the tenure; and it has ever been a fundamental principle of the law that when one makes a contract for personal services he cannot substitute another in his stead to perform the services, who may perhaps be less competent or skillful, or not agreeable to the person to be served; and in like manner, one who has agreed to perform a personal service for one cannot, without his consent, be required to do such service for another.   But when by the corruption of feuds, a payment of money or goods was agreed upon as a substitute for the personal services before performed, the relation lost its personal character, and the estate became in essence and in fact transferable so far as any objection by the lord was concerned; and accordingly we find it established, immediately after this corruption was introduced, that if the tenant alienated the whole of his land the alienee would be tenant of the lord of whom the land had been held, who would be compelled to receive the homage of the alienee (7).

As a rule, however, the tenants preferred to sublet their estates to others, who would hold of them as they held of their over-lords, whereby the fruits and advantages of the tenure would accrue to them instead of to their over-lords.   The over-lords immediately discovered how this worked to their disadvantage, both by the loss of the incidental feudal advantages of the new tenures thereby created, and also through impoverishment by the loss of the fruits of cultivation so that many times they could not pay their dues to their over-lords.   To avoid this result, it was provided by the Magna Charta of Hen. III (1217), c. 39, that "no freeman from henceforth shall give or sell any more of his land but so that of the residue of the lands the lord of the fee may have the services due him which belong to the fee."   It seems that the construction put on the statute by the courts and its operation in prac-

---

(7)   Maitland, Preface to Bracton's Note Book, p. 134; Digby, History of the Law of Real Property, 77.

tice were not very satisfactory to the over-lords. The better to secure the desired results it was provided by the statute of quia emptores, 18 Edw. I (1290), c. 1, that tenants in fee might freely alienate provided that the feoffee shall hold of the chief lord of whom his feoffor held, and should not hold of his feoffor. In this attempt of the lords to secure to themselves the feudal advantages, they removed the last semblance of restraint on alienation imposed by reason of tenure; and it has been impossible since that statute for anyone other than the king (who was not within its terms) to create any new tenures in fee.

§ 15. Alienation restrained by the right of the heir. The laws of Alfred the Great (890), cc. 37, 41, forbade the heirs to sell from their kindred land acquired by inheritance, if the ancestor purchasing it or the donor had provided against such transfer; and this remained the law with but slight alterations in the time of Henry II (1154-89), as we learn from Glanville (book 7, c 1), his chief justiciar. The plainest and most manifest meaning of a gift to "A and his heirs," is that the heirs are as much beneficiaries of the donation as A; it is not to him alone; the words "heirs" and "A" are co-ordinate, connected by the conjunction "and," which signifies in the clearest manner that A is not the sole donee, but only one of a class, appointed to take in succession; for the donor must be taken to have intended that the donees should take in succession and not jointly; because heirs is a general word, comprehending all generations; and as all the generations do not exist at the same time, he could not have intended that they would take jointly. No one but a lawyer would doubt that the heirs were to take under the gift; indeed, it would be difficult if not impossible to frame an expression which would include them more clearly than this one. But the notion that the heir had any rights direct from the donor, which could not be defeated, meant that the land must lie inalienable throughout all time to the last generation, a doctrine destructive of all liberty, enabling the dead and forgotten generation to bind the hands of the living throughout all time; a proposition too obnoxious to be tolerated, however plainly expressed.

§ 16. Same: Effect of judicial decisions. It may not be possible to specify the exact day on which this doctrine was overthrown; but the last hope of the heir as a purchaser under the original grant seems to have been blasted by the decisions of the courts in the early part of the reign of Henry III; and it is believed that the leading case on the subject is William De Arundel's Case (8) decided in 1225, in which the facts were that Ralph, the son of Roger, demanded of William De Arundel several tracts of land, and alleged that they belonged to Roger, his father and his heirs, and that he was the heir. William answered that he had it by descent from his father, who had it to him and his heirs by the deed of said Roger, which he produced in court. Ralph came and acknowledged his father's deed, but demanded the judgment of the court as to whether his father could give all the land

---

(8)   Bracton's Note Book, Case 1054.

he held and reserve nothing to his heirs. And because Ralph acknowledged the deed as his father's, and it proved that he rendered all the land for himself and his heirs, it was held that William go discharged and that Ralph be in mercy. The reasons for believing this to be the leading case are that the law was otherwise only a few years before, it was contended by Ralph's counsel then to be otherwise, the case was considered by Bracton to be so important that he included it in his Notebook as a noteworthy decision, and he declared that to be the settled law when writing his text afterwards. This has been indisputable law from that day to this; and in expounding the effect of a gift to one and his heirs, Bracton says (book II, c. 6, fo. 17): "And so the donatory acquires the thing given by reason of the donation, and his heirs after him by reason of their succession, and the heir acquires nothing by reason of the gift made to his ancestor, because he was not enfeoffed with the donatory." In later times conveyancers, thinking this to be a rule of interpretation, have tried to make the intention clearer by expressing it to be "to A for life and after his death to his heirs;" but even in such cases the courts held that A took the whole fee, that the heirs took nothing unless by descent from A, and that it was a rule of law, not of construction, that a grant expressly to the heirs of anyone will be given effect as a grant to him rather than to his heirs if he is given any estate of freehold by the same instrument. This doctrine is known as the rule in Shelley's case, and its effect is fully considered in the article on Title to Real Estate elsewhere in this volume.

§ 17. Fee conditional at common law. In point of time, the next scheme to create an inalienable estate that came to grief in the courts, after the determination that the heir had no rights as a purchaser under a donation to one and his heirs, as above described, was the attempt to confine the donation to a life estate till the particular tenant, the original donee, should have heirs of his body. The logic of the scheme was this: If land is given to A, and if he has heirs of his body then to his heirs, it would seem manifest that the having of heirs of his body is a condition precedent to the enlargement of the estate from a life estate to a fee.   Till A has heirs of his body he has but a life estate, he cannot sell more than he has, no one has heirs while he lives, and thus A would have no power to sell while he lived, and there would be no danger of his selling when he was dead.   The reasoning of the scheme is logical enough; but when it came to be tested in court, very shortly after it had been held that a gift to A and his heirs gave no rights to the heirs, it was held (which was a very strained and unnatural construction, made merely for the sake of defeating the intention to tie the hands of the donee) that as soon as issue was born to the donee the condition had been performed, and by his feoffment he could disappoint his issue, defeat the possibility of reversion to the donor for death without issue, and give to his feoffee an absolute fee simple.   The exact date of this ruling cannot be given; but it must have been some time in the early part of the reign of Henry III, for when writing on the subject about 1256, Bracton (book II, c. 6, fo. 17) says: "If heirs of this kind are procreated, they only are called to the inheritance; and if a person so enfeoffed has further enfeoffed some person, he holds the feoffment; and his (the first donee's) heirs are held to the warranty, since they can claim nothing except from the succession and the descent of parents; although it appears to some that they were themselves enfeoffed at the same time with their parents, which is not true. But if he shall have no heirs, that land shall revert to the donor, through a tacit condition, even if there be no mention made in the donation that it should return, or if express mention has been made in the donation. And so it will happen if there have been at some time heirs and they have failed. But in the first case, where there has been no heir, the thing given to the donee will always be a freehold and not a fee. Likewise, in the second case, until heirs have begun to exist, it is a freehold; but when they have begun to exist the freehold begins to be a fee.''

§ 18. **Fee tail.** The displeasure of the nobility at the subtle construction given by the courts to the fee conditional at common law is manifested in the preamble of the statute de donis, Westm. II, c. 1, 13 Edw. I, enacted in the year 1285 with the design to procure a more natural construction in such cases. The statute recites: ''Concerning lands that many times are given upon condition, that is, to wit, where any giveth his land to any man and his wife, and to the heirs begotten of the bodies of the same man and his wife, with such condition expressed that if the same man and his wife die without heir of their bodies between them begotten, the land so

given shall revert to the giver or his heir; in case where
one giveth lands in free marriage, which gift hath a condition annexed, though it be not expressed in the deed of
gift, which is this, that if the husband and wife die without heir of their bodies begotten, the land so given shall
revert to the giver or his heir; in case also where one
giveth land to another and the heirs of his body issuing,
it seemed very hard and yet seemeth to the givers and
their heirs, that their will being expressed in the gift was
not heretofore nor yet is observed. In all the cases
aforesaid, after issue begotten and born between them to
whom the lands were given under such condition, heretofore such feoffees had power to alien the land so given,
and to disinherit their issue of the land, contrary to the
minds of the givers, and contrary to the form expressed
in the gift. And further, when the issue of such feoffee
is failing, the land so given ought to return to the giver
or his heir by form of gift expressed in the deed, though
the issue, if any were, had died; yet by the deed and feoffment of them, to whom the land was so given upon condition, the donors have heretofore been barred of their reversion of the same tenements which was directly repug-
nant to the form of the gift. Wherefore our lord the
king, perceiving how necessary and expedient it should be
to provide remedy in the aforesaid cases, hath ordained
that the will of the giver, according to the form in the
deed manifestly expressed, shall be from henceforth observed, so that they to whom the land was given under
such condition shall have no power to alien the land so
given, but that it shall remain unto the issue of them to

whom it was given after their death, or shall revert unto the giver or his heirs if issue fail, either by reason that there is no issue at all or if any issue be it fail by death, the heir of such issue failing. . . . And if a fine be levied hereafter upon such lands it shall be void in law,'' etc.

§ 19. **Fines forbidden to bar entails.** The determination of the nobility to have their attempts to create perpetuities respected, and not defeated by the courts by the subterfuge of giving outrageous and distorted construction to deeds drawn for that purpose, is spoken in this statute in no uncertain language; and the judges did not at this time have the courage either openly to balk at giving effect to the will of Parliament so distinctly declared or to find other means of evasion. The lords who penned the statute had the foresight to see that resort might be had to fines to bar these entails, and declared such fines void for this purpose. The fines thus referred to were fictitious suits which had been brought by proposed buyers from the earliest times against proposed sellers, alleging that the defendant had agreed to sell to the plaintiff the land in question and had failed to perform his contract. The defendant would appear and admit the claim, whereupon the court would order the transfer made; and in this way the parties procured a perpetual memorial of the transaction in the records of the king's treasury—records, of which there was no occasion to fear any loss, and which by reason of their character were conclusive and admitted neither proof nor allegation to the contrary. The advantages of having such a record of transfer, sacred against dispute, destruction, or loss, can easily be appreciated in any times; but in such turbulent periods of war, insurrection, and pillage, before the days of public offices for recording land titles, the advantage was very much greater. In recent times a somewhat similar method of settling titles has been revived under the name of the "Torrens System" in a number of states.

§ 20. **Effect of statute** de donis. Before the statute de donis was enacted it had been settled that if a man made a transfer of land with warranty to the purchaser and his heirs for the seller and his heirs, the heir of the seller was bound to make good the warranty to the full extent of the property descended to him; and immediately after the statute the courts held that if the donee of an estate within the statute (which was called an estate tail,) enfeoffed it to another with warranty for the feoffor and his heirs, the heir of the body of the tenant in tail making the grant might recover the land from the feoffee or his heirs, but was bound by his ancestor's warranty to make good the loss to the feoffee or his heirs to the extent of all the assets he had by descent other than estates tail. This proved but a very slight relief from the operation of the statute; and it was noticed during the next two hundred years that treasons were encouraged, as the tenants knew that if they were convicted their estates could not be forfeited from their families; creditors were defrauded, since if the lands might be sold on execution the heir might thus be covinously defrauded; farmers were ousted of their farms leased from tenants in tail;

and children became disobedient and disrespectful to
their parents, knowing that they could in no wise be dis-
appointed of the inheritance; wherefore these estates
were justly branded as the common grievance of the
realm; and by degrees more and more land came to be so
held till nearly all the land of the kingdom was entailed.
Yet the nobility, because of the immunities above mentioned, were so fond of the statute that the House of
Lords resisted every effort to repeal it.

§ 21. **Common recoveries.** The extent of the evil of
entails being at last fully appreciated, and all hope of
relief from Parliament being abandoned, a means of de-
frauding the stubborn statute de donis was at last discovered in a collusive proceeding, which from its general
use later to defeat entails came to be known as a common recovery; and the cue to this proceeding was taken
from some remarks dropped by the judges in Taltarum's
case (8a) to the effect that the heir in tail would
be so barred; and the suggestion being immediately
acted on, the judges held that the heir in tail was thereby
barred; and since that time estates tail have been destroyed in that way whenever the tenant in possession
has desired to destroy them. The substance of a common recovery was this: Suppose A has an estate in tail
to himself and the heirs of his body, which he desires to
convey to B in fee simple absolute, and which A's heir
of his body could of course recover of B or anyone else
after A's death if A should make a direct simple conveyance. Now, in order to bar A's heir. A agrees with B

_____
(8a) Y. B. 12 Edw. IV, 19 (1473).

that B shall sue A for the land, and allege that the land
already belongs to B absolutely; this being done, A appears in court and says that he purchased the land of C
(who is the court crier or some other irresponsible fellow,
and not at all the one from whom the land was acquired),
whom he prays the court to summon to defend the suit in
his behalf; C being summoned, appears and asks for a
few minutes to confer with A, with a view to com-
promise, which courts always favor; this being granted,
the parties retire, and presently all but C return ready to
proceed; from C's default the court very naturally infers
that he has no defense to offer, and therefore judgment is
given that B is entitled to the land as he alleged; and a
judgment is given in favor of A against C for the value
of the land.   The courts held that this judgment against
A was binding on his heirs, and that the judgment
against C was an equivalent to the heirs for the land.
This proceeding, invented to defeat estates tail, soon
came to be one of the common, established, and unques-
tionable methods of conveyance.

§ 22.   **Conditions and limitations in restraint of alienation.**   Even before the invention of common recoveries
efforts were made to restrain alienations in fee, or in tail
with warranty, by inserting in the original gift a provision that if the donee should attempt to alienate the
estate so that it should not descend to his heirs, his estate
should thereupon become immediately null and void, and
that the land should thereupon revert to the donor or
should remain over to another.   If the provision were
that on the happening of the event the land should revert

estate to support them or even to take effect in defeasance of any estate before limited; and finally it was established in the case of Pells v. Brown (11) that these future estates could not be abated, discontinued, or barred, by common recovery or otherwise. These points being established, it was manifest that a way had been opened to the creation of an insuperable clog upon alienation of estates in fee, almost before the echo of Lord Coke's rejoicing at the unfettering of freeholds by Mary Portington's case (1614) had ceased to ring in the ears of the people. Unless some limit were set to the time when these future contingent estates might arise they might be limited to begin in a hundred or a thousand years from the making of the conveyance, or at the end of many generations, or on some uncertain future event; wherefore no one would venture to buy land limited subject to such estates, nor if he should could he be certain how long he would be permitted to enjoy it. See the article on Title to Real Estate, §§ 41-43, elsewhere in this volume.

§ 27.   **Rule against perpetuities..** The first great case which tended to set a limit to this time on the modern basis, was the Duke of Norfolk's case (12), in which the House of Lords of England in 1682 affirmed the opinion of Lord Chancellor Nottingham that such future estates should be sustained if they involved no more inconvenience than such estates as had been allowed by the common law; such as gifts to infants, who in the nature of things could not alienate till they became of age; or to in-

(11)   Cro. Jac., 590 (1620).
(12)   3 Chancery Cases, 1.

sane persons, who could not alienate during insanity, which might last as long as they lived, or in strict family settlement to persons in trust for the issue of a marriage now to be celebrated, which estate might remain tied up during the lives of the parties to the marriage and the subsequent minority of their children, and these might be born just before the death of their parents. The logic of this decision was worked out and applied in the decisions during the next hundred years, as the basis of determining in each case whether the limitation was too remote; and the principle thus established has been stated in the form of a rule, which has come to be known as the rule against perpetuities, which, with more propriety, might be called the rule against remoteness. It may be stated in some such form as this: Every future contingent estate limited to arise on an event that might possibly happen later than twenty-one years and the period of gestation after the death of persons living at the creation of the estate is void the day it is created. A gift to A and his heirs for ever would not violate this rule, for it would take effect at once and last forever. It is not the duration of the estate but the commencement of it which may violate the rule. A gift to A and his heirs, but if he should die leaving no children surviving him, or in case any of them should survive him and they should die without issue surviving them before they should be twenty-one years old, then the land is given to B and his heirs forever, would not violate this rule. A's estate is a present and not a future estate; and so there is no room for application of the rule to that. B's estate is not limited in violation of the rule; for if he ever gets the land at all it will be not later than the lifetime of A plus twenty-one years and the period of gestation. But a gift to such of the children of A as should live to the age of twenty-five years would be absolutely void the day it was made, except as to such children of A as were then twenty-five years old; for if he then had a son of the age of twenty-four years and other younger children and none older, it is clear that all these might die before becoming twenty-five years old, and a posthumous child might be born to A who might live to the age of twenty-five years; in which case, if allowed to take effect, this estate would arise more than the life-time of A plus twenty-one years and nine months after the making of the conveyance. In wills the time is reckoned from the death of the testator. By statute in some states the number of lives on which the estate may be contingent is limited to two or three.

SECTION 3.   RISE OF ESTATES LESS THAN FREEHOLD.

§ 28. **Fundamental distinction between freeholds and lesser estates.** It is very hard for the modern man unaccustomed to the feudal tenures, society, and notions of property to get a true idea of what the freehold of the early common law was. The idea involved both the interest of the person in the land and his social condition. This is indicated by Britton's definition (1292-1300) of a freehold as the "possession of the soil by a free man" (13). A villein could not have a freehold; delivery of seizin of the land to him as of freehold by his lord amounted to an implied emancipation, and made a free

––––––––––
(13) Britton, c. 32.

man of him. When in the course of centuries the holdings of the villeins acquired many of the properties of
estates in fee, and came to be known as copyhold estates,
simple estates of inheritance in copyhold lands were
likened to a fee simple by describing them as estates *as
of fee.* But originally a freehold was the possession of
the soil by a free man holding for at least the life of
himself or some other person. In reading this definition
we must not fail to observe also that it was the possession of the soil that constituted a freehold. This possession could be acquired and passed only by the formal ceremony of livery of seizin, or its equivalent—a proceeding
in a court instituted to pass or settle the right. A freehold was an interest in the very soil of the earth. It is
this aspect of the subject which is to be emphasized to distinguish the freehold from the tenancy for years, at the
will of the owner, or by his mere suffrance. The freeholder had an interest in the land itself, the tenant for
years had nothing but a contract or understanding with
the owner of that land, by which he was to be allowed to
occupy it for a stated time. He had no interest in the
land, only a contract right with the owner, even though his
contract was for 100 years. If that contract was broken
by the other party his only remedy was a suit on the contract for damages; he had no way of recovering the land
itself. If his contract was not in writing under seal he
had no remedy at all originally; for the action of assump-
sit, the remedy for breach of a simple parol contract, is
of comparatively modern origin.

§ 29. **Growth of the termor's remedies.** The action of covenant, the action peculiarly appropriate at common law for breach of sealed contracts, seems to have been invented to enforce leases. In other cases of action of covenant damages only were recoverable; but in actions on leases under seal in which the lessor had ousted the lessee during the term the courts came very early to award the termor recovery of his term as well as damages; which in this particular instance gave him the advantages of one having an interest in the land itself. This remedy was available only between the original parties, since others are not bound by their contracts; therefore, if the lessor sold the land, the lessee had no remedy against the purchaser, except by action against the lessor for breach of his covenant, and restitution from the purchaser could not be awarded. If the lessor sold and died, the lessee might sue the lessor's heir and recover damages to the extent of any land descended to him. If strangers ousted him without the lessor's consent, the lessor might recover the land of them by assize of novel disseizin and so make restitution, if he would, to the lessee; but this action did not lie in favor of the lessee himself, for his possession was not a seizin sufficient to sustain it.

To remedy this defect the action of quare ejecit infra terminum was provided about 1225. The following is the form of this writ as given by Bracton, writing about 1260 (14): ''The King to the sheriff (of such a county): Greeting: If A gives proper security, summon B to show

----

(14)   Bracton, Book 4, c. 36, to. 220.

cause why he ejects and keeps out A from so much land in such a township, which C demised to A for a term which is not yet expired, and within the said term said C sold the said land to B, by reason of which sale said B afterwards ejected A from the said land as he saith,'' etc. It will be observed that this action failed to give a complete remedy; it is by its form confined to actions against the lessor's grantees. Against the general ejector, the lessee was still without remedy. Where it was appropriate the remedy was complete, for the termor recovered not damages only but the restitution of his term also. This was another step in the direction of making the termor a qualified owner of the land, at least interested in it. However, this action was available against the lessor as well as against his assignee; and we have not yet mentioned the one fact which marked the greatest effect produced by the introduction of this new form of action. It is this: Whereas before there was no remedy against anyone, not even the lessor, unless there was a contract in writing, there is nothing about this writ which required that the lease should be in writing. It may be that actions on oral leases or written leases not sealed were rare, but the fact that the remedy now existed against the lessor and his grantee to recover both lease and damages in every case of ejectment by them of a termor having any valid lease, not necessarily under seal, is very important as to the scope of the remedy, and the nature of estate in the land created by a lease for a term; for the nature of the right in any case can properly be measured only by the remedy—the remedy is the essence of the right.

§ 30. **Same (continued).** As against the mere stranger who ejected him the termor was still without remedy; and the first remedy we find against him was in the year 1371, when the new writ of ejectione firmae (ejectment from the farm) was sustained; which was in the nature of a writ of trespass. By this writ the termor could recover damages from the stranger for being ousted of his term; but he still had no recovery of his term itself, which was the really valuable thing, because he had no freehold. Therefore termors so ejected went to the chancellor for redress. At this time the court of chancery was very aggressive in extending its jurisdiction, and quickly took this opportunity to grant against the lessor and his privies a specific performance of the covenant and damages also, and against strangers they granted to the termor a perpetual injunction that they should not disturb his possession. The law courts were at this time very jealous of the growing jurisdiction of the chancellor; and therefore, in order not to lose their jurisdiction in this class of cases, they took occasion about 1450 to 1500 to give the ejected termor judgment for restitution of his term from the stranger against whom he had brought this action of trespass in the form of ejectione firmae, as well as damages for the trespass; and this restitution was awarded without any warrant for it in the writ nor demand for it in the declaration. We have now arrived at a poirt where the status of the termor as owner of an interest in the land is almost com-

pletely reversed from what it was three hundred years
before. Instead of having only a contract with the
owner of the land, on which his only remedy is an action
against him for damages, he has become an owner of
land, able to try the title and ultimate right even with a
mere stranger to his contract of lease, and this, too, in a
much speedier and simpler manner than could be done by
the freeholder himself with his dilatory and technical
writs of right. This new advantage of the termor was
quickly recognized by land owners who had questions of
title to try, and it soon became the custom for them to
make leases in such cases for the mere purpose of getting
the advantage of trying the title in ejectment.

§ 31. Same (concluded). And yet the position of the
termor was not absolutely secure. By the lessor procur-
ing himself to be sued for the land by another claiming
the right, and suffering judgment to be rendered against
him, which is a common recovery, it was held that the
termor was bound by the judgment against his lessor in
a suit to which he was not a party, of which he had no
notice, and in which he had no standing to make any defense; because it was assumed that the owner of the fee
had a greater interest in defending the title than the
termor and represented him in interest and privity. It
was not till the statute of 21 Henry VIII (1529), c. 15,
that the position of the termor as a land owner was made
absolutely secure. This enacted that, notwithstanding
such recoveries, the termors should hold and enjoy their
terms and leases against all such recoverees, their heirs
and assigns, as if no such recovery had been suffered;

and if dispossessed might recover the mean profits by avowery or action of debt in like manner as their lessors might have done had. they not been parties to the recovery. Thus the estate of the tenant for years became a complete estate, but to this day leaseholds are treated as personalty which go to the administrator, like notes or promises to pay, and do not descend to the heir with the lands.

§ 32. **Rise of estates at will and from year to year.** Judge Littleton, writing in his Tenures about 1460-80, said that a "tenant at will is where lands or tenements are let by one man to another, to have and to hold to him at the will of the lessor, by force of which lease the lessee is in possession. In this case the lessee is called tenant at will, because he hath no certain nor sure estate, for the lessor may put him out at what time it pleaseth him" (15). The author then proceeds to say that the holding at will may arise by the tenant entering under an agreement for transfer of the freehold which is void for want of recovery, or the like. He also adds that if turned out suddenly the tenant at will may return to remove his goods or to cultivate and harvest crops planted before the holding at will was determined. The law in this respect remained with little change until about one hundred and fifty years ago. In the year 1701 it was declared by the chief justice of the court of King's bench that the tenancy at will might be determined at any time by either party, subject to the liability to lose the rent for the quarter commenced if terminated by the landlord, and to pay the

---

(15) Lit., § 68.

rent for the whole quarter then running if the estate was terminated by the tenant (16). But in the year 1769 it was decided by the same court that an action of eject-ment by the lord against the tenant at will was not main-tainable because the tenant at will had not been given the necessary notice to quit six months before the action was commenced (17). And in the year 1786 it was an-nounced by the same court that the law is averse to ten-ancies at will, and will seize any circumstance such as agreement for the payment of rent periodically to declare the estate to be one from year to year rather than at will; and that in this case the six months' notice to quit must be given at least six months before the termination of the rent period, and that the estate cannot be termi-nated till the end of a rent period at which the landlord has signified his intention by notice to terminate it (18). The matter is now further regulated by statute in all the states.

SECTION 4.   CHANGES IN THE LAW OF TRANSFER OF TITLE.

§ 33.   Ancient transfer by livery.   No branch of the law of real property has suffered more changes, and stands today at greater variance with its original posi-tion than the law of transfers. In every country where law prevails it is and always has been necessary to have some fixed formality in the transfers of land from one to another, in order to secure that certainty of grantor, grantee, estate, and thing granted, which are essential

---

(16)   Layton v. Field, 3 Salk., 222.
(17)   Parker d. Walker v. Constable, 3 Wilson, 25.
(18)   Right d. Flower v. Darby, 1 Term, 159.

to secure the title from future doubt and dispute, and which will guarantee that notoriety essential to enable the public in general to know to whom to look concerning the dealings with that land. Were our space not restricted it would be interesting to note how such things have been regulated in other systems of law; how "in former time in Israel, concerning redeeming and concerning changing, for to confirm all things, a man plucked off his shoe and gave it to his neighbor, and this was a testimony in Israel" (19); and how such things were done by the law of the Greeks and Romans. But let us look at the law of England.

The only method of transfer originally valid by the feudal law, under which England was governed for centuries, was by actual corporeal livery of seizin of the land, which was accomplished in some such manner as this: The feoffor, lessor, or his attorney, together with the feoffee, lessee, or his attorney (for this may as effectually be done by deputy or attorney as by the principals themselves in person), come to the land or to the house; and there, in the presence of witnesses, declare the contents of the feoffment or lease, on which the livery is to be made. Originally these witnesses were the vassals of the same lord or the tenants of the same barony; and the invention of charters to perpetuate the more effectually the memory of the transaction was no doubt due to the experience that the witnesses soon died or at least forgot the details of the transaction. The transfer was quite as valid without any writing at

(19)   Ruth, c. 4, v. 7.

all. The parties and witnesses being present, the feoffer picked up a clod of the ground, or a twig of a bush, or if it be of land containing a dwelling house he took the hasp or latch of the front door into his hand, and turning to the feoffee, donee, or lessee, said: "I now deliver these to you in the name of seizin of all the lands and tenements contained in this deed." While the livery was being made the land should not be in the possession of any other, but all the tenants should go out of the house and off of the land, so that the possession might be fully and perfectly delivered. The ceremony of livery being completed the purchaser would open the door and go in and shut the door again, to make sure that he had secure possession; then he might open it and let in the others as his guests. If the land lay in several parcels in the same county, one livery at the capital mansion-house was sufficient for all the land in that county; but if the land to be conveyed lay in several counties there must be a livery made in each county; for every jury to try titles must be summoned of the freeholders of that county, and the jury could not inquire what was done in another county. If the land was out in lease at the time of the transfer, the title of the feoffee was not complete till it was approved by the tenants accepting them as their new lord, which might be by paying him the rent, doing fealty to him, or the like. Moreover, there must have been a livery for each tenant of a part at least of the land he held. What has been mentioned above is livery in deed and fact, but there was also what was known as livery in law, which was by the parties going in person (for this could not be done by attorney) in sight of the land, and the feoffor saying to the feoffee: "I give you yonder land; enter and take possession." In this case the feoffee's title was not complete till he had taken actual possession.

This method of transfer was tolerable for a simple transfer among unlettered people; but it was wholly unsuited to the transfer of lands subject to complicated conditions, covenants, trust, and the like; wherefore resort was necessarily had at an early day to deeds and charters to accompany the transaction and define the estates.

§ 34. **Early transfers without livery.** In seeking for the origin of the idea that title could be transferred without livery, we are taken back to a time when nothing can be asserted with assurance. The first instances we find of this sort are the cases of devises among the Saxons. Some historians have asserted that lands were not devisable among the Saxons, except by virtue of a privilege especially granted with the original donation by the king or lord paramount, being what were known as "boclands" (book lands) as distinguished from lands not held by special charters. However this may be, it is fairly certain that these were the first transfers without livery; and whether the devise was given effect merely by virtue of the devise, or derived its operation from the original charter, we are brought to the same result—a transfer of an estate by reason of a mere declaration of the owner that it was his wish that at some future time unascertained, upon the happening of

an event specified (his own death, the death of his grantee testate, a livery to be made by his executor, or the
like), the title to the land should then pass from the
then owner to some other person, without any livery or
other contemporaneous act to witness, publish, and prove
the transfer. Though probably the common notion is
that such transfers were first introduced through adopting the doctrines of the courts of chancery into the law
courts by virtue of the statute of uses, 27 Henry VIII,
c. 10, the fact is that transfers without livery were admitted by the law courts to be good in the cases above
mentioned long before the recognition of uses by the
law courts, and even before they had acquired any system and established rules even in the chancery. But
while the judges recognized that the validity of such
transfers had become established beyond question, they
marveled at their being allowed in violation of the principles and reason of the common law. An idea of how
such transactions were regarded by the law courts is
conveyed by a remark of Chief Justice Babington of the
court of common pleas in 1431, as follows: "The nature
of a devise where lands are devisable is that one may
devise that the land shall be sold by his executors; and
this is good, as has been said, and is marvelous law in
reason; but this is the nature of a devise, and devises
have been used at all times in this form; and so one may
have a lawful freehold from another who has nothing,
just as one may have fire from flint and yet there is
no fire in the flint; and this is to perform the last will

of the devisor" (20). While these instances of purely legal estates transferred without any livery at the time of creation of the state furnished ample precedent for the extension of the principle of transfer in the future by mere declaration of the owner that such is his wish, it remained for the statute of uses, 27 Henry VIII, c. 10, enacted in the year 1535, to extend this principle by transplanting it into the law with the whole code of rules worked out by the court of chancery in developing the doctrines of uses, the fundamental maxim of which was that the use follows the consideration except as executed with transmutation of possession on a different intention. We must therefore now go back to trace the development of the doctrine of uses and their establishment as legal estates.

§ 35. **Origin and development of the doctrine of uses.** We are told that the Franciscan friars had lands conveyed to others to hold to their use as early as the reign of King John (1199-1216), because the rules of their order did not permit them to own property; but the general introduction of the practice is credited to a later period, when the statute de religiosis, 7 Edw. I (1279) declared that any term for years, or other title to land whatsoever, conveyed to any bishop or other religious person, should be at once forfeited to the lord of the fee, or on his default to the king; conveyances to the religious houses having been declared forfeited by the provisions of the Great Charter of Henry III, c. 43

---

(20) Farington v. Darral, Y. B. 9, Henry VI, 23b.

(1217). To evade these statutes the clergy resorted
to taking conveyances to their use. Such conveyances
were not within the letter of the statutes and so not subject to forfeiture. The trust reposed in the feoffee was
purely at his mercy at first, as there was no recognition
of it by the law courts, and the court of chancery had not
yet developed. Such conveyances were also made by
dishonest debtors to defraud their creditors, and for
many legitimate purposes. Later, when the chancellor
began to take upon himself the jurisdiction to give relief
in all cases in which there was no remedy in the law
courts, resort was made to him for relief against such
feoffees if they refused to devote the property to the
uses declared in the conveyance to them; and he compelled the feoffees to obey the use. Before this time
the only protection the feoffor or other person entitled
to the benefits (called cestuy que use) had was the honor
of the feoffee, or such advantage as he might acquire by
making the conveyance to a number of persons jointly
instead of to one. When it became known that the chancellor would enforce observance of the use such conveyances became very common for many purposes, such
as to provide for disposition of the estate after the
death of the beneficiary (who could not devise the land
by the common law, but could convey the land to be held
to such uses as he might appoint and then by will appoint the uses); or to provide for the issue of a marriage to be presently solemnized. During the wars in the
reigns of Henry VI and Edward IV, known in history
as the Wars of the Roses, from the emblems on the

armor of the leaders, no man could tell when his property would be declared forfeited for treason, no matter on which side he aligned himself, for each side was alternately victorious; so, to provide against this nearly all the land in the kingdom was conveyed to a number of persons to be held for the use of the real owner. If the owner of the use was declared a traitor and executed, the land was not forfeited, since it belonged to the feoffees, who would hold to the use of his heirs. If one of the feoffees was declared a traitor, the land was held by the others by survivorship still subject to the appointed uses.

§ 36. **Various incidents of the doctrines of uses.** Originally uses were enforcible only against the feoffees themselves, but in the reign of Edward IV the chancellor began enforcing the trust against the heirs of the feoffees and such of their alienees as took with notice of the use, or without payment of value. The king from his sovereignty, and corporations from lack of conscience and body to be taken in execution, could not be held to obey the use. The lord taking by escheat from the feoffee, the husband or wife taking by curtesy or dower from the feoffee, were not bound by the use. The widow of the cestuy que use took no dower of the use, the husband no curtesy; it was free from feudal burdens, being held of nobody; if the cestuy que use was attainted his heirs took the use, or if he had none the feoffee held the land discharged of the use, and there was no escheat; his creditors could not reach his interest to satisfy his debts; the feoffees might deprive him of the use by sale to an

innocent purchaser or by excluding him until he should
be compelled to sue in chancery; and in like manner
might refuse to make a transfer till the proposed purchaser should be gone, unless a suit in chancery to compel
the transfer could sooner be perfected.

To remedy these evils, numerous statutes were enacted;
it was enacted that the creditors of the cestuy que use
might take the land on execution (21); the lord was given
wardship and the feudal perquisites in general (22); his
conveyance without the concurrence of his feoffees was
made good and effectual (23); lands held by anyone to
the use of another were declared the absolute property
of the cestuy que use upon the trustee becoming king
(24).   But these statutes did not suffice to remove the
evils.   The feoffees to use could still sell to defraud the
cestuy que use, who could also sell; and so it happened
that one would sell to one, the other to another, sometimes playing against each other, sometimes by collu-
sion to defraud the purchasers; no one could be sure of
his title; farmers were ousted of leases taken bona fide;
women lost their dower, men their curtesies; lands were
held to the use of aliens; feoffments were made to fraudulent and secret uses.

§ 37.   Statute of uses.   Finally a statute was passed,
27 Hen. VIII, c. 10 (1535), which, after reciting the above
grievances and others, declared, that "for the extirping

(21)   50 Edw. III, c. 6.
(22)   4 Henry VII, c. 17; 19 Henry VII, c. 15.
(23)   1 Rich. III, c. 5.
(24)   1 Rich. III, c. 1

and extinguishment of all such subtle practices feoffments, fines, recoveries, and errors heretofore used and
accustomed in this realm to the subversion of the good
and ancient laws of the same, and to the intent that the
king's highness or any other of his subjects of this realm
shall not in any wise hereafter by any means or inven-
tions be deceived, damaged, or hurt, by reason of such
trusts, uses, or confidences," it was enacted "that where
any person or persons stand or be seized, or at any time
hereafter shall happen to be seized of and in any honors,
castles, manors, lands, tenements, rents, services, reversions, remainders, or other hereditaments, to the use, confidence, or trust of any other person or persons, or of any
body politic, that have or hereafter shall have any such
use, confidence, or trust, in fee simple, fee tail, for term
of life or for years, or otherwise, or any use, trust, or
confidence in remainder or reversion, shall from henceforth stand and be seized, deemed, and adjudged in lawful seizin, estate, and possession of and in the same honors, castles, manors, lands, tenements, rents, services,
reversions, remainders, and hereditaments, with their
appurtenances, to all intents, constructions, and purposes
in the law, of and in such like estates, as they had or
shall have in use, trust, or confidence of or in the same;
and that the estate, title, right, and possession that was
in such person or persons that were or hereafter shall
be seized of any lands, tenements, or hereditaments, to
the use, confidence, or trust, of any such person or persons, or of any body politic, be from thence forth clearly
deemed and adjudged to be in him of them that have or

hereafter shall have such use, confidence, or trust, after
such quantity, manner, form, and condition as they had
before in or to the use, confidence, or trust that was in
them.''

§ 38. **Effect of statute of uses upon titles.** This statute thus executed the use, that is conveyed the possession
to the use, and converted the use into possession, thereby
making the cestuy que use complete owner of the lands
and tenements at law as well as in equity. It will be observed that by this statute uses were not abolished but
established and increased by the annihilation of the intervening estate of the feoffees to use and throwing the
whole title upon the cestuy que use; so that uses are now
legal and not merely equitable estates. The law courts
now began to take cognizance of uses instead of sending
the party to the chancellor for relief; and considering
them now as a mere method of conveyance they adopted
many of the rules concerning them that had before been
established in chancery; the same persons were capable
of holding to uses, the same considerations necessary to
raise them, and they could exist only as to the same
hereditaments as before. But in many respects they
were now entirely changed: the use, which was now the
land itself, could no longer be devised, was subject to
dower and curtesy, could no longer be alienated by the
feoffees discharged of the use, and was not liable to
escheat or forfeiture for the act or default of the feoffees
to uses, because the estate did not rest in them for a
moment but was wholly drawn to the cestuy que use. On
the other hand, the rule of the chancery enforcing ob-

servance of directions as to the use at any time, whereby the feoffee might be required to hold for the use of the feoffor for a time and then for the use of another, or at some future designated time make a conveyance or permit a use to certain named persons, now was soon recognized as a principle of law pertaining to uses; wherefore, unlike remainders, they needed no particular estate to support them, might be limited to arise at any certain or uncertain future time, without any prior estate or in defeasance of any prior estate. But the design of the statute to unite the legal and equitable title indissolubly in one person was soon defeated by one or two hasty decisions of the law courts, which held that the statute executed only the first use, from which it followed that if a grant was made to A for the use of B in trust for C the legal title stopped in B, who was required by the chancellor to permit the enjoyment of the profits to be taken by C. In this way the whole system of uses before the statute as equitable estates cognizable only in the chancery was soon revived with ten-fold increase under the new name of trusts, which are to this day purely the creatures and subjects of the equity courts wherever such courts exist.

§ 39. **Effect of statute of uses upon conveyancing.** However, the changes of greatest importance produced on the law of real property by the statute of uses related to the matter of conveyancing. It will be remembered that originally livery of seizin actually made on the land or in sight of it was necessary to a valid transfer, and that the only change in this respect (except as to lands de-

visable by special custom) made before the statute of
uses was the establishment of the custom **of** conveyance
in a court of record by means of fine, invented as early
as the reign of Henry II (1154-1189) if not before, and
by the similar proceeding of common recovery, which is
thought to have been first used by the ecclesiastics in **the**
reign of Edward I (1272-1307), to evade the statutes of
mortmain. But now, by virtue of the statute of uses,
which made the confidence before enforced by the chancellor a legal estate, it was possible to make transfers
of estates of any sort in lands by merely agreeing that
the title should pass now or at some future time, provided
that agreement has a sufficient consideration to support
it; and even without any consideration to support the
use it was enforcible if the title had passed out of the
owner by any common law conveyance (livery, fine, recovery, etc.,) at the time he declared the use; for he to
whom the title had passed without consideration, subject
to the agreement to hold to a certain use, had no standing
to oppose the use and claim the beneficial estate to himself. The only case, in which it is intended to state that
the use would not be enforced for want of consideration
to raise it, is where the owner merely declared the uses
to which he would hold it and there was no consideration
to support the declaration.

Another important change produced by the statute
was the power it gave the vendor to mold the estate
granted to suit the exigencies of his case. The utmost
that the common law would allow in this respect was **a**
condition inserted in the original conveyance by **which,**

on specified events, the grantor or his heirs might re-enter and possess themselves of his *whole* original estate; or a defeasance, which differed in nothing from a condition except that it was not in the original conveyance, and that was void if not made at the same time with the transfer first made. On the other hand, a conveyance by way of use might merely declare that the uses thereby declared were subject to revocation, modification, etc., at a specified time, or at any time, by the vendor or by any other person specified, and in such manner (deed, will, etc.,) as the deed creating the use may authorize. Note that the condition or defeasance had to specify the terms upon which they should have effect; but in the case of conveyances by way of use, this might be left to be determined by future desires and exigencies. Further, in the case of the condition or defeasance, the estate could only return to the grantor or his heirs entire, for, on the defeasance or entry for breach of condition, the grantor or his heir was in possession of the original estate; but on the exercise of the power under the conveyance by way of use the estate might be given over to another, or split up, or modified, as convenience might require. Thus was established the modern law of conveyancing, and on this statute of uses the whole notion of conveyancing today depends, except that the idea has been extended and modified by various statutes enacted in each state of this country.

§ 40. **Operation of various deeds under the** statute. The principal deeds operating by virtue of the statute of uses were the bargain and sale, the covenant to stand

seized, and the lease and release. The bargain and sale
was merely the contract, whatever it was, which before
the statute had sufficed to raise the use. For example,
suppose that before the statute was passed A had agreed
with B to sell him Whiteacre for so much, which B had
paid to A; now, by virtue of the agreement and the payment of the price, B became in equity and good conscience the owner; in other words, A was seized to B's
use, and on B's complaint the chancellor would compel
A to make transfer of the legal title as he has agreed.
What is the effect of the statute on this transaction? It
simply makes the transfer for A which the chancellor before the statute would have compelled him to make. A
agrees to sell to B and B pays the price, that raises a
use in B, and thereupon the statute conveys the legal
title to the use, turns the use into a legal title, and the
land now belongs to B. Again, suppose that B owns land
in fee and conveys it to A by livery of seizin (as the custom was before the statute) to hold to B's own use; now,
the minute that the title passes to A holding for the use of
B, the statute operates immediately to throw the legal
title back upon B, and so would defeat the purpose of the
transfer; but in this case the law courts allowed that if
the feoffee had active duties to perform or equity required it, the legal title might remain in A, and the use
remain unexecuted by the statute to be protected and
executed as a trust in chancery.

The covenant to stand seized, as its name implies, had
to be in writing under seal, and was valid only when the
covenantor and beneficiary were related to each other by

blood or marriage or partly by one and partly by the other; and if A should covenant with B to hold the land to the use of A's son, wife, brother, father, brother's wife, son's wife, or the like. Upon the making and delivery of the deed the title passed to the beneficiary by virtue of the statute as soon as the use arose; and the deed might provide that the use should arise in the future, as if made upon a marriage to the use of the children of the marriage when born.

The lease and release were two deeds to make one conveyance; first, the lease, for a valuable consideration, by one seized would raise a use in the lessee, which the statute would by a sort of parliamentary magic convert into an actual possession, and put the lessee in an imaginary possession of the land he may never have seen and which may be miles away; but this implied possession was held by the court sufficient to enable the lessee to take from the lessor immediately afterwards a common law deed of release, which would pass the rest of the lessor's title to the lessee and make him absolute owner. To appreciate the logic of this transaction it should be remembered that no livery could be made to one who had the possession already, and therefore a release to him was good at common law without livery; but no one could take a release unless he was in possession before he had the release. This double conveyance was invented to evade the enrollments act, mentioned in § 41, following.

§ 41. **Statute of enrollment of conveyances.** As has been suggested before, there was no provision at common law for the enrollment of title deeds, so that one could

be sure of not losing proof of his title, nor in purchasing
could assure himself by examination of any public records that the person of whom he was purchasing had any
title to sell. This was in part avoided in the city of
London and perhaps other places by special provision of
the city's charter or by ancient custom, providing for enrollment in the office of the sheriff, mayor, or elsewhere;
and by resort to the courts of record by collusive suits
called fines and recoveries, for the sake of getting the
matter on record, or to accomplish some other special
purpose. But when the statute of uses was passed it
was immediately seen that it gave great facility for
making a secret bargain and sale, perhaps by word of
mouth only; and to prevent such secret transfers, it was
enacted by statute passed at the same session of Parliament, and known as the statute of enrollment, 27 Henry
VIII, c. 16, that no lands or tenements shall pass or
change, whereby any estate of inheritance or freehold
shall be made or take effect by reason of any bargain
and sale thereof, except the same be by writing indented,
sealed, and enrolled in one of the king's courts of record
at Westminster, or in the county where the lands affected lay, and the enrollment made within six months
after the date of the writing. It will be noted that the
statute applied only to conveyances of a freehold estate,
and it has been suggested that perhaps the omission of
terms for years was occasioned by the fact that the effect
of the statute permitting termors to defeat fraudulent
recoveries (mentioned in § 31, above), which made such
interests indefeasible, and was enacted only six years be-

fore, had not yet come to be generally appreciated. However that may be, the fact is that the omission enabled secret transfers without livery, by the lease and release invented for that purpose shortly after the statute was passed, which is discussed in § 40, preceding. This statute has furnished the suggestion for our American recording acts, which require all land titles to be recorded or that they shall be void as to innocent purchasers whose deeds are first recorded.

TRANSFER OF TITLE TO REAL ESTATE

BY

ALBERT MARTIN KALES,
A. B. (Harvard University)
LL. B. (Harvard University)

Professor of Law, Northwestern University.

TRANSFER OF TITLE TO REAL ESTATE.

§ **1.** **Outline of subject.** 1. The title to real estate is most commonly transferred by an act of conveyance done with the consent of the owner. This happens in the ordinary case of transfer by deed or will, which is familiar to all. 2. The title of the owner may, however, be transferred without his consent, for example, by a sale on execution to satisfy a judgment. 3. The title of the former owner may not pass at all, and yet without his consent his title may be extinguished and a new and original title may arise in another. This happens when

63

B obtains title and A loses title because of the running of the statute of limitations in favor of B against A. 4. There may be cases where the land in question had no former owner at all and where B derives a new and original title to it. This occurs where accretions form on the shores of the sea, a lake, or a river and the riparian owner becomes the owner of the new-made land. These four ways in which title to real estate may be acquired will be discussed in the following article (1).

---

(1) Transfers at death by intestate succession and the formal requisites of transfer by will are treated in the article upon Estates of Decedents in Volume VI of this work. The *estates created* by transfers, whether by deed or will, are treated in the present article (see § 15, below).

PART I.

TRANSFER OF TITLE WITH CONSENT OF OWNER.

CHAPTER I.

FORM OF CONVEYANCE AND DESCRIPTION OF PROPERTY.

§ 2. **Policy of the law in regard to transfer of land.** It is the policy of the law to allow owners of land the greatest freedom possible in carrying out their wishes regarding the transfer of that which belongs to them. Hence, any form of conveyance of title which expresses an intention of the owner to convey to another will be sufficient, except so far as certain formalities are positively required upon particular grounds. These required formalities differ considerably according to the subject-matter of the transfer.

§ 3. **Surrender by tenant to landlord.** If a tenant is giving up his lease to his landlord so as to extinguish the tenancy, no formality is, apart from statute, required other than the expressed intent to give up the tenancy and the assent of the landlord to receive it. The landlord and tenant may meet casually on the street and upon a moment's conversation the lease may be gone and the tenant free to move out and pay no more rent. The temptation to both landlord and tenant to commit perjury,

which this situation furnishes, has been deemed so great
that many legislatures have required that the surrender
by a tenant to the landlord shall not be effected unless
evidenced by a writing, signed by the party against whom
it is sought to enforce the surrender.

But even under such acts a surrender may still occur
by "operation of law" without a writing. Many are
the niceties as to what is a surrender by operation of law.
Thus, if the tenant accepts a new tenancy in place of the
old, though for but a shorter and less advantageous term,
the old lease is surrendered (2). So, if the tenant gives
up possession to his landlord and the landlord accepts the
possession, there is a surrender by operation of law (3).
This last comes very near letting in all the evils which
existed before surrenders were required to be evidenced
by a writing and signature. For instance, the tenant
appears and places the keys to the leased premises in
the landlord's hands and says that he gives up possession.
If the landlord assents and receives the keys, he cannot
recover for the loss of rent during the balance of the
lease. It may, of course, be very easy for the tenant to
swear against the landlord that the landlord did accept
the possession. The temptation for some one to commit
perjury is very acute. The only safe course is to do
business with the tenant before witnesses or by letter,
making it perfectly clear that the landlord does not accept
possession, but that possession is thrust upon him
against his will; and that if he re-lets the premises it is

(2)   Whitley v. Gough, Dyer, 140b.
(3)   Dodd v. Acklom, 6 M. & G., 672.

merely to keep down the damages which the tenant may have to pay. See Landlord and Tenant, §§ 118-19, in Volume IV of this work.

§ 4. **Term for less than one (or three) years.** In every state short leases (from one to three years according to the statutes) are valid without a writing. No formality is required in these cases, except either an entry upon possession by the tenant, or the giving of a consideration, however slight, by the tenant.

§ 5. **Longer term for years.** Where the subject matter of the transfer is an estate for years, for the term of a year or more, or in some jurisdictions, three years or more (according to the statutes mentioned in § 4, above), the additional formality of a writing and signature by the party to be bound is required by statute.

§ 6. **Life estate or fee, in personal possession of grantor.** If the subject matter of the transfer be a life estate or a full ownership in fee (§ 17, below), which the transferor enjoys in actual personal possession (not merely possessed by his tenant), there must be a writing signed by the transferor. This is a statutory requirement. At common law the transfer of a freehold estate (§ 16, below) in the possession of the grantor was accomplished by livery of seisin, actually or symbolically putting the purchaser in present possession. See the article on History of Real Property, § 33, elsewhere in this volume. At present, in addition to a writing, at least one of two other formalities must be observed. Either the instrument must have a seal, or the transferee must have given some consideration, however small, in return for the transfer.

§ 7. **Same: Is a seal necessary?** If the instrument has a seal, its effectiveness is principally due to statutes, common to most jurisdictions where the law is founded upon the common law, which make sufficient and effective all conveyances which are sealed in addition to being in writing and signed. Perhaps most courts would say, or have actually held, that the seal is indispensable. But this, it is believed, may be successfully controverted as a matter of logic in most jurisdictions, for the following reasons: The statutory provisions regarding the effect of a seal are not compulsory, but only permissive, leaving a conveyance without a seal valid provided it were valid on any ground apart from modern statutory provisions. As an historical fact, an instrument without a seal was valid to pass title if founded upon a consideration, however slight, given by the transferee to the transferor for the conveyance, by virtue of the statute of uses of Henry VIII which became law in England in 1536. That statute is either expressly or impliedly incorporated into the laws of practically all the jurisdictions of the United States. It is true that there was a later statute of the same year, known as the statute of enrollments, which required a seal, but that was a statute which on its face was local to England and could not, and it is submitted, has not applied to or become incorporated into the law of the colonies or the different jurisdictions of this country. It is a matter of frequent observation by laymen that an instrument of conveyance contains the recital of one dollar in hand paid by the grantee, and that this dollar is in fact never paid, and that where the conveyance is by way of gift, no consideration whatever is paid. The effectiveness of this untrue recital is due to the fact that it being a recital in a deed—that is to say, an instrument under seal—it cannot be denied by the parties that some consideration passed, and since that fact cannot be denied, the conveyance may be valid and effective under the statute of uses of Henry VIII just referred to. By reason of this fact the recital has come down to us as the result of many centuries of habit on the part of conveyancers. Today, under our modern statutes, the deed would be good with a seal without any consideration or recital. The modern deed containing the recital and also sealed is therefore sufficient both by reason of the statute of uses of Henry VIII and by our modern legislation respecting conveyances under seal. See § 41, below.

§ 8. **Vested future interests. Reversions and remainders.** Suppose the subject matter of the conveyance is a future interest, as distinguished from a present one; and suppose the owner of land is not in possession, but a tenant of his is. The landlord then usually is what is called a "reversioner." He has a future interest. It does not take effect in possession until the tenancy has expired. But it is a future interest which is subject to no contingency whatever, other than the termination of the tenant's lease. So, if there is a life tenant in possession, the owner may be what is called a reversioner or a remainderman (§ 31, below). In either case we will suppose that the owner's interest is subject to no contingency whatever, other than the termination of the life estate. All the future interests of the sort here described may

be transferred only by an instrument under seal. It is usually assumed that such an instrument must be signed also. In the middle ages where there was a transfer by the owner of the reversion or the remainder, the tenant in possession was obliged to attorn to or acknowledge the transferee before the conveyance was valid and effective. But this is no longer a requirement of the law in England, and has not been since the reign of Queen Anne, and is not the law in any jurisdiction of the United States (4), unless it be by some curious survival.

§ 9. Contingent future interests. Now suppose the actual possession of land be in A, and B have a future interest that is subject to a condition precedent in form and in fact to its taking effect in possession, and that this condition is something other than the termination of the preceding interest by its natural expiration. Thus, suppose after a life estate in A, there is a future interest in B, provided A dies. without children him surviving. B's interest during the life of A was not, apart from statute, directly transferable to one other than A by any form of conveyance. The same was true of other contingent future interests in real estate. In England by an act of 1845, and in many jurisdictions of this country, this prohibition on the alienation of future interests has been removed and the contingent future interest, such as it is, is made freely alienable.

But these contingent future interests can be "released," as it is called, to the person in possession, provided the release be made by the person next entitled to

(4) Perrin v. Lepper, 34 Mich. 292.

the person in possession (5). The release is in form nothing more than an instrument in writing and sealed. It is usually assumed that it must be signed also. As a matter of custom it is in the form of what is known as a quit-claim deed.

§ 10. **Usual form of conveyances. Various kinds of deeds.** So far we have dealt only with the bare requirements for transfers of title to real estate. The usual form of conveyance.is a deed or instrument under seal. Long usage has developed a somewhat stereotyped form of conveyance of real estate. Deeds are catalogued as "warranty deeds," "special warranty deeds" and "quit-claim deeds." The first have full covenants of warranty, which are elsewhere more fully explained (§ 95, below). The second contain covenants of warranty only against the acts of the grantor. The last contain no covenants of warranty at all. Deeds, whether warranty deeds or quit-claim deeds, are also catalogued as indentures and deeds poll. The former are executed in duplicate and are properly used where by reason of the deed containing covenants by the grantee, it is proper for the grantee to sign. The identure is most commonly used in leases, which it will be observed, contain many covenants by the tenant. The term indenture is, of course, derived from the fact that formerly the two parts of a deed were executed on parchment and then severed upon an irregular or identical line, so that by fitting the two parts together upon that line they could be identified as duplicate

(5) Williams v. Esten, 179 Ill. 267.

originals. Deeds poll on the other hand, are those executed only by the grantor.

§ 11. **Different parts of a deed.** Every well drawn
deed of conveyance has at least a suggestion of the following parts:

1. The premises: In a deed poll the premises are
"Know all men by these presents, that I," or "To all to
whom these presents shall come, Greeting! Know that
I." Indentures on the other hand, recite that "This Indenture, made this ...... day of .... by A. B.,
party of the first part, and C. D., party of the second part,
Witnesseth."

2. The recitals: After the premises follow the recitals or introductory matter, preceded by the word
"Whereas." The statement of the consideration is also
properly classed with the recitals. The making of recitals in a deed must be done with care, because the parties are not permitted to deny the truth of the recitals. A
qualification of this may be stated with respect to the recital of the consideration. Neither of the parties can
deny that some consideration passed, but they are not
bound by the particular figures mentioned as the consideration in the deed.

3. Words of conveyance: These include (a) the
description of the property granted; (b) the words which
indicate what estate is created; (c) the covenants for
title; (d) the release of the wife's dower or husband's
curtesy; (e) the release of statutory exemptions; (f)
the witnessing clause, signature, and seal; and (g) the
acknowledgment.

§ 12. **Description of property granted.** Competent conveyancers spare no pains to see that the description of the property conveyed is without ambiguity or uncertainty. It is often compared and re-compared with a known correct description in an abstract of title, or with a surveyor's description and plat. The reason for this is obvious. If the description is defective, the whole conveyance fails. No other part of the instrument is so vitally important. But even if the description is not wholly bad, the conveyancer is blameworthy who allows any question of construction or ambiguity to arise in respect thereto. Nevertheless, some often repeated difficulties have arisen respecting descriptions and in respect to such difficulties some more or less definite rules have been announced by the courts.

§ 13. **Same: Some rules of construction.** If the premises conveyed are described by lots and blocks in regularly laid out and platted subdivisions the description is according to the monuments of the subdivision duly noted on the plat, and in the case of subdivisions properly platted by competent surveyors, very little question as to description can arise. If, however, the premises must be described by metes and bounds, then it must be observed that if any conflict occurs between the monuments and the distances, or between the monuments and the courses, or the monuments and the contents, the monuments always govern (6). If there is any conflict between distances, courses, and contents, there is no rule, but the words of the deed and all the surrounding circumstances

(6)   Pernam v. Wead, 6 Mass. 131.

which throw light upon what the parties meant by the words they used must govern. If the result is still in doubt, resort may be had to the rule that the deed will be construed most strongly against the grantor, and whatever description will convey the most to the grantee will be taken.

A case which arises with comparative frequency is this: A being the owner of "the northeast quarter of the northeast quarter of section ten," makes a deed or will in which he conveys or devises "the southeast quarter of the northeast quarter of section ten." He has no such property as he describes and never had, and we will assume that it is proved that he never intended to acquire it. Nevertheless, there is such a tract as is described. From all the surrounding circumstances it is clear that the "northeast quarter of the northeast quarter" was intended to be conveyed. Let us suppose that the grantor is now dead and that his heirs are claiming the northeast quarter of the northeast quarter as against the grantee or devisee. It seems clear that where there is some other expression in the deed or will which designates the land conveyed as "land which I now own," the courts are ready to find that the words actually used in fact describe the northeast quarter of the northeast quarter which the grantor or testator intended to convey (7). But when no such additional words appear, the courts, while clear as to what the testator meant by the words used, yet have difficulty in finding that the words used are such as will

(7)   Patch v. White, 117 U. S. 210.

actually bear the meaning attempted to be imposed upon them.

§ 14. **Boundaries on waters and on ways.** In many jurisdictions the ownership of the bed of rivers, even rivers navigable in fact, is in the riparian owner. If he owns on one side only he will usually own only one-half of the bed of the stream. It is usual also, especially in rural districts, for owners abutting on the highway to own to the center of the highway, subject to the rights of the public to use the strip as a highway. When the owner abutting on the river or the highway transfers his holding, it is very common either to leave it entirely ambiguous as to whether the fee to the middle of the way or river will pass, or else to use language which would seem to positively exclude any part of the way or the river. In the former case the rule is that the title to the center of the way or the river will pass. Thus if the grantor bounds the premises conveyed "along the river," or "by the river," or "along the way," the universal holding of the courts is that the title to the center of the river or the way will pass. If the grantor bounds "to an oak tree on the river," or "to a stake or stakes on the side of the way and thence along the river or along the way," it is generally held that the title to the center of the river or the way will still pass. Now suppose the grantor bounds "along the river *shore*" or "along the *side* of the highway." Here the authorities divide. In some jurisdictions the courts declare that the literal meaning of the words must be followed, and that the expressions used are too strong to cause the title to the center of the

stream or the highway to pass (8).   In others, the courts
insist that title to the center of the river or the way will
still pass, and declare that even stronger expressions
than the above must be used to prevent this result (9).
This rule is based upon the public policy which seeks to
prevent leaving a title outstanding to some strips of land
which are of no use to the grantor or his heirs, except to
annoy the grantee or his heirs or assigns whenever the
way is vacated or the river suddenly changes its course at
some remote time in the future.   It may be observed that
the alteration of the natural meaning of a man's words in
an instrument of conveyance on grounds of public policy is generally dangerous and unjustifiable.   While the
authorities are not all harmonious, it is held that rules of
construction which cause the title to the center of a way
to pass apply even though the way is not a public way,
but only a private way or intended way or street (10).

---

(8)   Starr v. Child, 20 Wend. (N. Y) 149; 4 Hill (N. Y.) 369; Buck
v. Squiers, 22 Vt. 484.

(9)   Sleeper v. Laconia, 60 N. H. 201; Salter v. Jonas, 39 N. J. L. 469.

(10)   Bissell v. New York Cen. R. R. Co., 23 N. Y. 61.

CHAPTER II.

ESTATES AND INTERESTS CREATED.

§ **15. Estates** created in both wills and deeds **considered.** While Part I of this article is devoted primarily to the transfer of title to real estate with the consent of the owner, excluding, however, transfers upon the death of the owner by descent or by will, nevertheless, with respect to estates created the same questions arise in deeds and wills and are in both sorts of instruments settled to so large an extent by the same rules, that it is advisable to treat the creation of estates in both instruments together.

§ **16. Classification** of estates. Estates in real property are commonly classified as follows: (A) Freehold, comprising (1) estates of inheritance [divided into (a) fee simple and (b) fee tail], and (2) life estates; (B) Less than freehold, comprising (1) estates for years, (2) estates from year to year, (3) estates at will, and (4) estates at sufferance. A further subdivision of estates tail and of life estates will be found in § 20 and § 23, below.

A freehold is an estate of uncertain duration, which may continue as long as some particular human life, and which is not terminable solely at the will of the grantor or owner of the reversion. See the article on History of Real Property, § 28, elsewhere in this volume. An estate of inheritance is a freehold which on the death of the owner will descend to his heirs if undisposed of by will. An estate for 1,000 years is not a freehold (save by statute), though much longer than a life, because its duration is not uncertain. An estate until A marries, or as long as he continues to dwell in a certain place, is a freehold because its duration is uncertain and it may also last as long as A's life.

SECTION 1.　CREATION OF PRESENT ESTATES.

§ 17.　**Fee simple. Use of word** "heirs." The most complete estate of ownership is known as a fee, or estate in fee simple. It is a freehold in perpetuity. It was formerly necessary in a deed, after the words of conveyance to the grantee, to add the words "and to his heirs," and if the word "heirs" was not used, only a life estate passed, no matter how clearly an absolute interest was intended and expressed (1). The rule was not quite so strict with respect to the creation of a fee simple in a will. There, if "heirs" was not used, a life estate was devised unless other words showed a contrary intent (2). Modern statutes have changed all this, so that a simple gift to A, whether by deed or will, prima facie is effective to confer a fee simple upon the grantee or devisee, and other words must be found to cut down the interest to a less estate. Conveyances to modern business corporations confer a fee without the use of any words beyond the name of the corporation. It is customary, however, to put after the words of conveyance to the corporation "and to its successors and assigns forever," so as to in-

---

(1)　Littleton, § 1.

(2)　Co. Lit. 9b, 10a.

dicate more clearly an intent to confer an absolute interest.

§ 18. **Fee tail.** A fee tail, or estate tail, is an estate which descends to the heirs of the body of the first grantee, and so on indefinitely to the heirs of the body of each taker so long as any such line of lineal heirs continues to exist. As originally permitted by the statute de donis of Edward I, it was absolutely inalienable by any tenant (holder) in tail for the time being, except for the life of that tenant in tail. During the fifteenth century, however, the English courts found a devious way of enabling the tenant in tail to turn the estate tail into a fee simple. By English legislation of the nineteenth century this method was simplified. In such jurisdictions of this country as still permit estates tail, a simple conveyance in fee by the tenant in tail will operate to transfer a fee simple. In most states statutes, which began in this country about a century ago, abolish estates tail entirely and declare that whatever would have been an estate tail according to the rules of the common law, shall be a fee simple. Other statutes provide that he who would have been a tenant in tail by the rules of the common law shall have a life estate, and that on his death the remainder shall pass in fee simple absolute to the person or persons to whom the estate tail would on the death of the donee in tail first pass "according to the course of the common law." Under this latter form of act a very strange result has been reached. By the course of the common law an estate tail descended, if the tenant in tail had a son, or several sons and daughters, to the eldest son. Such was the "course of the common law." Under the above statute, therefore, it would logically follow that where an estate tail was created the tenant in tail would have a life estate, and, upon his death leaving a large family of children, sons and daughters, the eldest son only would have the remainder in fee. Such is the result actually reached under the Missouri statute (3). In this way the rule of primogeniture has by accident been preserved.

§ 19. Same: **Use of** word "heirs." By the common law of England it was an absolute requirement for the creation of a fee tail by a deed that the word "heirs" should be used, followed by any words of procreation which limit heirs to the lineal descendants of the transferee (4). In wills the rule was more relaxed, and it was not absolutely necessary to use the word "heirs," but any form of expression which indicated an intent that the lineal descendant of the first taker should enjoy in infinitum, was sufficient to create an estate tail. These rules, it is believed, will be found to be still generally in force in this country.

§ 20. **Classes of estates tail.** There were several recognized divisions of estates tail (5). An estate in general tail was to A and the heirs of his body. Any children of the grantee or donee by any lawful wife might inherit it. An estate in special tail was to A and the heirs of his body by B, his wife. Children of A by another wife, or

(3)   Frame v. Humphreys, 164 Mo. 336; Burris v. Page, 12 Mo. 358.
(4)   Co. Lit. 20a, b.
(5)   Littleton, §§ 13-19, 21-24.

of B by another husband, could not inherit it. Estates in tail male were limited to male issue of the donee, and in tail female to female issue. These divisions might be combined, as an estate to A in general tail male, or one to A and B in special tail female.

§ 21. **Life estates.** Any words expressing an intent to confer upon a grantee or devisee an estate for the life of the grantee or devisee, or for the life of another, will be given effect. It should be noted, however, that life estates include much more than estates for the life of any individual, or the lives of any individuals, for if an estate is created for any uncertain period, which is not an estate terminable at the will of the grantor or reversioner, it is technically classed with life estates. Thus, an estate for so long as the possessor shall please, is technically classed with life estates and not with estates at will (6).

§ 22. **Life estates by implication.** Difficult and important questions arise as to whether a life estate has been created by implication. Thus, suppose there is a devise to B to take effect from and after the death of A, with no direct gift to A. Will a life estate be implied to A? The English judges of the eighteenth century and early part of the nineteenth century were much inclined to imply the gift of a life estate to A rather easily. As, however, they have become more exact in construing language, a tendency has developed to restrict the earlier holdings. Within the last twenty-five years the higher courts in England have drawn the line very rigidly upon the implication of life estates in the circumstances men-

(6)   Beeson v. Burton, 12 C. B. 647.

tioned. The rule now seems to be that no life estate in A will be implied where the gift "from and after the death of A" is to all the heirs of the testator and one outsider, or where the gift "after the death of A" is to all the heirs at law of the testator but one (7). The implication of a life estate is restricted to the one case where the gift from and after the death of A is to the *heirs of the testator,* and to them alone. The implication of a life estate in this one case is justified upon the ground that there is such an absurdity in the heirs who are expressly excluded until after the death of A coming in before that time, that a life estate must be implied to A in order to carry out the intention of the testator that his heirs at law shall not take until after the death of A. The rule seems to be settled that in this one case the life estate will be implied. In all others, no matter how nearly they may approximate the one case described, the English judges, at least, refuse to make any implication of a life estate. American courts would probably be more inclined to rely for a different result upon a special context in the will (8). But see §§ 76-77, below.

§ 23. **Classification of life estates.** Life estates are usually divided into two classes: (A) conventional (created by act of the parties), including (1) estates for the life of the grantee, and (2) estates pur autre vie (for another's life). (B) Legal (created by operation of law), including (1) curtesy, (2) dower, and (3) tenancy in special tail after possibility of issue is extinct. A grant to A for his life, when conveyed by A to B becomes in B's

(7)   Ralph v. Carrick, 11 Ch. Div. 873.

(8)   Anders v. Gerhard, 140 Pa. 153; Holton v. White, 23 N. J. L. 330.

possession an estate pur autre vie (for the life of A).
Estates by curtesy and dower are treated in §§ 137-38,
below. Upon a gift to A and the heirs of his body by B,
his wife, if B died without issue it is evident that the possibility of heirs within the limitation is extinct, and that
A's estate will now cease with his life. It is therefore
for certain purposes reduced to a life estate by operation
of law.

§ 24. **Estates for years, from year to year, at will, and
by sufferance.** An estate for years was a grant for any
definite period of time, long or short. An estate at will
was terminable at the will of either party. An estate by
sufferance is a mere holding over after the termination of
a previous right to possession. All of these are fully
treated in the article on Landlord and Tenant in Volume
IV of this work. The estate from year to year needs a
word of explanation. It is not improbable that at all
times in all countries the leases of small renters have
been made with the utmost informality. Formality costs
money, and the cheap tenancy will not bear the expense.
With ignorant or dependent tenants, the tendency is for
the landlord merely to let them into possession at a certain rental, with no terms as to the length of tenancy
being specified. On its face this must be regarded as a
tenancy at the will of both parties. Such a construction
of the transaction, however, may cause hardship to the
tenant, for he may be put out of possession at any time.
The English courts began very early to rule that when
the tenant paid rent by the year or by any aliquot part of
a year, as quarterly or half-yearly, the tenancy was one
from year to year, and that neither the tenant nor the

landlord could terminate the lease without giving six months' notice before the end of any yearly period (9). In the absence of such notice the tenancy was continuous, and the tenant protected. See the article on History of Real Property, § 32, elsewhere in this volume. More recently we have begun to have the tenancy from month to month, and even from week to week. These occur upon the taking of possession by a tenant and the paying of rent by the month or by the week, without any stipulation as to the termination of the tenancy. The notice here required is a whole month's notice (10), or a whole week's notice, before the end of any monthly or weekly period. See the article on Landlord and Tenant, §§ 111-12, in Volume IV of this work.

§ 25. **The "premises" and "habendum."** Instruments granting or conveying estates in describing the estate created customarily contained what were called "premises" and an "habendum." Thus, a conventional conveyance would read "to A and his heirs [these were the premises] to have and to hold to him and his heirs forever" [this last from the words "to have and to hold" being called habendum]. The premises had, it is believed, no special significance or efficacy in a will. But when the premises occurred in a deed it was a rule of somewhat ancient and technical character, that, if any inconsistency occurred between the premises and the habendum, the words of the premises must prevail. The application of this rule was to be found, of course, in informally drawn instruments which would read "to A and

---

(9) Right d. Flower v. Darby, 1 T. R. 159.

(10) Steffens v. Earl, 40 N. J. L. 128.

his heirs to have and to hold to A for life.'' Frequently there was much to induce the belief that the latter words expressed the real intent of the grantor. In fact, there is a natural inference that of two inconsistently expressed ideas the one contained in the clause which repeats in varied form what has gone before, is the one which really expresses the writer's intent. Such a principle is applied in construing inconsistent clauses in wills where the two cannot be reconciled, and it is thought unnecessary to invalidate the whole on the ground of uncertainty. The rule of law, however, with respect to the habendum in deeds seems to have been inexorable—in case of such an inconsistency as that just put, the premises must prevail, and A would be entitled to a fee simple and not to a life estate (11). There has, however, been much relaxation of this rule in this country, and our courts now seek to carry out what appears to have been the really expressed intent, with the result that the language of the habendum will not infrequently be found prevailing over the language of the premises (12).

§ 26. **Joint ownership.** The only joint interests now in common use are joint tenancies and tenancies in common. The joint tenancy has the attribute of causing the whole interest to remain in the hands of the surviving joint tenant when any joint tenant dies. Thus, if a conveyance be made to A, B and C as joint tenants, and A dies, B and C are joint tenants of the whole estate and A's heirs or devisees take nothing. When B dies C has

---

(11) Winter v. Gorsuch, 51 Md. 180.
(12) Miller v. Mowers, 227 Ill. 392.

the whole estate, and on C's death the title passes by descent to his heirs, or by devise according to his will. On the other hand, when A, B, and C are tenants in common, each has an undivided separate interest which upon his death he may devise, or which will pass to his heirs by descent. It should be observed that one joint tenant during his life may alienate his share, and his alienee then becomes a tenant in common with the remaining joint tenants, who still remain joint tenants as between themselves. The alienee might then transfer back to his alienor, who then would be a tenant in common with the other tenants. This was known as "severing" the joint tenancy. It was resorted to for the purpose of obtaining the benefits of the separate ownership which the tenancy in common afforded.

Nowadays joint tenancy is usually desired where title is taken by a husband and wife, and where each desires the other to have the real estate in case he or she dies first. In such cases it is most convenient to convey to both as joint tenants. Where, however, the grantees are husband and wife it may satisfy their desires to become tenants by the entirety, which is like joint tenancy only that there is no right of severance and one spouse alone can convey no interest without the joinder of the other. The nature of estates by the entirety and whether they can be created, is considered in another place. See the article on Domestic Relations and Persons, § 36, in Volume II of this work. In making a conveyance to one or more persons it should always be specified whether the estate is to be a joint tenancy or a tenancy in common. If nothing is stated the inference now is that a tenancy in common is meant, though the old common law rule was otherwise. To create a joint tenancy it is necessary therefore to say in terms that A and B are to hold as joint tenants. Conveyancers frequently add the words ''and not as tenants in common.''

Other forms of joint ownership are co-parcenery and partnership. Co-parcenery is like tenancy in common except that it must be created or continued by descent. Any other form of transfer turns it into a tenancy in common. Partnership is a form of joint tenancy, the special characteristics of which are discussed in the article on Partnership in Volume VIII of this work.

SECTION 2. CREATION OF EASEMENTS.

§ 27. **Quasi easements.** Closely associated with the creation of estates by deed is that of the creation of easements in deeds transferring title to a part of the estate belonging to the grantor, while the grantor retains the balance. Suppose, for instance, that A is the owner of lots one and two and uses a way for his residence on lot one over lot two to the highway thus:

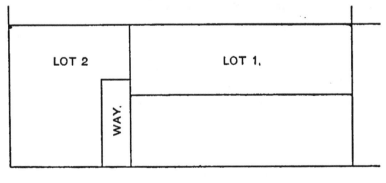

The way from lot one over lot two is not an easement, because of the unity of title in A. A cannot have an easement over his own land. The user, however, of the way in connection with lot one and over the other is very properly called for convenience a quasi easement, and lot one is the quasi dominant estate and lot two the quasi servient estate. See the article on Rights in Land of Another, §§ 30, 36, in Volume IV of this work.

§ 28. Conveyance of quasi dominant estate. If A conveys lot one to B, it is important that B have the same right to use the way over lot two that A always had. Otherwise he may have no access to the highway. The proper course for B to pursue is to require A in his deed expressly to grant him a right of way over a defined strip to the highway. It will be enough, however, if A grant to B as appurtenant to lot one "all ways as then used and enjoyed" (13). But it will not be a sufficient express grant of an easement to B to convey to B lot one "together with all and singular the hereditaments and appurtenances thereunto belonging" (see note 13). Suppose, then, that A uses insufficient words to create an express easement in favor of lot one over lot two. Under certain circumstances B will nevertheless have such an easement by operation of law without words. Thus, in the case put, if B upon taking lot one would be left without any right of access to the highway, unless he has a way over lot two, so that the way is what may be called a way of necessity, B will secure the easement of the right

---

(13)   Saunders v. Olifi, Moore, 467.

of way by operation of law without words (14). If in
our original case the way is not one of necessity to lot one
because of another highway at the back of lot one, still B
will have an easement or right of way over lot two by
operation of law, provided the way over lot two was in
fact used continuously and apparently by A before and at
the time of the conveyance to B (15).

§ 29. Conveyance of quasi servient estate. If A conveys lot two to B, it is important for A himself to secure
the grant of an easement to himself from B at the time
B becomes by the conveyance the owner of the quasi servient estate. The safe and proper way to do this is to use
a deed, in form an indenture, containing a distinct grant
to the party of the first part of an easement over lot two
by the party of the second part (the grantee of lot two)
in favor of lot one, and then to have this deed signed and
sealed by the grantee as well as the grantor. In this way
the grantee B, by the same instrument by which he receives title to lot two, duly and properly creates an easement over it in favor of the owner of lot one. In this
country, however, it is believed that such care and exactness in conveyancing is unusual, especially in rural districts, and grantors like A are accustomed to execute
deeds poll signed and sealed by themselves alone, merely
reserving to themselves an easement over the lot conveyed. The theoretical difficulty with this sort of an instrument is that easements generally can be created only
by instruments under seal or at least by a writing signed

(14)   Clark v. Cogge, Cro. Jac. 170.
(15)   Martin v. Murphy, 221 Ill. 632; Watts v. Kelson, L. R. 6 Ch. 166.

by the person creating the easement. Since the real character of the transaction between A and B demands the grant back of an easement by the grantee, no easement can be created without his seal and signature, or at least without his signature. In England this theoretical difficulty is insurmountable and the seal at least of the grantee is essential, and no easement is created by mere words of reservation on the part of the grantor without also the seal of the grantee (16). In this country, however, the efficacy of the words of reservation to create the easement in favor of the grantor is very generally recognized, although there is no seal or signature on the part of the grantee (17). One jurisdiction at least in this country gives effect to the words of reservation where there is no seal or signature of the grantee, only providing the user of the quasi easement existed at and before the time of the conveyance from A to B (18).

§ 30. **Same: Creation of easement by operation of law.** Even, however, where no words at all are used the easement may be created in favor of the grantor by operation of law. This occurs where the easement is one of necessity (19). Where the easement is not one of necessity the English cases require that the user of the quasi easement exist before and at the time of the conveyance by A to B, and that the user of it by A be continuous, apparent

---

(16)   Gale on Easements (7th ed.), 71.

(17)   Haggerty v. Lee, 54 N. J. L. 580; Druecker v. McLaughlin, 235 Ill. 367.

(18)   Ashcroft v. Eastern Ry. Co., 126 Mass. 196.

(19)   Packer v. Welsted, 2 Sid. 39, 111.

and reciprocal (20). This last element would exist in the case put if the right of way in question, instead of running wholly on lot two, ran to the highway one-half on lot two and one-half on lot one—that is to say, along the boundary line between the two lots. In this way the user of the way would be reciprocal, i. e., the user of the way by the owner of lot one would involve the user of the land of lot two, and the user of the way by the owner of lot two would involve the user of the land of lot one. Many jurisdictions in this country require the same elements (21). The reason for requiring the element of reciprocal use in the case of implied reservation or grant back, and not in the case of implied grant, is that the deed must be taken most strongly against the grantor, and that he cannot be permitted so easily to derogate from his conveyance by the creation of an easement in himself in the property granted as he can to grant an easement over his own land by implication in favor of the land granted. But many American jurisdictions hold that it is enough to cause the creation of an easement by operation of law in the grantor, if the quasi easement was continuous and apparent, thus refusing to recognize any distinction between implied reservation and implied grant of an easement (22).

---

(20)   Union Lighterage Co. v. London Graving Dock Co., L. R. (1902) 2 Ch. 557.

(21)   Mitchell v. Seipel, 53 Md. 251; Wells v. Garbutt, 132 N. Y. 430; Toothe v. Bryce, 50 N. J. Eq. 589.

(22)   Powers v. Heffernan, 233 Ill. 597; Geible v. Smith, 146 Pa. 276; Fremont v. Gayton, 67 Neb. 263.

SECTION 3. CREATION OF FUTURE INTERESTS.

§ 31. Classes of future interests. Future interests in land are those not at present enjoyed in actual possession, but which may be, if at all, some time in the future. The future interests recognized by the common law were reversions, remainders, rights of entry and possibilities of reverter, and the marital rights of dower and curtesy. A *reversion* was the estate left in a party after he had conveyed away less than a fee, as in a transfer by X to A for life or for years. X has a reversion after the termination of A's estate. After a reversion has been thus created it may be transferred by X to another and will remain a reversion. A *remainder* was an estate created by the same transfer as a preceding estate and taking effect immediately upon the termination of that estate. There could be several successive remainders. A transfer by X to A for life, then to B for life, and then to C in fee, creates remainders in B and C. A *right of entry* and *possibility of reverter* were not estates, but were rights that might produce estates. A transfer by X to A in fee, on condition liquor is never sold on the premises, gives X and his heirs a right to regain the estate by entering on it for condition broken. A similar transfer to A until liquor shall be sold on the premises revests the land in X, without entry, as soon as liquor is sold. This is a possibility of reverter. For dower and curtesy see §§ 137-38, below.

§ 32. Vested and contingent future interests. A remainder is "vested," as the phrase goes, if, throughout its continuance, A, or A and his heirs, have the right to immediate possession, whenever and however the preceding estates may determine (22a). Reversions are always vested. No other future interests are always vested. Remainders may be vested or contingent (see § § 38-39, below). A transfer to A for life, or for ten years, then to B for life or years, and then to C in fee, gives vested remainders to B and C. There are no conditions precedent to their rights to immediate possession as soon as the preceding estates end. B may die before A, and so never actually enjoy his life estate, but this is only because his life estate itself has come to an end. "Throughout the continuance" of B's life estate there was no condition precedent to his right to possession, except the existence of the preceding estate in A. A transfer to A and his heirs until B's marriage, and then to B, gives B a contingent remainder, subject to the condition precedent of his marriage. So, a transfer to A for life, remainder to the first son (now unborn) of B. Until B's son is born the remainder is contingent. As soon as he is born it vests in him, and takes effect in possession at the end of A's life estate. Rights of entry and possibilities of reverter are, of course, always contingent interests.

§ 33. Modern freedom to create future interests. The alienability of future interests has already been somewhat discussed (§§ 8-9, above). The more interesting and difficult question is how far future interests can be created at all, so that the transferee who is to enjoy in the future will be entitled when the time arrives. At the present day the layman may safely start with the idea

---

(22a) Gray, Rule Against Perpetuities (2d ed.), § 101.

that he can create any sort of future interest which he desires. The land is his. It is his natural idea, confirmed in him by the spirit of the law today, that he can create such interests in it as he pleases, subject only to restrictions imposed by modern public policy (§§ 59-71, below).

Thus, you can transfer to A a fee simple, subject to a condition of forfeiture upon the happening of which the transferor or his heirs will be entitled to possession again as the full owner in fee (23). Such conditions of forfeiture are of everyday occurrence in the ordinary lease for years. You can give an interest to A, and then to B, and then to C. A's interest may be a life estate or a term for years, with an interest after A's death or at the end of the term to B; or B may take on the contingency that A die without any child surviving him or upon any other contingency, with the exceptions hereinafter mentioned (§§ 59-71, below). A's interest may be a fee simple, and B's may take effect in the event that A dies without issue, him surviving, or upon any other condition or contingency, subject to those exceptions. An interest may be conveyed to B to take effect contingently or at a certain time in the future, without any previous interest being expressly conferred at all; or A may be given a life estate for a term of years, and it may be provided that a year after A's death B shall be entitled.

§ 34. **Same: Further illustrations.** Even stranger things than these may be done. Land may be transferred to such persons and in such estates as A shall ap-

---

(23) Gray v. Chicago, Mil. & St. P. Ry., 189 Ill. 400.

point, and upon A's appointment the appointee will take the title appointed. A rather striking use of this power of appointment was made in England, when land owners desired to retain the title to their properties free from the necessity of obtaining the wife's waiver of dower in case the land owner conveyed his estates during the wife's lifetime. The result desired was obtained in this way: A, being the owner in fee of Blackacre, and about to marry, would, prior to the marriage, convey to himself in fee with full power to appoint by deed or will, and in default of appointment, to himself in fee simple. He then married. His wife became entitled to dower in the property which he owned in fee simple, but upon his appointment, A was not obliged to secure the wife's waiver of that dower, because the appointee took by virtue of the original instrument which created the power and this was made before A was married, and hence was not subject to the dower interest of any wife (24). So, a title may be conveyed to A with power in the grantor to revoke at any time and, upon revocation, A will lose his title and the transferor will have it again. Land may be transferred to A and his children born and to be born, and the children as thereafter born will come in and share the estate. A land owner may even transfer to himself an estate. Of course there is no object in this unless the transferor desires to create a power of appointment in himself, as in the example above given, where A was seeking to cut his future wife's dower interest off, or unless he desires to confer upon himself a life estate with future

---

(24)   Sugden on Powers (8th ed.), 144.

interests in others. The usual case which one meets in practice is where the grantor conveys to his children, reserving to himself a life estate. In short, it seems as if every possible vagary in the creation of interests in land that a grantor or testor could think of might be validly created—always provided, however, that there are observed certain limits to be hereafter mentioned (§§ 59-71, below).

§ 35. **Early importance of seisin of land.** This great freedom in the creation of future interests which we enjoy today is a unique attribute of English law. It is the result of an evolution in the English law of real property continuing from the middle ages to the present time. In the middle ages when feudalism still prevailed in England, the seisin, or possession of land by one claiming a freehold (§ 16, above), was of very great importance. He who had it even had claims to consideration at the hands of the law as against one out of possession who today would be called the rightful owner. In other words, far more than today the person in possession claiming a freehold, even wrongfully, was preferred to the rightful owner. The reason for this is not difficult to understand. The feudal system depended upon the rendering of the feudal services and the payment of the feudal dues by the feudal tenant in possession. The exacting of those services and dues could be enforced practically only against those in actual possession of the freehold. This possession or seisin, therefore, carried with it feudal burdens. It was not unnatural, therefore, that what today we call the absolute ownership should be less important; that actual possession, under a claim of freehold, and the performance of the feudal duties was more important; and that the law should protect the latter much further than it does today.

§ 36. **Creation of future freeholds limited by necessity** of livery of seisin. As livery of seisin (formal putting in possession—§ 6, above), was necessary to the transfer of a freehold, X could not directly transfer to A an estate for life or in fee to begin five years from that date. He could transfer a term of five years to P, followed by a freehold remainder to A, by making livery of seisin at once to P on behalf of A. A thus obtained a present seisin, and P was his tenant. Successive future estates after a freehold were not open to this objection, as the seisin was transferred to the first freehold tenant for the benefit of all succeeding estates created at the same time, and passed to each successive owner as he came into actual possession of the land.

§ 37. **Feudal objections to creation of future interests.** While seisin was so important an element in the feudal system, it was natural that few, if any, future interests should have been permitted. It was natural that no future interest should be permitted which left a gap between a present estate in possession and a future interest. Thus, if an estate were given to A for life, and five years after A's death to B, the estate in B was entirely invalid. During the five years there would be no one to perform the feudal duties, and, if this might be so for five years, it might be so for longer. It was no answer to this to say that the creator of the interests would have the right to possession during the interval, for, even if he had this right, there was no probability that he would exercise it and assume the feudal burdens for any such temporary occupation; and, even if he did, the disorder likely to ensue upon his being forced at the end of the five years to give up his possession and seisin to the one next entitled, was to be avoided if possible. The feudal rule became firmly established that interests to take effect in possession in the future after a gap were wholly void from the start (25). If the attempted creation of estates were to A in fee and if A died without issue him surviving to B in fee, there was not a gap between the two estates, but a lapping over of the second estate upon the first. This was objectionable from the feudal point of view because if the first taker took possession and performed the feudal duties, there was a fair probability of trouble when his heirs at the end of his life were asked to give up the estate to B. If A did not take possession and perform the feudal duties for the possibly short and precarious term of his life, then there was a gap in the seisin or possession and a consequent failure in the performance of feudal services and dues. Hence, any future interest which overlapped upon or interrupted the preceding interest in possession was wholly void. It followed from these feudal principles that there could be no such thing as the creation of a future interest by the exercise of a power, and that a conveyance to A and his children born and to be born, would be wholly ineffective as to children born after the conveyance took effect.

---

(25)   Buckler v. Hardy, Cro. El. 585.

§ **38. Vested future interests unobjectionable.** One sort of future interest was, however, unobjectionable. That was an interest after a life estate, which, by the expressed provision of the creator of it, stood ready at all times during the continuance of the life estate to take effect in possession, whenever and however the preceding estate determined. This was a vested remainder (§ 32, above). Thus, estates might be created to A for life, with remainder to B and his heirs. Here there is no possibility of a gap between A's and B's interests and no possibility of a lapping-over. B's interest stands ready to take effect, whenever and however the preceding estate determines. Thus, the objection of the feudal system to future interests of the sort above described were avoided.

§ **39. Introduction of contingent remainders. Their destructibility.** Suppose now that the interests attempted to be created were to A for life and then to A's eldest child if he reaches twenty-one. Here the interest in the child of A does not as expressly limited, stand ready at all times to take effect in possession whenever and however the preceding life estate determines, for if A dies before his child reaches twenty-one there would be the same sort of a gap as in the case first put. On the other hand, in the case first put there is the absolute certainty of this gap, while in the case of the interests limited to the eldest son of A if he reaches twenty-one, there is a chance that there will be no gap, for the son may reach twenty-one before the termination of A's life estate. Up to 1430 the feudal law refused to recognize the validity of the interest to A's eldest son in the case put, and held it wholly void because of a possibility that a gap might occur. No doubt this was in accord with the strict spirit of the feudal system. But by 1430 feudalism as a system was weakened and declining, and the modern policy of carrying out the intent of the landowner in creating estates was gaining strength. In 1430, therefore, it is not surprising to find the rule promulgated that the interest in A's oldest son provided he reached twenty-one, would be valid providing the event upon which the interest was to take effect in possession happened before or at the time of the termination of A's life estate (26). In short, the future interest was valid if, before or at the time of the termination of the previous life estate, it came into a position where it stood ready to take effect in possession, whenever and however the preceding estate determined; thereby becoming in all respects like the future interests which the feudal system had always regarded as valid. In time the form of the rule was changed to this: The interest in the eldest son of A as put above would fail or was void unless the event upon which it was limited happened before or at the time of the termination of the preceding estate. This was familiarly called the rule of destructibility of contingent remainders. The later history of this rule and its abolition by modern statutes is hereafter considered (§§ 46-47).

§ 40. **Future interests created by trusts before statute of uses.** Such, then, was the feudal law with regard to the validity of future interests. It only remains in this

---

(26)   21 Law Quar. Rev. 118, 125.

brief historical sketch to indicate how the future interest after a gap, or limited so as to overlap the preceding interest, which the feudal law refused in any way to recognize, became possible by means of trusts before the statute of uses of Henry VIII, and how they became valid legal estates by virtue of that statute.

While the feudal law of real property was being administered by the law courts of England in all its strictness, there grew up beside it and inimical to it, the practice of creating trusteeships. The feudal legal title was placed in A, B, and C as joint tenants in fee, but they were directed to hold this legal title to the use of certain persons, or upon trust for certain purposes specified. At first these trusts were enforced by no secular authority whatsoever, but, by the time of Henry VI, the king's authority as exercised by his chancellor, was used to compel the trustees to carry out the terms of the trusts. The scope and object of these trusts were numerous, and not to be described here. It is sufficient to say that the beneficial interests were not subject to feudal rules. Hence, where the trustees were directed to hold for the benefit of B after five years from date; or for the benefit of A for life, and one year after A's death for B in fee; or for A absolutely, and if he died without issue him surviving, then for B absolutely; or where the trustees were directed to hold to such uses as the creator of the trust should by his last will appoint these trusts would be carried out according to the intention of the creator of them, although as legal estates they were forbidden by the feudal rules.

§ **41. Effect of statute of uses (1536).** In 1535 there was passed the statute of uses, which in substance declared that whenever a trustee was seized of the legal title to the use of another, that other should have the legal estate to the extent that he had the use or beneficial interest. By this act what was, before the statute of uses, an equitable estate or trust, became a legal estate. Therefore, where the land was conveyed to X and his heirs to the use of B after five years from date; or to the use of A for life, and one year after A's death to B and his heirs; after the statute of uses B had a valid legal estate beginning in the future, or taking effect after a gap, though in direct contravention of the principles of the feudal law. So, if after the statute of uses the conveyance was made to X and his heirs to the use of A and his heirs, but if A died without issue him surviving, then to B and his heirs, again B would have a legal future interest taking effect by way of interruption or overlapping upon A's estate and in direct contravention of feudal principles. But the landowner could dispense with the conveyance to a third party, such as X, and could covenant to stand seized of the land to the use of A for life, and one year after A's death to B and his heirs; or for A and his heirs, and if A died without issue him surviving to B and his heirs; and by force of the statute in both cases A and B would have the legal estates limited, in direct contravention of the principles of the feudal law. To the validity, however, of a covenant to stand seized it was necessary either that the covenant should be under seal and in favor of a blood relation, or that there should be a money consideration actually paid or expressed to be paid. It was but a step from this to the rule of construction that any deed (under seal) purporting a direct conveyance to a blood relation, or, if not, containing the recital of a money consideration, was to be construed as a covenant to stand seized, if necessary in order to carry out the expressed intent (27). Hence, if an ordinary deed such as is in use today, under seal and with the recital of a consideration of one dollar in hand paid, purports to convey an estate to A for life, and one year after A's death to B in fee; or to A in fee, and if A die without issue him surviving to B in fee; it may, if necessary to give validity to the estates attempted to be created, be read as a covenant to stand seized to the use of A for life, and one year after A's death to B and his heirs; or as a covenant to stand seized to the use of A and his heirs, and if A die without issue him surviving to B and his heirs. Upon precisely the same reasoning, by the ordinary deed in common use today powers of appointment may be created, and, when the appointment is made, a legal estate by way of appointment will be created. So, a deed purporting to convey to A and his children born and to be born, is valid to let in to the benefits of the conveyance after-born children of A. For a full account of the effect of the statute of uses upon conveyancing, see the article on History of Real Property, §§ 37-40, elsewhere in this volume.

§ 42. **Effect** of statute of wills (1540). But this freedom in the creation of future interests would have been still very much restricted had it been confined only to

(27) Roe v. Tranmer, 2 Wils. 75.

the creation by deed of such future interests as the feudal law would not permit. To complete the freedom in the creation of such future interests it was necessary that the rules which obtained in conveyances inter vivos to uses under the statute of uses should prevail also where the estates were created by will. This was accomplished, for no sooner were devises of land permitted by will, by the statute of wills of Henry VIII in 1540, than the same liberty with respect to the creation of future interests created by will was permitted as obtained in the case of conveyances to uses.

Prior to the time of Charles II it is probable that the creation of future interests such as were prohibited by the feudal law were not common. About the time of Charles II, however, the beginnings of modern English conveyancing began to appear and from then to the present time there has been a constantly increasing enjoyment of freedom in the creation of future estates.

§ 43. Classification of future interests arising under statutes of uses and of wills. Where a future interest took effect under the statute of uses just as a common law remainder would, that is, exactly at the determination of the preceding estates, it was variously called a "future use," a "contingent use," and a "use by way of remainder." The same rules were applicable to it as to ordinary remainders, including, if it were contingent, its destructible character. When a future use of a freehold was limited to begin in the future, or after a gap following some precedent estate, it was called a "springing use." When it cut short a preceding estate by overlapping it (§37, above) it was called a "shifting use." Similarly, devises that could take effect like common law remainders did so, with all the usual incidents of remainders, and were often called "devises by way of remainder." Devises that could not take effect as remainders, but were analogous to springing and shifting uses, were called "executory devises."

SECTION 4. MODERN LIMITATIONS UPON CREATION OF FUTURE ESTATES.

§ 44. **Classification of such limitations.** The principal obstacles to an owner's complete freedom to create future interests in land as he pleases, today, are as follows: 1. Some survivals from the feudal system of land law. 2. Difficulties of construction due to ambiguous language in creating complicated interests. 3. The rule against perpetuities. 4. Rules making invalid conditions by way of forfeiture and restraints on alienation. These will be considered separately below.

A. *Feudal survivals.*

§ 45. **Rule in Shelley's case.** There are still left as historical survivals from the middle ages some rules which are founded upon no sound public policy today, and which defeat the grantor's or testator's clearly expressed intention. For instance, formerly most famous —now most notorious—the rule in Shelley's case, which dates back to the year 1324. That rule is that where a life estate is given to A, with a future interest to A's heirs (the use of the particular word "heirs" being necessary), the whole gift is construed as one "to A and his heirs," at once giving an estate to A in fee. In 1769

Lord Mansfield tried to turn this into a rule of construction which would give way if the grantor or testator was sufficiently emphatic about saying that he intended A to have only a life estate (28). But Lord Mansfield was overruled and the rule in Shelley's case remains what it always was, a rule defeating the testator's intent; and today no matter how clear it is that A is intended to have only a life estate, if the rule applies, A will have the fee. In many states the rule in Shelley's case has been abolished by statute. Conveyancers, however, are apt to like it because by it inconvenient future interests can be gotten rid of and an absolute title vested in a living person, usually of age, who has a marketable title to dispose of.

§ 46. Rule of destructibility of contingent remainders. By what is known as the rule of destructibility of contingent remainders, if A has a legal life estate and B has a legal future interest after A's life estate, which is not to take effect in possession until a certain contingency has happened, which may happen either before, or at the time of, or after the termination of A's life estate; then, unless the event happens at or before the termination of A's life estate, B's future interest is void (§ 39, above). Thus, if a wife be given a life estate by will with a future interest to such of her children as reach twenty-one, and the wife dies before any child has reached twenty-one, the gift to the children is void; or if the wife has a life estate and the gift after her death is to such children of hers as survive her, and the wife's life estate is

---

(28)   Perrin v. Blake, 1 W. Bl. 672.

prematurely terminated before her death by being forfeited, the gift to her children will fail. This rule also is
of feudal origin and dates back to the fifteenth century. It
has been abolished in England wholly since 1877, and in
many states of the Union at an earlier date. Some courts
have refused to apply it even in the absence of statute (29). Yet it is likely applied even today in jurisdictions where it has not been formally eliminated by the
legislature (30).

Of course, this rule of destructibility of contingent remainders is a rule which absolutely and unequivocally
defeats the intention of the testator or settlor. The case
which resulted in its total abolition in England is striking
proof of this. In Cunliffe v. Brancker the limitations were
in substance to A for life and then to such of A's children
as survived A and his wife B. A died first. An eminent
English equity judge held that the gift to the children
entirely failed (31). So great was the popular outcry at
so harsh and unjust a rule that Parliament at once passed
an act to abolish the rule of destructibility.

§ 47. Use made of rule in resettling estates. If, however, this rule be in force, it may at times be taken advantage of to effect convenient results without doing injustice to any one. Suppose, for instance, a testator devises the legal title of lands to his daughter for life and
then to such of her children as survive her in fee. The
daughter has a life estate with a contingent remainder in

---

(29) Hayward v. Spaulding, 71 Atl. 219 (N. H.).
(30) Bond v. Moore, 236 Ill. 576.
(31) 3 Chan. Div. 393.

fee to her children. The reversion will descend in the
meantime to the testator's heirs at law, who are, we will
assume, the daughter and her brother. If then the daughter and brother will convey all their reversionary interest
and the daughter her life estate to any third party, the
life estate will "merge" (32) in the reversion in fee and
terminate prematurely before the death of the daughter.
The contingent remainder in fee in the children of the
daughter will then be destroyed under the usual rule of
destructibility. The third party will thus obtain the entire fee, and according, of course, to a previous arrangement, he will then proceed to re-settle the property by a
conveyance to trustees with full powers of sale, etc., to
hold for the benefit of the daughter for life and then to
such of her children as survive her in fee, and in default
of such children, then to herself and her brother in fee
equally as tenants in common—i. e., exactly as the beneficial interests were indicated under the will of the testator. The only difference will be that while under the will
the title was in impossible shape for purposes of alienation or mortgaging to make improvements, under the re-
settlement the trustees will have such powers as will enable them to deal to the greatest advantage with the legal
title, either selling it, if a good price is offered, and in-
vesting the proceeds, or mortgaging it to make necessary
improvements, and otherwise having that control of disposition which is frequently necessary to the profitable
management of an estate.

---

(32) Merger is the absorption of a less estate into a greater when
held by the same owner.

§ 48. **Pseudo feudal rules invalidating future interests.**
From unfamiliarity with the history and principles of
the law of future interests, courts even in recent times
occasionally promulgate rules which defeat the testator's
or grantor's clearly expressed intention. Thus, some respectable courts today, following a decision of Chancellor
Kent of New York, hold that when the limitations are to
A in fee, with a gift to B if A dies intestate (i.e., without
having transferred the title by deed or will), B's interest
is absolutely void (33). No reason, either in history or
logic, can be perceived for this arbitrary and unjustifiable
rule. At least one court has held that a conveyance by
deed to A in fee, and, if A die without children him surviving, to B in fee, gives B no interest whatever (34);
and the same court decided that a conveyance to "A and
his heirs, born and to be born," likewise conferred no
interest upon the after-born children of A (35). Such
holdings as these are also without justification.

B. *Difficulties of Construction.*

§ 49. **Carelessly drawn instruments.** The drafting of
a coherent scheme of future interests is a work of art, requiring very great experience and training. The inex-
perienced or ignorant will raise in a few words trouble-
some questions of construction, which may result in much
expense to the estate afterwards to settle. One of the
shortest wills that ever came to the writer's attention
raised the greatest number of difficult questions and was

(33) Wolfer v. Hemmer, 144 Ill. 554; Jackson v. Robins, 16 Johns.
(N. Y.) 537.

(34) Palmer v. Cook, 159 Ill. 300.

(35) Morris v. Caudle, 178 Ill. 9; Miller v. McAlister, 197 Ill. 72.

subject to the most bitter litigation. It was executed by
a mother who merely devised "all my property to my
son A, for life, and then, if he die without issue, to my
heirs at law." Upon this will the following questions
arose: (1) Did the son take as one of the testatrix's
heirs at law, if he died without issue (§§ 57-58, below)?
(2) Did "die without issue" mean die without issue in
the testatrix's life or after her death (§§ 53-54, below)?
(3) If "die without issue" meant die without issue after
the testatrix's death, did it mean an indefinite failure of
issue, so as to make the gift to "heirs" void for remoteness as to the personalty, and give the son an estate tail
as to the realty which a statute would then turn into something else (§§ 57-58, below)? (4) If "die without issue"
did not mean an indefinite, but only a definite failure of
issue, was there a gift by implication to any issue which
the son might have, or did the property descend to the
testatrix's heirs at law at her death, including the son if
he died leaving children or issue? (5) If the issue of the
son did have an interest by implication, was it contingent upon their surviving the son, or not? (6) If
any implied gift to the son's issue were contingent upon
such issue surviving the son, could that interest, together
with the gift to heirs of the testatrix if the life tenant died
without issue, be destroyed by the premature termination
of the life estate by uniting it to the reversion to the testatrix's heirs, pending the happening of the events upon
which the future interests were limited (§ 46, above)?
The reader may not understand or appreciate all of these
difficulties but they will perhaps convince him that there
are terrors even in a will of the fewest possible words.

§ 50. **Same: Further illustrations.** The instances of prominent lawyers, who have drawn their own wills so as to raise questions which were the subject of long and costly litigation to settle, are numerous. Samuel J. Tilden's will was the subject of a great deal of important litigation in New York (36). A prominent lawyer of Chicago a few years ago, who drew his will in his own hand, after creating a trust fund for the benefit of his wife during her life in a fifth of the estate, then devised the residue of his property from and after his wife's death to his children. Thereupon ensued litigation as to whether the children could take immediately as to so much of the residue as the wife did not have a life estate in, and only after her death as to that which she did have a life estate in; or whether the distribution of the entire estate must await the death of the widow; and, if so, what became of the income of four-fifths of the estate in the meantime. Did the widow have a life estate by implication, or did the income pass as intestate property, not being devised at all; or should it accumulate and be added to the principal?

A few of the more important and usual questions of construction which even good lawyers are apt to raise in drafting deeds or wills are worthy of brief mention.

§ 51. **Effect of words of condition.** The words "on condition" are often so used as to make it ambiguous whether an estate on condition is meant or merely a promissory obligation on the part of the transferee of the land. Suppose, for instance, the conveyance be made "on the

---

(36) Tilden v. Green, 130 N. Y. 29.

express condition that the grantee shall not build upon the premises nearer than ten feet to the front lot line.'' Does this mean that the estate is subject to a condition of forfeiture upon the breach, or does it mean merely that the grantee accepting the deed with such a clause, agrees that he will not build nearer than ten feet to the front line? The difference in result is very great. The grantee can borrow money on his title in the latter case, but not usually in the former—to say nothing of the difference between the grantee having his title taken away from him and merely being sued to enforce the agreement. Yet the language is ambiguous. The court leans against its being construed as a condition, yet the use of the word ''condition'' stares the court in the face and makes it difficult to say that a condition of forfeiture was not meant.

It should always be made clear whether a condition or a promissory obligation is intended. If the former is desired always add a clause of re-entry giving the grantor in express terms a right to re-enter and forfeit the estate of the grantee in case of breach. If a promissory obligation only is intended, omit the word ''condition'' entirely and put it plainly that the grantee covenants. Sometimes the point whether a condition or a covenant is meant is left ambiguous from design. The grantor knows that if he puts in a straight condition of forfeiture with a re-entry clause, the grantee cannot be induced to become a purchaser. The grantor then puts in all the words of condition he can without frightening the purchaser, and, having sold his lots, holds an extra club over the purchaser by insisting that he may forfeit the title upon the breach of what he calls a ''condition.'' If this will not suffice he at least has a promissory. obligation of the grantee which he can enforce.

§ 52. **Conditions of survivorship.** Grantors and testators in creating future interests often fail to make it clear whether the future interest is to take effect at a specified time and subject to no other contingency except the arrival of the time specified, or only if the person who is to take *survives* that future time. Thus, suppose A be given a life estate with a future interest to B in fee. If B is to take at all events and he die before A, then B's heirs or devisees will take in B's place at A's death, but if B is to take only if he survive A, then, if he die before A, his heirs and devisees can never take. There is no more fruitful source of litigation over questions of construction of wills than whether B is given an interest dependent upon his surviving A or not. All sorts of ambiguous phrases creep in owing to the testator or grantor contemplating that of course B will survive A and will take in that event, without remembering that events may turn out the other way; and that, if they do, it is necessary to make it clear what the testator or grantor intends shall happen.

§ 53. **Difficulties with the phrase ''if A die without issue.''** Grantors and testators frequently, after a gift to A, make a gift to B in fee, provided ''A dies without issue.'' This simple little phrase is filled with difficulties. First, there is the question what period ''die'' is to be referred to. Is it die before the testator's death without issue, or after the testator's death without issue? If the latter, is it die without issue surviving at the death of A, or does it mean when A is dead without issue in any generation hereafter, so that if A die today and his issue do not become extinct until the tenth generation hereafter, he will only then be dead without issue or have died without issue? What the layman usually means is that "if A die either before or after the death of the testator without issue him surviving at that time." This should always be fully expressed, for a long line of English and American cases support a meaning to the expression "die without issue" which is contrary to the sense in which most testators probably use it. Thus, if the gift be of real and personal property to A for life and, if A die without issue, to B absolutely; "die without issue" means die without issue either before or after the testator's death. But "die without issue" also has, under the line of decisions mentioned, been held to mean die without issue in any generation. This makes the gift of personal property to B void by reason of the application of the rule against perpetuities (§ 60, below). As to the real estate, another rule of construction applies which turns A's life estate into an estate tail and makes B's interest a valid future interest after an estate tail, but subject to be destroyed by A's turning his estate tail into a fee simple (§ 18, above).

§ 54. **Same: Statutory interpretations.** Of course, under the modern statutes in this country which abolish estates tail, such rules as those just mentioned applying to real estate are utterly incongruous. Why use an artificial rule which practically always defeats the testator's express intention, for the purpose of producing an estate tail which a statute turns into something else, so that you obtain ultimately a result doubly removed from the testator's expressed intent? Legislators in many states have seen the absurdity to which the old construction of the phrase "die without issue" results, and have passed statutes which declare that the phrase "die without issue" shall primarily mean a definite failure of issue in the first generation—that is to say, it will be equivalent to the phrase "if the first taker dies without issue him surviving." By this simple means all the difficulties above pointed out are avoided. The gift of personal property to B if A dies without issue is no longer void by reason of the rule against perpetuities. A's interest is not turned into an estate tail so far as the real estate is concerned, and B's interest in the real estate is valid and takes effect at the same time as his interest in the personal property, if at all. In at least one state where no such legislation exists, the highest court has on several occasions intimated that it would adopt as the regular rule of construction this meaning of "die without issue" (37).

§ 55. **Determination of classes.** It is very common in wills to find gifts to a class, as a gift to the children of A, or to the grandchildren of the testator. The one using these general phrases seldom observes the difficulties of meaning which are inevitably raised. Suppose there is a

---

(37) Summers v. Smith, 127 Ill. 645.

gift "to all the grandchildren" of the testator. Does this mean all the grandchildren of the testator who are in being at the testator's death, or does it mean all grandchildren of the testator born and to be born? We might fairly surmise that the testator meant the latter. But to give the words such a meaning would result very inconveniently, because no final distribution to the members of the class could be made till the death of all the testator's children made it certain there could be no more grandchildren. As a matter of convenience the rule of construction is that when the time of distribution is the testator's death and the testator has grandchildren living at his death "all grandchildren" means all living at the testator's death and not all who may be born at any time (38). If, however, the testator had no grandchildren at the time of making his will or of the date of his death, "all grandchildren" will mean all grandchildren of the testator born at any time (39). So, if the testator devised to his child for life and then to his grandchildren, "grandchildren" regularly includes those in being at the death of the life tenant, but none born afterwards (40). In short, the principle is that the class is not allowed to increase after the time for distribution arrives.

§ 56. Same (continued). Suppose that the devise is "to such grandchildren of mine as may reach twenty-one." Here again, if the testator means all grandchildren born at any time, perhaps no final distribution can be

(38)   Arnold v. Alden, 173 Ill. 229; Lancaster v. Lancaster, 187 Ill. 540.

(39)   Weld v. Bradbury, 2 Vern. 705.

(40)   Ayton v. Ayton, 1 Cox, 327.

made amongst the grandchildren until twenty-one years after the death of the testator's male children and the time when the female children shall have passed the child-bearing age. This is thought to be a great inconvenience for a small chance of benefiting someone. According to the regular rule, therefore, the class must close when the first grandchild reaches twenty-one, that is to say, when the first period of distribution arrives (41). But if there is a specific sum given to each member of the class, then the class must close at the testator's death, for if it were allowed to increase until even the first child reached twenty-one it would postpone the settlement of the entire estate and the distribution of the residue until that time (42). This it was thought would be an intolerable inconvenience. Suppose the testator devises to his grandchildren when all of them reach twenty-one, or when the youngest reaches twenty-one. What does "all," or what does the "youngest" include? Of course it includes all the grandchildren born up to the time the youngest living at the testator's death reaches twenty-one. It probably goes beyond this and includes all grandchildren living at any one time who have reached twenty-one. It is very doubtful whether a court should go further than this and hold that "all" means all grandchildren who may be born at any time. To go to such a length would be to hold up the final distribution to the class a great length of time on a very slight chance that any more grandchildren

---

(41)   Andrews v. Partington, 3 Bro. C. C. 401.

(42)   Ringrose v. Braham, 2 Cox 384; Storr v. Benbow, 2 Myl. & K. 46.

would be born. The cases where a grandchild is born after the youngest grandchild has reached twenty-one are rare.

§ 57. **Difficulties with gifts to the testator's "heirs at law."** A testator frequently makes a general gift to his heirs at law, after a life estate to his child, A. Then it often happens that A is also one of the testator's heirs at law at the time of his death. An inference at once springs into the minds of the testator's other heirs at law that A was not included in the gift to "heirs," but is confined to the express life estate which is indicated. The settlement of this difficulty is complicated by certain rules of construction. It seems fairly well settled that, in the case put, where the child is one of the testator's heirs at law at the time of his death, he is entitled not only to a life estate but to a share in the remainder as one of the heirs at law (43). On the other hand, it seems equally well settled that if the child in the case put is the sole heir at law of the testator, he will be excluded from any share in the remainder (44). The foundation for the difference is the absurdity of the child taking not only a life estate, but the whole of the remainder as heir at law, when in fact he was by the express language of the testator limited to a life estate.

§ 58. **Same (continued).** With these rules in mind what shall be done where the gift is a residuary one of real and personal property to the testator's widow for life, with remainder to the testator's heirs at law; and the tes-

(43)   Holloway v. Holloway, 5 Ves. 399.
(44)   Johnson v. Askey, 190 Ill. 58.

tator dies childless, so that the widow is (under some statutes) the sole distributee as to the personalty and heir to one-half of the realty, with collateral relatives of the testator as heirs to the other half? The first point to be determined is whether the word "heirs" is to be taken distributively or in the fixed meaning which it bears when applied to real estate. That is to say, does it mean the widow solely as to the residuary personalty and the widow and collateral relatives as to the residuary realty, or does it mean the widow and collateral relatives, one-half to each as to the realty and personalty together? Clearly the latter is the sound construction. The word "heirs" being applied to a mixed fund of realty and personalty, cannot with any propriety mean one thing as to one part and another thing as to another part. It clearly means one thing as to the whole. The primary meaning of the word is that which it bears when applied to real estate. Hence, the widow, if entitled in remainder at all, is entitled only to one-half the personalty and realty together. Such is the view of well considered authorities (45). The case, therefore, comes fairly within the rule that where A, the life tenant, is only one of several heirs at law of the testator, A can share in the remainder as one of such heirs, and, in the absence of a special context requiring a contrary result, the widow in the case put must be entitled to share in remainder as to one-half the real and personal property.

---

(45) Allison v. Allison, 101 Va. 537; Olney v. Lovering, 167 Mass. 446.

The questions of construction mentioned in this and the preceding sub-sections are but a very few of the questions which arise in the creation of future interests. The books on the construction of wills are filled with minute analyses of hundreds of questions of construction, with many distinctions so nice that lawyers and laymen alike are constantly confounded. The test of good draftsmanship is not to permit them to arise at all.

C. The rule against perpetuities.

§ 59. **Modern public policy in limiting creation of future interests.** In carrying out the principle that the landowner can do as he likes with his own and so create what future interests he pleases, we must not overlook the fact that there should be some limit to this liberty. It will not do to permit landowners to designate rigidly the persons who shall enjoy property during many generations to come. It is most desirable that, when the landowner undertakes to transfer, during his life or at his death, to some living person, he should be allowed to do so. It is fair and proper that he should designate that after that person's death his children who may hereafter be born shall take; but it will not do to go on to the third and fourth unborn generations and designate who amongst them, if they ever come into existence, shall enjoy. To permit that is to prevent property from coming into the hands of one with absolute power to direct the beneficial ownership according to his individual desires, based upon conditions which he personally observes. In short, it is not for the interest of future generations that one man shall direct all future ownership in a given property, though it may be proper that he should designate the ownership for such generations as are near enough to his life to be practically known to him.

§ 60. **Statement** of rule against perpetuities. The technical rule which carries out this public policy is known as the "rule against perpetuities." The history and reason of the rule are given in the article on History of Real Property, § 27, elsewhere in this volume. Its final form was settled in England in 1833 by the decision of the House of Lords in Cadell v. Palmer (46). The rule may be stated thus: Every future interest is void unless it must be enjoyed in possession, if at all—or must be or come into a position where it stands ready, throughout its continuance, to take effect in possession, whenever and however a preceding interest less than an absolute interest may determine, otherwise than by being prematurely cut short by the express provision of its creator— not later than 21 years after some life in being at the time of the creation of the future interest. Thus, a devise to take effect 10 years after the probate of the will is void, because the will may not be probated for 12 years, and 10 years from that time would be more than 21 years after the testator's death; and, since no lives are mentioned, none can be counted.

By the rule as above stated, it is sufficient to avoid its violation that the future interest must, if at all, not later than 21 years after some life in being at the creation

(46) 1 C. L. & F. 372.

of the interest, stand ready throughout its continuance to come into possession, whenever and however a preceding interest less than an absolute interest may determine in its natural course. This covers the case of a gift to A for 30 years and then to B in fee. Here the interest in B is valid, because B's estate stands ready throughout its continuance to take effect in possession, whenever and however A's term for years determines. If the term ends before 30 years, as by forfeiture or surrender, B's interest takes effect in possession at once. But a gift to B to take effect absolutely after 30 years, or after the marriage of some unborn child of A, is void, because B's interest here may not take effect in possession until after 21 years; and, since no lives in being are mentioned, none can be counted. Furthermore, B's interest at no time can come into a position where it stands ready to take effect, whenever and however any preceding interest less than an absolute interest determines in due course. Suppose further, A is given a life estate, with a future interest to A's unborn son for life, and then to such children of B as survive A. B's children may possibly not be entitled to possession until after the death of A's unborn son, which is possibly more than 21 years after A's death. But B's children, who survive A, will at A's death stand ready, throughout the continuance of the estate for life of A's son, to come into possession whenever and however the life estate of A's son shall determine; and the children of B, who survive A, will get into that situation at the death of A, which is within lives in being. The interest of the children of B is therefore valid.

§ 60a. **Historical reasons for rule.** If the historical view with respect to the validity of future interests, heretofore given (§§ 35-43, above), be kept in mind, the reason for that part of the rule covering the cases last above given will occur to the reader. It will be observed that the language of the rule in question operates to take away its application from all future interests in land which by the feudal law were wholly valid. So long as a future interest was not of this sort, the rule against perpetuities inexorably required that it be void, unless it took effect in *possession* within the proper time, or unless it came into the situation within the proper time where it would have been a valid future interest according to the feudal law. It was natural that such a qualification should obtain, when it is remembered that the rule against perpetuities arose several centuries after the feudal law had come to recognize the entire validity of those future interests limited after a life estate or a term for years, which stood ready to take effect in possession whenever and however the preceding estate might determine. Considerations of convenience later required that future interests of the same sort in personal property be exempt in the same way from the application of the rule against perpetuities Thus, that part of the rule became general which declares valid the future interest which must, if at all, not later than 21 years after some life in being at the creation of the interest, stand ready throughout its continuance to come into possession, whenever and how-

ever the preceding interest less than an absolute interest
may determine, otherwise than by being prematurely cut
short by the express provision of its creator.

§ **61. Corollaries to the rule.** For the purposes of the
rule, a child conceived but not yet born is treated as a
life in being; and any number of practicably identifiable
living persons may be used as the measure of such
lives (47). Thus, an estate may be limited to begin
21 years after the death of a large number of persons,
whether specified individually or as a class. Of course a
gift taking effect within a gross term of years (not exceed-
ing 21), regardless of preceding lives, is valid (see note
46, above).

§ **61a. Illustrations of violation of rule.** It is very easy
to violate the rule and thus wholly defeat a testator's intended gift. Thus, a gift to take effect ten years after
the probate of the will is void, because the will may not be
probated for twelve years and ten years from that time
would be more than twenty-one years after the testator's
death, and, since no lives are mentioned, none can be
counted. So, also, suppose a testator devised to his adult
unmarried son for life, then to any wife the son may have
for her life if she survive him, and then to such children
of said son as may survive the survivor of the said son or
his wife. Here the gift to the grandchildren is void, because the grandchildren to take must survive the son's
wife, and the son's wife may not be in being at the testator's death and might not be born within twenty-one
years after the testator's death. For instance, the son at

---

(47) Thellusson v. Woodford, 11 Ves. 112.

the age of sixty, twenty-four years after the testator's death, might marry a woman of twenty-two, born after the testator's death, who might outlive her husband twenty-two years and then die leaving grandchildren of the testator her surviving. Not till that time, then, would it be determined who were to take, and that is more than twenty-one years after the death of the testator's son, who is the only specified life in being. However improbable it may be that this chain of fortuitous events would occur, yet the *possibility* will make the gift to the grandchildren void. The rule against perpetuities requires it to be an absolute certainty that gifts will take effect, if at all, in the required manner within lives in being and twenty-one years.

§ 62. **Application of the rule to gifts to classes.** This requires some additional explanation. Suppose the testator devises to his son for life and then to such children of said son as reach the age of twenty-five years, and suppose at the testator's death there is one grandchild six years old who does in fact subsequently reach the age of twenty-five years. The result reached by the courts in such a case is well settled. The gift to all the grandchildren, including the one in being at the testator's death and six years old, is void (48). The reasoning in support of this involves two distinct steps: First, the gift to the class as a whole cannot be split up so that the gift can be regarded as separate gifts to individual grandchildren for the purpose of applying the rule against perpetuities. The reason for this is not any corollary to the rule, but

_____

(48) Leake v. Robinson, 2 Mer. 363.

rather the result of a principle of construction that you must take the estates and interests which the testator has created as he has created them. You must deal with *his* will, not with a will which you have made over for him. In this view the gift to a class is an entire gift to the whole class. It is not a collection of separate gifts to different members of the class. All are included. It is not for any judge or any court to say that the testator intended an older member of the class to take in preference to a younger or vice versa. This being established, one comes secondly to the application of the rule against perpetuities. That rule simply requires that the gift as limited, whatever it is, be absolutely certain to take effect in the manner required within the proper time, or fail entirely. Hence, in the case put, the whole gift to the grandchildren must fail. There is a possibility that the only child to reach twenty-five will be born after the testator and be less than four years old when its father dies. Hence, there is a chance that the whole class to take under the gift as made by the testator will not be ascertained until more than twenty-one years after lives in being at the testator's death.

§ 63. Same: **Part of class ascertained in time.** The same result obtains where part but not all of the members of the class have actually been ascertained in time. Thus, suppose a devise to A for life, and then to such children of A as reach twenty-five. At the testator's death a child of A has reached twenty-five. That child has, therefore, a present absolute right to a share. Individually the gift to him does not offend the rule, but the taking effect of the whole gift to the class may possibly not occur until twenty-four years after the death of A. The class may increase in numbers until the death of A. At the death of A there may be grandchildren in being not born until after the death of the testator and one year old at the death of A, and those may die just prior to reaching the age of twenty-five, or more than twenty-one years after lives in being at the testator's death, and not until that event has happened can the gift to the class as a whole be regarded as finally determined and ascertained. In short, while the minimum number of the class is known at the testator's death, the maximum number cannot be ascertained until possibly more than twenty-one years after lives in being. This possibility defeats the gift to the entire class, provided in applying the rule against perpetuities the gift to the class must be regarded as a whole and not split up into separate gifts to individuals. The courts refuse to consider the gift to the class as other than a single gift which cannot be separated without making the testator's will over for him, and hence the logical result is reached that the gift to the entire class, including the share of the grandchild who had reached twenty-five, is void (49).

§ 64. **Same: Postponed enjoyment.** In the preceding cases the gift itself to the grandchildren was contingent upon their reaching twenty-five. Suppose now the gift is to the grandchildren of A, and as such is a gift to take effect immediately upon the death of the testator, so that

(49) Pitzel v. Schneider, 216 Ill. 87. But compare Edgerly v. Barker, 66 N. H. 434.

it is subject to no condition precedent whatever except the actual birth of grandchildren of A. Suppose, however, there is what is called a ''postponed enjoyment'' clause added—that is to say, there is a trusteeship and the trustees are directed not to pay over any share of the principal to any grandchild of A until such grandchild reaches twenty-five. Here each member of the class has an absolute interest as soon as born which he cannot be deprived of, but no member of the class can obtain payment of the principal until he reaches twenty-five, or, if he dies before that age, his estate is not to take it until he would have reached twenty-five. Suppose now a grandchild of A is in being at the testator's death who is not over three years of age. Here again, individually considered, that child's interest does not violate the rule against perpetuities, yet, since the class may increase until the eldest reaches twenty-five or would have reached twenty-five had he lived, the maximum number of the class or the minimum amount of each share will not be ascertained in the proper time, and the whole gift to the grandchildren must be void were it not for one other consideration which saves it. By a rule quite distinct from the rule against perpetuities, the postponed enjoyment clause will not be enforced if it involves the possibility of keeping up of a trusteeship in favor of one having the absolute indefeasible interest for longer than lives in being and twenty-one years. That is exactly what the postponed enjoyment clause here does. It may possibly, for twenty-two years after lives in being at the testator's death, make it impossible for a grandchild absolutely and indefeasibly entitled to obtain a distribution of the principal from the trustee. Hence, the postponed enjoyment clause is unenforceable and the only ground for the class being allowed to increase until the eldest grandchild reaches twenty-five fails. The devise therefore stands simply as a gift to the grandchildren of A, the class is determined at the testator's death, and the one grandchild three years old at the testator's death, takes the entire estate (50).

§ 65. **Application of the rule to rights of entry and contracts to buy** land. It will occur to the reader that most deeds that he has seen, containing conditions of forfeiture of the fee conveyed, violate the rule against perpetuities so far as the right of entry for the breach of the condition is concernd. Thus, a deed upon a condition of forfeiture if the premises conveyed shall be used for the sale of intoxicating liquors clearly contains a provision of forfeiture upon a condition which may not be violated until many years after lives in being at the time it is created. Is it then void? The English courts have said yes (51). Curiously enough the application of the rule has not been perceived by courts in this country, and very frequently such conditions are held valid and enforceable, though they clearly violate the rule. So common have such decisions been that a professional, and prehaps a judicial opinion can be said to have been established, that the rule against perpetuities does not apply to rights of entry for condition broken (52).

---

(50)   19 Harv. Law Rev. 598.

(51)   Dunn v. Flood, 25 Ch. Div. 629.

(52)   Wakefield v. Van Tassel, 202 Ill. 41; Gray, Rule against Perpetuities (2nd ed.), § 304 ff.

It has been held in England, too, that the rule against perpetuities applies to options or contracts for the purchase of land. Thus, a contract by the purchaser from a railroad that he would re-sell the land to the railroad again when it was needed for railroad purposes could not be enforced by the railroad so as to require a re-conveyance to it, because the railroad's option was upon a condition which violated the rule (53). It should be assumed that a similar rule would be enforced in this country. Observe, however, that the rule only prohibits the purchaser from obtaining a specific enforcement of the contract by an actual conveyance from the seller. It does not prevent a recovery of damages for the breach of the contract (54).

D. *Rules against restraints on alienation.*

§ 66. Conditions of forfeiture on alienation: Estates of inheritance. It was stated above (§ 33), that estates in fee simple might be made subject to a condition subsequent, upon the breach of which the estate could be forfeited and terminated by the creator of the estate, or his heirs. It was stated also that an estate might be given to A in fee, and then taken away from A upon a certain event and given to B in fee. In both cases and in other examples that might be put, the condition which deprives the first holder is a condition of forfeiture upon the event named. To the general assertion that these conditions of forfeiture and gifts over by way of forfeiture, attached to a fee simple, are valid, must be added the general quali-

---

(53)   London & S. W. Ry. v. Gomm, 20 Ch. Div. 562.

(54)   Worthing Cp. v. Heather, (1906) 2 Ch. 532.

fication that the condition must not be one imposing a forfeiture in case the first holder in fee alienates or attempts to alienate. If the condition is one of forfeiture on alienation or attempted alienation, it is void and the first taker will retain the fee regardless of the breach of condition. This is the application of a rule quite distinct from the rule against perpetuities, and yet one resting upon a very strict public policy against limiting a landowner's freedom of alienation.

§ 67. Same: **Estates for life and years.** This public policy against conditions of forfeiture upon alienation is not applicable, however, when the first taker has only a life estate or a term for years, and the landowner has a reversion in fee. In such cases the landlord has a vital interest in who is to occupy the leased premises. Conditions of forfeiture if the tenant alienates are, therefore, entirely valid. The most common of all of these conditions of forfeiture is that contained in the ordinary lease for years that the tenant shall not assign or sub-let without permission of the landlord, and, if he does, that the term may be forfeited and the landlord re-enter. Forfeiture is a harsh weapon, however, and its severity has been mitigated by the law in several ways. All doubtful language will be construed against a forfeiture; and, even when the language is clear and a breach of condition has occurred, certain conduct on the part of the landlord will easily waive the forfeiture by operation of law. A forfeiture due merely to a brief delay in the payment of money will often be enjoined. All of these matters are fully discussed in the article on Landlord and Tenant, Chapter III, in Volume IV of this work.

§ 68. **Restraints on alienation.** Sometimes the grantor or testator, instead of attempting to create a condition of forfeiture on alienation whereby the holder of an estate may alienate, but, if he does, is liable to have the estate forfeited or go over to another, simply declares that the estate created shall not be alienable. This is an attempt to prevent the operation of the usual laws permitting alienation. If this were effectual the holder of the estate could not get rid of it. Such attempted restraints on alienation are, however, wholly void and unenforceable. It makes no difference whether the interest subject to the attempted restraint be a fee simple, or a life estate or a term for years. The restraint is void. Whatever interest one has in land he may transfer, and his creditors can take it from him for the satisfaction of his debts.

§ 69. **"Spendthrift trusts": In England.** Within the last century and a half in England, however, conveyancers have been called upon to devise some way, consistent with the above rule, by which the spendthrift member of a family might have the benefit of an income which he could not waste and which his creditors could not reach. This is the best they have been able to do: The grantor or testator can transfer property to trustees to pay the income wholly, or in part, or not at all, to such one or more of A, his wife, and children, during the life of A, as the said trustees in their discretion shall see fit; and, in case the whole or any part of the income is not paid to any person, to accumulate the part not paid and add it to the principal. Then the grantor provides for the distribution of the principal after A's death. The above settlement leaves A with nothing. If he becomes bankrupt the trustees can refuse to give A anything, and A's creditors will get nothing. The trustees can then begin to pay the income to A's wife and children. Of course, in that event A is deprived of all income. That cannot be helped, but at least A's family is protected against A's creditors (55). It is important in carrying out this plan that A be given no rights whatever that he can enforce, for if A has any such rights his creditors can reach them. Thus, where the trusts were to use the income to purchase clothing, board, and lodging for A, A could compel the trustees to use their discretion in expending the money for him in the way specified, and the creditors could reach that right for their benefit (56).

§ 70. **Same: In the United States.** In the United States courts have very generally, perhaps universally, held valid the restraint on alienation when it is attached to an equitable life estate, i. e., when the property is transferred to trustees to hold for A for life, not subject to any claim by A's creditors or to any power of alienation by A. This is called a "spendthrift trust." It has the advantage for A, over the only scheme available in England, in that A can have the income for his support and maintenance while his creditors go unpaid. It has the disad-

---

(55) Lord v. Bunn, 2 Y. & C. C. C. 98.

(56) Green v. Spicer, 1 Russ. & M. 395.

vantage of enabling a debtor to enjoy luxury and idleness
to which he is not morally entitled. The policy of the
spendthrift trust has been attacked with the greatest
vigor by high authorities in this country (57).

§ 71. **Trusts indestructible for limited periods.** A testator with a family of young children and no wife, and a
considerable property, frequently finds it convenient to
devise to his children absolutely in equal parts. This absolute gift takes effect at once upon the testator's death.
If, however, the gift contemplated an immediate distribution upon the testator's death there would have to be a division of the estate, and a guardian must be appointed for
each minor. All this would involve expense and the division of the property into small shares might be injurious
to its income-producing power. The testator, therefore,
naturally and properly appoints trustees and charges
them with the management and care of the property while
the children are young. Very naturally also he does not
wish the trusts to end with the bare majority of the children. At that time they will still be immature so far as
the management of property is concerned. The sons may
be completing their educations or starting in business or
professional life. It is unwise to thrust upon them at
such a time the absolute control of the investment and
care of their share of the estate. The age of twenty-five
would be a better period to fix for a division of the principal. The sons will then be fairly started in their occu-
pations, and the daughters may have married. The testator, therefore, directs that the trustees shall not distribute

---

(57) Gray, Restraints on Alienation, Preface to second edition.

the principal of the estate until each child reaches twenty-five. What harm is there in this? The children's creditors are not defeated, for they may reach the equitable interests of the debtor. The children may even alienate their equitable interests after they come of age, so there is no restraint on alienation. Such a postponement might be unwise if the child became a spendthrift and insisted upon selling his equitable interest at a sacrifice, but the postponement is not designed for a wayward child but assumes a well-regulated and intelligent family who are merely too much occupied in obtaining a higher education, coming out in society, or starting in business or professional life, to undertake the care of investments of money and property. It is believed that the refusal of the English courts to enforce the postponement after the child reaches twenty-one is unnecessary, and that the universal favor with which the postponement is treated in this country is sound (58).

§ 72. **Same: Probable limits of this.** Of course, the liberty to use such a postponement or clause creating indestructible trusts should not be abused. It would not do to permit trustees and their successors to insist upon a trusteeship forever or even for a very long period of time. The courts in this country seem to be moving very rapidly toward the general announcement of the rule that trusts of absolute indestructible equitable interests cannot be made to last for longer than lives in being and twenty-one years, and that any provision which may by any possibility postpone the term of the trusteeship for longer

(58)   Kales, Future Interests, §§ 228-294.

than that period is wholly void from the beginning. Thus
the trusteeship and the equitable interests are left as limited, but without any authority on the part of the trustees
to continue the trusteeship beyond the minority of the
beneficiary (59). This, it should be observed, is not the
application of the rule against perpetuities, but of a rule
which merely controls the length of time that trusts may
be made indestructible.

SECTION 5. GENERAL PRINCIPLES OF CONSTRUCTION.

§ 73. **Principles of construction to determine the estate
created.** In some of the preceding subsections certain
difficulties of construction in determining what estate has
been created have been touched upon (see particularly
§§ 49-58). In all, however, the difficulties being of a conventional type and often repeated, the solution has been
aided by more or less conventional rules concerning what
certain phrases mean. There are, however, a host of sit-
uations where no such rules are applicable and where the
difficulties must be solved afresh by the application of
general principles of construction relating to written instruments and more especially to wills.

§ 74. **Distinction between contracts and wills.** The
expression ''more especially to wills'' is used because, in
the beginning, a distinction must be taken between instruments in which two parties join, such as a formal contract, and one which contains the act of a single party,
such as a will. The instrument executed by two parties,
in which there are mutual obligations, must be construed
according to a standard in the use of language which is

---

(59)   Armstrong v. Barber, 239 Ill. 389.

common to both. Neither is permitted to say that he understood the words one way. Both must abide by the meaning according to the common standard—that of the ordinary man under the circumstances. But in a will, which is wholly the act of the testator, the test is what did the *particular individual* mean by the words he used. What meaning did *he* place upon the words which he used? In what sense did *he* use them? The matter of the meaning is personal to him. Within limits he may make his own standard. He may indeed go to considerable lengths in placing an unusual meaning upon a common word, and if it can be shown that he has done so his unusual meaning must prevail.

§ 75. Use of extrinsic evidence to identify subject matter or object of devise. This has led naturally and inevitably to the proposition that, in construing a will, you may introduce evidence of facts outside the will to prove the meaning which the testator put upon particular words. It should be noted, however, that direct declarations by the testator of what he meant are always excluded except in the one case hereafter mentioned. Under this rule all sorts of facts surrounding the making of the will may be introduced in aid of its interpretation. In cases where the difficulty is in ascertaining the *subject matter* of a devise or the *object* which is to benefit by the devise, such outside evidence becomes extremely valuable and often controlling. Thus, where a testator in devising certain specified land misdescribes it and describes instead another parcel of land which he does not own, evidence of facts surrounding the will may be conclusive in showing that the testator meant, by the words he used, to devise the land which he actually owned, and not other land which he did not own. So, where the testator devises to his nephew John Jones and he has no nephew by that name, but the outside evidence shows that he had a nephew whom he called by that name, the outside evidence would probably be conclusive that that nephew was the one meant by the words used. So, if he had two nephews of the same name, the evidence outside the will may make it clear which nephew he meant, and here, because there are two objects each answering to the description used, direct declarations of the testator's intention are admitted.

§ 76. **Effect of similar evidence to show estate created. Illustration.** The foregoing matters have been thus particularly pointed out in order to emphasize the statement now to be made. In endeavoring to ascertain *what kind of an estate* a testator intended to devise, all the outside evidence that can possibly be introduced is of practically no value in most or all cases. In short, when a testator becomes obscure about whether a particular individual is to have any gift or what estate or interest he or she is to have, the introduction of outside evidence does nothing more than furnish the ground for a cheap and easy speculation founded upon a most inadequate view of what went on in the testator's mind. It merely gives the court an opportunity to peek in behind the scenes and to find out who *"ought"* to win, and then get the result which the judge deems right.

Thus, the will involved in a recent Georgia case made a gift to the testator's daughter in the following words: "It is my will that my infant daughter, Sarah Alberta Addison Alexina Telfair Cobb, should she live to attain the age of twenty-one years, become then the *absolute owner* of all the estate, real, personal, and mixed, including choses in action, to which I have a lawful title, *to have and to hold the same, and her heirs forever.*" Then there is a gift, if the daughter died without leaving issue, to the testator's next of kin living at the death of the daughter. The daughter marries and all the estate which she has under her mother's will comes to her husband by conveyance or by reason of the marriage. The husband is a dissipated spendthrift, and in due course of time transfers the title to the property devised by the will to a manufacturing corporation and squanders the proceeds. Subsequently the daughter dies, leaving children surviving her, and they now seek to recover the property from the corporation. It is a hard case. The children have been deprived of their inheritance by the folly of a wicked father. But what can be done? The daughter plainly had an absolute interest. This was to be taken away from her only in the event that she died without leaving issue surviving her, and she has died actually leaving issue. It would seem, therefore, by the plainest reasoning, that the corporation had the fee simple absolute and that the grandchildren of the testator must fail. The recent graduate of a reputable law school would say that the case was hopeless on behalf of the children. The wise and experienced practitioner would say it was far from hopeless. He would work into the record all these outside circumstances, and, having carefully shown up the fire-side equities, would offer as an excuse for a decision on behalf of the children the argument that because there is a gift over if the daughter died without issue, it must be taken that the daughter was intended to have only an estate during her life; and that, therefore, the language by which the daughter is given an absolute interest is nullified or disregarded and she takes a life estate. Also, from the fact that there is a gift over if she dies without leaving issue, it would be argued that there is a gift by implication to her issue if she leaves any. By this simple process the court may arrive at the result that the daughter had only a life estate and that there is a remainder in fee to her children if she leaves any. The corporation, therefore, upon this view would obtain through the medium of the husband only the daughter's life estate, and, she being dead, her children are entitled. These arguments were accepted by the Georgia supreme court, and the corporation was defeated in favor of the children (60).

§ 77. **Such evidence should be disregarded.** The course of action typified in this Georgia case is subversive of all law, but unhappily it is constantly going on. It throws a large and important class of cases affecting the rights of individuals outside the realm of law, and places property rights in the power of a judge's discretion. Each time the impropriety is committed, it furnishes a precedent for the commission of a like impropriety in another case,

(60) Wetter v. Hydraulic Cotton Press Co., 75 Ga. 540.

where superficially the facts are the same but where equitably they are entirely different. The whole course of construction, difficult enough at best, is beset with additional pitfalls and "no case is hopeless and no case secure." Every case, even the simplest, must be sent to a court for construction at a considerable expense of time and money. Only the callow youths at the bar undertake to give opinions on the meaning of wills in advance of a court decision. It is believed that a great evil in the way wills are construed would be remedied, if judges and courts would observe that, when the difficulty of construction has to do with the *state or character of the interest created,* outside evidence of the state of the testator's family and other circumstances surrounding the making of the will, while legally admissible for what they are worth, are worth nothing except to induce a prejudice for one construction because it would be more likely to do justice between the parties, and to furnish the basis for wild speculation, without adequate proof, that the testator meant the words in the sense which to the court's mind would do this justice between the parties.

SECTION 6. DRAFTING A WILL.

§ 78. **Introduction.** The subject matter of the preceding sections is, it will be observed, very closely connected with the art of drafting wills. In fact, most of the questions discussed arise in connection with the constructions of wills and the estates which may be created by them. The matter presented does not, however, give one any idea of the practical art of will-drawing or of making family settlements. To obtain that one must come at the

subject from the practical point of view of what is best to
be done, and how to do it so as to avoid the very difficulties that have been discussed in the preceding sections.
No better method of introducing the reader to the niceties
of the practical art of will-drawing exists, it is believed,
than that of letting him in behind the scenes to observe
the actual mental processes of the draftsman in getting
up a typical instrument for a typical testator, and examining the actual phrases which the draftsman uses in making the instrument.

§ 79. **The typical testator.** The typical testator selected is a man of moderate fortune. He has at least a
country house or a town house—perhaps both. The capital of his estate consists of lands and personal property in
suitable proportions. A proper proportion of the real
estate is productive, and the personal estate is invested
suitably in public securities, mortgages, bonds of railway
corporations, and some of the better-known and readily
salable stocks. Our typical testator is forty years of age,
and neither a bachelor nor a widower. Both are abnormal
variations at this age. Furthermore, there is no question
of race suicide. He is the father of three young children
—two boys and a girl—and has a fair prospect of more of
each kind.

§ 80. **Evolution of methods of conveyancing appropriate for the typical will.** The typical testator probably
does not know that the best testamentary disposition
for him to make has been settled, like the rules of law, by
generations of experience and experiment on the part of
trained specialists. The results of this experience and

experiment, as well as the evolution which it has produced, are to be found in the form books of the English conveyancers of every generation since the reign of Charles II. The plan prescribed for him in the seventh volume of the last edition of Bythewood or in the fourth volume of a recent edition of Davidson's Precedents is the crowning effort of an evolution which dates back to the latter part of the seventeenth century. The founder of that school of conveyancers which has produced the form we are about to consider in detail was no other than Sir Orlando Bridgeman, afterwards lord keeper of the great seal from 1667 to 1672. He is called the father of modern conveyancing. Since the time of Bridgeman there has been a succession of conveyancers, conveyancing counsel, and chancellors who have added to, pointed the way for, or insisted upon improvements in the form of family settlements. To the American lawyer the names of Fearne, Preston, Butler, Smith, Hayes, Davidson, Bythewood, Jarman, and such chancellors as Lord Hardwick, Lord Eldon, and Lord St. Leonards, are familiar (61).

We are to consider then what this evolutionary process has settled as the best course for a typical testator to take.

§ 81. General outline of the will. This has long since been settled. After the gift of specific legacies, the wife shall have an interest in the whole of the residue for her life or until she marries again, and, after her death or remarriage, the whole property shall be divided equally

---

(61) See "History of Settlements of Real Estate," 1 Juridical Society Papers, 45, 54.

among the children of the marriage. Nothing could be more direct and simple than this, and yet the infinite care and attention to detail with which the English conveyancers since the time of Charles II have worked out this typical form of will makes it today a wonder to behold.

§ 82. **The will in detail: Specific legacies.** The first care of the draftsman is to allow the testator to bequeath as he pleases a few specific chattels—a watch to one, a picture to another, books to a third, and so forth. There is only one restriction upon the testator here. He must make his gifts absolute. He must not attempt any gifts of chattels to one for life and then to another. Such gifts are valid, but extremely annoying to both parties interested and unwise from other points of view. If the testator has any poor female relative or relatives whom he wishes to provide for he may then charge upon his estate or direct the purchase of a small annuity for their benefit. At this point the personal choice or preference of the testator largely, if not entirely, ceases.

§ 83. **Gift of household effects to the widow.** Here some difficulties in the use of language must be faced. It is, of course, impracticable to put into the will an inventory of all the household effects which are to go to the widow, for they might all wear out and be replaced by the time of the testator's death. General descriptive language must be employed. The articles must be described with reference to their existence at a certain locality or without reference to locality. The former is a very usual method and the one adopted in the will of the late Marshall Field. In either case, however, difficulties arise.

If the clause be drafted so as to leave all the residue of the testator's effects which shall be in and about a certain dwelling at the time of his death, he may include much more than he intends, viz., money, or securities for money, bonds, stocks, and other personal property of that nature, in a private safe upon the premises. It is well, therefore, after a general gift of "all my wines, consumable stores, household furniture, household linen, plate, china, books, and other effects which shall be in and about my house at ...." to except "money, securities for money, stocks, evidences of indebtedness, and documents of title." In the will of the late Marshall Field this same object was effected by the following enumeration: "Furnishings and equipments of every kind, including furniture, paintings, library, bric-a-brac, horses, carriages, and all other personal property which may be used in connection with said residence at the date of my death." If the testator does not restrict the gift to articles at a given locality, he must still use some general word such as "effects." This may include too much, viz., the whole personal estate of money, stocks, bonds, notes, etc. The general words must, therefore, be selected with the greatest care. Experience has suggested the following, after an enumeration of the ordinary household articles: "The last mentioned bequest shall comprise all effects, though not strictly household, which are applicable to personal or domestic use, ornament, occupation, or diversion and are not hereinbefore specifically bequeathed."

§ 84. Same: Absolute gift or life estate? The usual practice of English conveyancers is to make the gift of effects to the wife an absolute one. A gift to her for life was valid enough, but the practical inconveniences of it were too great. In the first place, the subject matter of the gift is to a very considerable extent perishable, so that the one ultimately entitled cannot in the usual course expect to enjoy it. This gives rise to the requirement that effects of a certain character must be sold, the proceeds invested, and the income only used by the widow during her life. Difficult questions arise as to what articles must be treated in this way. Finally, there is always the opportunity of friction between the life tenant and those entitled afterwards. If the testator insisted upon the widow having a life estate only in these chattels, it was customary to bequeath all such as were of a permanent character and not likely to wear out or disappear in the using to trustees to permit the widow to use them during her life or widowhood (62). It is a matter of remark, therefore, that in the will of the late Marshall Field the gift of household effects to the widow includes all sorts of effects, both those likely to be consumed in the using and those of a permanent character, and creates in the widow an interest for life without the intervention of trustees.

§ 85. **Disposal of the residuary estate: Powers to trustees.** The first step is to devise all the rest and residue of the estate, real and personal, to trustees who are named, and to expressly provide what powers they shall have. Here experience has constantly added provisions which enable those administering the estate to proceed with the least possible inconvenience. The trustees rep-

---

(62) Davidson's Precedents (1880), Vol. IV, p. 67.

resent the estate to the outside world. Whatever acts the holder of such a property must ordinarily execute in its profitable administration, the trustees must be given express power to perform. There must be power to lease, to sell, to exchange, to mortgage, to pay off encumbrances, and to make a voluntary partition of lands which the testator may hold in common with others. In their relation to the trust estate the trustees must be given directions as to the investments to be allowed, whether within a restricted, fair, or comprehensive range. There then must be a power to vary investments, to buy land, and to sell the same again. It was wise, also, to confer power upon the trustees to apply the proceeds of any sale of real estate to pay off encumbrances upon the property sold or any other property in the trust estate. Powers to partition the trust premises among the beneficiaries at the time of distribution and to allow the widow to reside in a particular residence of the testator during the time when she was entitled to the income from all or any part of the trust estate by the terms thereof, without paying rent, were appropriate and advisable.

§ 86. Income from trust estate to be paid to widow: Support of children. It is of course expected that the widow will support, maintain, and educate the children out of her income so long as they remain minors, yet the conveyancer, who left nothing to chance, gave the children a legal right to such support, maintenance, and education, by charging the widow's income with the expense of such as she in her discretion might deem it proper they should have. The principal question, however, which arises in regard to the trust for the widow is: How long shall the income be paid over to her? Shall it be during the remainder of her life, or merely during her widowhood, i. e., so long as she remains unmarried? For many generations the English conveyancers seem to have had but one opinion about this—that the widow's interest should terminate with her second marriage. There can be only two results of continuing the whole income to the wife after her second marriage: either she will have more than she properly needs, or the income will make up the deficiency in her second husband's income. It is the somewhat usual American practice, however, to give the income to the wife so long as she lives.

§ 87. **The widow's special power of appointment: Hotch-pot clause.** The English form books usually provide for a special power in the widow to appoint such part or all of the residuary estate among her children as she shall see fit. In drafting such a clause some care is required. It must be clear that the widow may appoint to one or more exclusively of the others, otherwise an appointment of the whole interest which leaves out any one will be wholly void. The power must be to appoint not only to children, but to more remote issue, and in such manner and form as the widow shall deem best.

The existence in the will of a power in the widow makes necessary, at a later stage of the will, what is known as a "hotch-pot clause." According to the usual course the widow appoints something to the daughters when they marry, or to the sons when they reach twenty-one or twenty-five. It not unfrequently happens, therefore, that out of a family of say four, the first three have received appointments at the death of the widow. Let us suppose that these appointments have amounted to $20,000 apiece and that at the death of the widow there is a balance of $60,000 in the estate. This latter sum must be divided among all the four children, so that the three who have already received appointments will have altogether $35,000 apiece, while the youngest child must be satisfied with only $15,000. This is neither what the testator intended nor as the widow planned. The hotch-pot clause is designed, under the exigencies described, to effect an equal division as nearly as possible. It, therefore, provides that no one who took by appointment should (in the absence of an express direction in the appointment to the contrary) share in the unappointed part without bringing his appointed share into the general fund—that is, into hotch-pot—to be distributed as in default of appointment.

§ 88. **Same: Expediency of such a power.** As to the expediency in general of giving the widow this power of appointment, opinions may differ. Its use may be most salutary. It enables the widow to retain control over the children. She may alter the disposition of the property according as events turn out. If the daughters marry well their shares may be reduced. If a son is wild his portion may be cut down to a life estate, with clauses which will save the estate from his creditors and provide for his wife and children. On the other hand, if the testator's children are normal individuals, but the widow proves flighty or partial, or lives to a great age and falls under the influence of some single child who lives with her when all the others have moved away, great disturbance in the family may result from the existence of the power. The American tendency has been to omit the power, unless there is some very strong reason for it.

§ 89. Gift to children in default of appointment after termination of widow's interest: Objects sought. The testator is apt to think only of a simple direct gift to his children. When, however, he is reminded that his family is a young and growing one, it will occur to him that the trust must not terminate for each child till he or she comes of age, and perhaps he may desire that it shall not end for the different shares except as the children reach twenty-five. Should any of the children die under twenty-five he will wish their children, if any, to take the parent's share; and the shares of his childless children dying under twenty-five are to be divided among the other children who reach that age. The problem is to effect these desires as simply and conveniently as possible.

§ 90. Same: Accomplishment by postponed vested gift. Scientific modern conveyancing recognizes that these objects may be accomplished in just two ways, which must be kept absolutely distinct and separate. The first method is to make a direct gift to all the children to take effect immediately upon the death or remarriage of the widow. That will give each child what is known as a vested interest (§ 32, above). Each will have a share at once upon the testator's death, subject to the provision for the widow. Then there will be a clause simply postponing the termination of the trust and the payment over of the principal of each share, till the beneficiary of that share reaches twenty-five. If the will stopped here each child would have full power to alienate after it came of age, by deed or will; and upon the child's death intestate at any time the share would descend to its next of kin. If, then, any child of the testator dies under twenty-five, leaving children, there is no reason why the child's right of alienation should be interfered with, for he will naturally alienate to his children by will or the share will descend to them. The deceased child's portion may, therefore, be left to descend or to pass by will. On the other hand, if a child of the testator dies without leaving issue, it is proper that the share of the child so dying should go to the other brothers and sisters. This requires a special provision, known as a clause of "accruer," declaring: "In case any of my said children shall die without leaving issue surviving them, the share hereinbefore given to the child so dying, including any further share or shares accruing under this present clause, shall go and accrue to my other children."

§ 91. **Same: Accomplishment by contingent gift.** The second plan for the gift to the testator's children is to describe the class who are to take, and to make it, as far as possible, contingent upon each member of the class reaching the age of twenty-five—the time of distribution. According to this plan the devise will read:

"To such child or children of mine as shall survive me and attain the age of twenty-five, and to the child or children of any child or children of mine who shall be dead at my death or shall die under the age of twenty-five; provided that the child or children collectively of any child of mine dead at my death or dying under the age of twenty-five shall take only such share as his, her, or their parent would have taken, if such parent had lived to take a vested interest.''

Both these plans—that of a vested gift with a clause of accruer and that of a contingent gift—accomplish precisely the same result, but by quite a different series of clauses which must not be mixed with each other or hopeless confusion and litigation will result. The English conveyancers now almost wholly prefer the second plan, and its further development has been carefully worked out.

§ 92. Same: Development of latter plan. The reader will observe that, while the gift to the children of the testator was made contingent on their reaching twenty-five, the gift to the child of any deceased child of the testator is made to it absolutely. The reason for this is that a gift to the child of any deceased child of the testator, on such grandchild reaching the age of twenty-five, would be in violation of the rule against perpetuities (§ 60, above), as it might take effect more than twenty-one years after the death of the widow and all the testator's children. Nevertheless, the general plan requires that all gifts be postponed, if possible, till the legatee reaches twenty-five. The ingenuity of more recent conveyancers has devised this clause, which does the work simply and effectively:

"Provided always: That if any grandchild or grandchildren of mine should attain the age of twenty-one years before the expiration of twenty-one years from the time of the death of the survivor of my children and more remote issue (if any) living at the time of my death, then the vesting of the share of each such grandchild shall be postponed to the expiration of such time of twenty-one years, or until the attainment by such respective grandchild to the age of twenty-five years, whichever shall first happen.'' Then follows a clause giving the shares of grandchildren, who died before obtaining a vested interest, to their children, if any.

§ 93. **Disposition of income prior to time of distribution.** Whichever plan be adopted—the one where the gift is vested or the one where it is contingent—the provision for the children and other issue is still incomplete. As none are to take till they reach twenty-five (except in the case of great-grandchildren) what is to happen between the termination of the widow's interest and that time? Obviously the income upon the vested or expectant share of each child or grandchild is to be used for its maintenance and education. This is accomplished by a general direction to the trustees thus to apply such part of the income as seems best, or to pay it to the parents or guardians of the persons entitled, to be by them thus applied. If all of the income of any share is not thus spent, it may be directed to be accumulated for the benefit of its share, subject to any future use for maintenance and education of the one entitled authorized by the trustees. Power should also be given the widow and trustees to use for similar purposes any necessary part of the principal, or even to make an advancement to children on certain occasions.

§ 94. Routine clauses. Summary. The balance of the will contains some routine clauses, declaring that the gift to the wife shall be in lieu of all interest which the law allows her, providing a method of supplying the place of a trustee who dies or becomes incapable or refuses to act, and naming executors.

This, then, as Davidson says in his Precedents, is an outline "of a will of the simplest and most ordinary description." It is nothing but a gift to the widow for life or during widowhood, and then to the children. It is what testators do or are planning for every day. Almost anything, however, is more easily conceivable than that the layman who contemplates such a testament should ever imagine the perfection of form and detail to which an instrument on these simple lines can be brought. Through experiments and mistakes of the past, generations of a trained, experienced and skilful professional class have evolved what is best for the purpose. With a will drawn according to the ideal thus wrought out, the question of testamentary disposition may in most cases safely be dismissed from his mind by the testator during the remainder of his life.

CHAPTER III.

COVENANTS FOR TITLE. EXECUTION OF DEEDS.

SECTION 1. COVENANTS OF TITLE.

§ 95. **The modern covenants of** title. These are as follows: 1. *Covenant of seisin:* This is a covenant that the grantor is seized at the time of the grant. In most jurisdictions this covenant is only satisfied by a lawful possession of the grantor. In some jurisdictions, however, it is satisfied (by reason of the survival of the feudal definition of seisin) by a wrongful possession of the grantor. 2. *Covenant of the right to convey:* This is not the same as the covenant of seisin, because one may have a right to convey under a power to appoint, for instance, and yet not have any seisin or possession. 3. *Covenant against incumbrances:* This is self-explanatory. It is a covenant that there are no incumbrances upon the land conveyed. 4. *Covenant for quiet enjoyment:* This is a covenant that the grantee shall not be disturbed by any one claiming through the grantor. It is only broken when one enters claiming under the grantor. 5. *Covenant for further assurance:* This is not so common in this country as in England. It is a covenant to make further conveyances to remove clouds or clear up the title. 6. *Covenant of warranty:* This is peculiar to the United States. In scope it is similar to the covenant for quiet enjoyment, except that it is a covenant that the grantee shall not be disturbed by any one claiming a superior title. It is the general warranty of good title as against all the world.

Formerly all these covenants were spelled out at length in the draft of every warranty deed. The prolixity of deeds thus engendered was unnecessary, because the form and substance of the covenants were the same in all instruments. A sensible reform has been effected by means of statutory forms of conveyance, wherein the use of the one word "warrant" in the phrase "warrant and convey" is sufficient to introduce into the deed practically all of the covenants above mentioned except perhaps the covenant for further assurance. Frequently statutes provide that the use of the words "grant, bargain, and sell" in a deed will operate to incorporate into the instrument a covenant of seisin, a covenant against incumbrances, and a covenant of quiet enjoyment against any claiming under the grantor.

§ 96. How far covenants of title run with the land? In general. It is a matter of no particular remark that the original parties to the covenant for title can sue and be sued. It is, however, one of the special attributes of these covenants for title that the benefit of suing on them exists not only in the original grantee, who was a party to the deed in which the covenants were contained, but also in any other person to whom the original grantee conveys his title and to whom his title comes by a regular chain of conveyances from him. The benefit of the covenants is thus said to "run with the land." The doctrine that the benefit of covenants for title runs with the land is, however, subject to some subtle and annoying qualifications, which will be explained in the succeeding subsections.

§ 97. **Same: Broken covenants.** Suppose the covenant has been broken. That occurs with respect to the covenants of seisin, right to convey, and against incumbrances, if at all, when those covenants are made. The English courts now allow the *breach* of the covenant to run with the land until some holder of such title as passes has suffered, as the phrase goes, the "ultimate damage," for instance, in the case of an incumbrance by way of mortgage, until some holder of the title has been obliged to pay off the mortgage to protect his possession (1). The American cases, on the other hand, generally insist that a covenant for title cannot run at all after it has been broken (2). In cases, then, where the original covenantee has conveyed after the covenant has been broken, his transferee who wishes to take advantage of the covenant must sue in the name of his transferor, who is the original party to the covenant sued upon (3).

§ 98. **Same: Effect of the lack of title.** Suppose when the covenants were made the covenantor had no title whatsoever, so that no title passed at all to the grantee. The English courts, relying upon an old dictum uttered in 1595 (4) hold that the benefit of the covenants cannot run with the land because no title to land passes for them to run with. This prevents the running of the benefit of

(1) Kingdon v. Nottle, 4 M. & S. 53.
(2) Greenby v. Wilcocks, 2 Johns. (N. Y.) 1.
(3) Cole v. Kimball, 52 Vt. 639.
(4) Noke v. Awder, Cro. Eliz. 373, 436.

the covenants of quiet enjoyment, covenants for further assurance, and covenants of warranty, if any, which are not broken when made. The American courts, with more liberality, seem to adhere to the doctrine that if there is a regular chain of title from one transferee to another, and at the same time a passing of possession from the original covenantor to his grantee and then on from each transferee to the other, the benefit of the covenant which has not been broken will run (5). At least one jurisdiction seems to have gone so far as to dispense with the requirement that possession must pass from one transferee to another (6). This position seems very sensible from the point of view of policy. It seems absurd that at just the time when one desires the warranty most—that is, when no title has passed—he should be told that the covenant will not run.

§ 99. Same: Burden of covenants for title. The preceding subsections have dealt with the running of the benefits of covenants for title. The burden of the covenant—that is, the duty to respond in damages upon its breach—remains in the grantor during his life. How far does it bind his heirs? The rule of the common law was that, since the covenant was in an instrument under seal, if it puported to bind the covenantor's heirs and assigns, as it practically always did, the covenantor's heirs would be bound to the extent of assets descending to them from the covenantor. To that extent, then, the burden of the covenant passed to others than the covenantor.

---

(5)   Beddoe v. Wadsworth, 21 Wend. (N. Y.) 20.
(6)   Wead v. Larkin, 54 Ill. 489.

§ 100. **Estoppel** by deed: **Two** theories. The rules concerning estoppel by deed, as it is called, are so closely connected with the operation of covenants for title that it seems appropriate here to consider them in connection with covenants for title.

Suppose A, having no title, conveys to B, and then acquires the title from X. According to the view of the English, and some American courts, B has no title, but only a right (in case A has conveyed to B with covenants of warranty or representations as to his having a good title) to compel A to transfer his present good title to B (7). In this country more generally, where A has purported to convey to him with covenants of warranty, B is regarded as having at once the legal title without any action or proceeding against A. The after-acquired title of A, which he derives from X, is said to enure to the benefit of B by way of estoppel (8). In some cases there is no difference in result between the view of the English cases and the view of the American cases. Thus, if A sues B for possession, B cannot on either theory defend upon the ground that B received no title and that A has the right to possession. Under the English theory B is denied the right to set up that defense and may be enjoined from setting it up, and in this country B can claim that he has the legal title. In either case the result of the litigation is the same—B prevails over A.

§ 101. **Same: Differing results** of theories. The difference in result between the American and English view

(7) Burtner v. Keran, 24 Gratt (Va.) 66.
(8) Somes v. Skinner, 3 Pick. (Mass.) 51.

of the way in which B's obvious rights are to be enforced
becomes important in two cases. Suppose, after A has
acquired the title from X, B attempts to maintain ejectment against M, a stranger who happens to be in possession, but who has no title and does not claim from X, A, or
B. B must then succeed, if at all, on the strength of his
own title, and not at all on the weakness of M's. B will
fail in England because he has no title. He will succeed
in this country because he has. So, after A conveys to
B, if A then acquires title from X and conveys it to C, a
bona fide purchaser for value, in England C must prevail
because he takes the legal title free and clear from B's
mere right to compel A to transfer to him. In this country, however, if our courts adhere strictly to the theory
that the title passes to B by way of estoppel, as soon as A
acquires it from X, B should prevail over C. This problem in this country, however, is complicated by the application of the recording acts, and had best be discussed
later (§§ 115-16, below) in that connection.

The American courts have not always been able to adhere strictly to the theory that B obtains title by estoppel
when A acquires the title from X. For instance, B, having been ousted from his possession by X, the holder of
the superior title, makes a claim against A on his covenants of warranty for the return of the purchase price.
Suppose A is able to buy in the title from X at a greatly
reduced price, can A then force his after-acquired title
upon B by estoppel? The courts hold that he cannot (9).
If, however, A can buy in the outstanding title, however

(9) Blanchard v. Ellis, 1 Gray (Mass.) 195.

cheaply, while B is still in possession and before he has
suffered any damage, perhaps B will be forced to take the
after-acquired title by estoppel, even against his will.

SECTION 2.   EXECUTION OF DEEDS.

§ 102. Statutory provisions regarding execution of
deeds. The differing detailed provisions of the laws of
the different states relative to the execution of deeds
make any attempt to state the law fully and precisely out
of the question. This subsection consists rather of a
series of conveyancer's cautions than an attempt to state
the rules of fifty different jurisdictions.

A conveyancer always remembers that a deed of conveyance of land must be executed according to the formalities of the state where the land is situated. He knows
the law of his own state. What does he do when he
wants to know the law of other states? He may, of
course, consult the statutes of another state, but that
would be a long and difficult task, because a great many
different provisions might affect the execution of deeds,
and they may be widely separated under different heads
in the statute books. They are not apt to be all known
or readily referred to except by local practitioners who
have all their lives been in contact with the law of that
particular jurisdiction. If the matter is of very great
importance the conveyancer desiring to draft an instrument in conformity with the laws of a neighboring jurisdiction may take the advice of local counsel in that jurisdiction. If, however, it is a small matter, like the formalities of a warranty deed conveying a fee simple, he
will frequently obtain full satisfaction by consulting the

current volume of a legal directory or mercantile agency. That contains a summary of the law of each state with respect to the formalities for the execution of deeds. It purports to be prepared by competent local attorneys, and the profession has come to rely upon that fact.

There will be found a great variety of provisions about seals. Some jurisdictions require seals and some do not. Some states that require seals will not take a pen scroll for a seal, but insist upon a wafer being attached. In other states a pen scroll is enough. In some a seal printed on the blank form of deed is sufficient, and in others it is not. The different provisions for waiver of a wife's dower or a husband's curtesy, and the waiver of statutory exemptions of homestead property; the different forms for the acknowledgment of a deed by the parties; and the different modes of insuring the recognition of acknowledgments taken in a neighboring jurisdiction, all present a variety of detail which it is impossible to state in the mass.

§ 103. **Delivery and acceptance necessary.** The signing and sealing of a deed—even the signing, sealing and acknowledging of a deed—does not make it effective as the legal act of the grantor. To do that there must be a *delivery*, and, with some qualifications to be hereafter noted, an *acceptance*.

§ 104. **Delivery to grantee.** There can be no delivery till the instrument has been placed entirely out of the control of the grantor. This usually occurs by the final handing of the instrument to the grantee or his agent.

Many difficulties of fact arise as to whether the deed has been placed out of the control of the grantor, especially where the transaction is between a husband and wife. After the death of the husband the deed is recorded, and the question is raised whether it was delivered before the husband's death. The wife is practically always an incompetent witness as against the heirs of the husband, so that the whole question comes down to one of circumstantial evidence with respect to the place where the unrecorded deed was kept. Often the testimony is of a picturesque character. The question turns upon whether the instrument was kept in the top bureau drawer with the wife's lingerie, or in the second drawer with the husband's red shirt. But observe that the placing of the instrument in the hands of the grantee does not necessarily constitute a delivery, unless by that act the instrument is placed entirely out of the control of the grantor. Thus, if the instrument be placed in the hands of the grantee as the grantor's messenger or servant or agent, to take the instrument to town and there hand it to another agent of the grantor, there is no delivery. On the other hand, delivery may possibly occur without any actual physical removal of the deed from the grantor's hands. For instance, if he in the presence of the grantee says: "Here is the deed; I deliver it to you, but if you wish I will keep the instrument safe for you. Here is my receipt to you for it, and you may have it at any time on demand. In the meantime I will keep it in my safe for you." Under such circumstances the grantor has turned himself into the bailee or custodian of the paper for the

grantee, and the delivery is complete (10). But the cases
where this actually appears are rare.

§ 105. **Delivery upon condition to third party: Escrow.**
The placing of the instrument in the hands of a third
party, to be delivered by him finally to the grantee upon
the happening of certain conditions, is frequent. Thus,
where the deed is placed in the hands of a third party and
absolutely beyond the legal right of the grantor to recall
the instrument except upon the non-happening of the condition, the grantee is entitled to the deed upon the happening of the condition and the title is good in the grantee
by relation back to the time of delivery to the third party.
The delivery upon condition to a third party in this manner is called a delivery in escrow, and the third party is
the escrowee. There are two principal difficulties which
arise in regard to escrows, which are considered below.

§ 106. **Same: Violation of condition by escrowee.** Suppose the escrowee delivers the instrument in violation of
the condition to the grantee, and the grantee conveys to
one who pays full value and has no notice of the improper
action of the escrowee. Does such bona fide purchaser
for value obtain any rights as against the grantor who delivers the deed in escrow? The older law, which proceeded upon the premise that no title passed until there
was a delivery by the escrowee pursuant to the condition,
was obliged to say no (11). Respectable courts are to
be found, however, which insist upon protecting the bona

---

(10) Doe d. Garmons v. Knight, 5 B. & C. 671.
(11) Smith v. South Royalton Bank, 32 Vt. 341.

fide purchaser for value (12), though the precise theory does not yet authoritatively appear.

§ 107. **Same: Ambiguous delivery.** Great inconvenience and often expensive litigation ensues when the grantor, who delivers his deed to a third party, leaves it ambiguous whether he has placed the instrument absolutely out of his control or has reserved a right to recall it. This ambiguity arises in the cases where a father, not wishing to hazard the uncertainties of will-making, makes a deed conveying his farm to his children equally. He keeps the matter secret, and, not wishing to be deprived during his lifetime, he places the deed in the hands of some neighbor or justice of the peace or lawyer, with instructions to deliver it to his children at his death. If at this time he reserves the right to recall the instrument, as he frequently does, the instrument cannot be valid as a deed at his death, because it was never delivered before his death. The instrument was never put out of the control of the grantor beyond his right to recall it. As a matter of fact, the whole transaction on the part of the grantor is an attempt to make a will. He has attempted to dispose of his property at the time of his death and he has made that disposition revocable at any time during his life. This precisely complies with the definition of a testamentary act. The difficulty is that the deed is not attested and executed as is required in order to make it effective as a will. Even if it be properly attested and executed as wills are required to be, yet at least one respectable court has held that since it is in the form of a

---

(12) Schurtz v. Colvin, 55 Oh. St. 274.

deed it cannot be proved as a will (13). In any event, the
old man who so carefully set out to avoid the terrors and
uncertainties of will-making, has succeeded in attempting to make a will without the slightest effort at complying with the requirements, which he probably knew something of and would have fulfilled had he only known what
he was doing.

Such is the logical result where the grantor does reserve a right to recall the instrument in the case just put.
The determination of the fact whether he did reserve any
such right is a matter which depends upon conversations
between the alleged escrowee and the grantor at the time
of the delivery to him. At that time the grantor may
have used phrases which are ambiguous beyond the hope
of satisfactory interpretation. The person to whom the
deed was entrusted may not remember what was said, or
he may honestly or corruptly state what was said inac-
curately or falsely. After long and expensive litigation
the whole question of fact may still be obscure and the
final result depend upon nothing definite or satisfactory.

§ 108. Delivery upon condition to grantee. There is
one technical and dogmatic rule regarding delivery upon
condition which must be noted. The grantor cannot deliver upon condition to the grantee. If he does so the title
passes in spite of the fact that the condition has not been
performed (14). There is a modern tendency, not yet

---

(13)   Noble v. Fickes, 230 Ill. 594.
(14)   Whyddon's Case, Cro. El. 520; Shep. Touch. 58, 59.

very well defined, to protect the grantor against the grantee in such a case. But if the grantee has conveyed to a bona fide purchaser for value it is believed that the grantor must stand the loss.

CHAPTER IV.

REGISTRATION OF TITLE.

Section 1. Registration under Recording Acts.

§ 109. The recording statutes. There is some diversity in the provisions of the recording statutes in this country. Some provide that an unrecorded deed shall be ineffective against all the world, except the grantor and those who take from him with actual notice and record first. This makes the unrecorded deed invalid against attaching judgment and execution creditors, and subsequent transferees who did not pay value, provided they had no actual notice. Others provide that the unrecorded deed shall be void only against the subsequent purchaser for value without notice who records first. This makes the unrecorded deed good against judgment, execution and attaching creditors. Other acts combine the features of these two sorts of statutes, making an unrecorded deed void against judgment, execution and attaching creditors and purchasers for value who record first. A rather clumsy form of statute is one which only requires recording within, let us say, six months, and only fixes the character of the deed as an unrecorded deed if it has not been filed for record within the six months. Thus, if A receive a conveyance in January and records it in May, he can claim ahead of B, who purchased for value without notice and received a conveyance in February and recorded the same day. A rather extreme form of statute is one which makes the unrecorded deed void against the subsequent purchaser, whether he has notice of the previous unrecorded deed or not. The provision of local statutes must be ascertained when the necessity arises.

§ 110. **Recording gives notice of what is recorded.** Whether our acts say so in terms or not, they are construed as providing that what is properly recorded is notice to all the world. Thus, if A agrees to sell land to B, and then A sells to C, who is a bona fide purchaser for value; in the absence of all recording, C will prevail over B. Now, if B records and the statute thereupon gives constructive notice of B's contract to all the world, C ceases to be in law a purchaser without notice. C is chargeable with notice of the contract, and B will prevail. Such, it is believed, is the universal attitude of our American courts toward the recording acts. This is in sharp contrast to the attitude of the English courts toward a recording act passed in the reign of Queen Anne. That act might have been treated in the same way as our American courts have treated the American statutes. Nevertheless, the statute of Anne was held to give no notice of the instrument recorded, and hence, in the case put, B, although he records, would not prevail over C, who was in fact a purchaser without actual notice. Naturally the English registry act of Queen Anne's time was not successful in introducing a general registry system. It is to the single fact that the American recording acts are statutes which make properly recorded instruments notice to all the world that the success of our registry system may be largely ascribed.

§ 111. **Unauthorized recording.** Formerly, it was usually a statutory requirement that, before an instrument was entitled to be recorded, it must be acknowledged before a notary or other public officer. The reason for this was that the recording acts usually allowed a certified copy of the record to be introduced in evidence by way of proof of the original, where a proper foundation had been laid that the original had been lost. Hence, for this purpose, it was expedient that the deed be proved by acknowledgment before it was recorded. The requirement of acknowledgment had no particular connection with the effect of the record as notice to all the world, yet the courts were inclined to hold that if the deed were not acknowledged, although it was duly recorded, it was not notice by the record to any one. Statutes, however, have now been very generally passed remedying this defect and making an unacknowledged deed actually recorded, constructive notice, like a deed properly acknowledged and recorded.

§ 112. **Errors of record.** Suppose A, owning lots 4, 5, and 6, conveys 4, 5 and 6 to X by deed. The recorder erroneously copies the deed so as to make it appear that lot 5 had not been conveyed, and thereafter A conveys lot 5 to Y, a bona fide purchaser for value. So far as the statute will permit it, Y ought to be protected. It is not usual or natural for a grantee to look at the record to see if his deed has been correctly recorded, yet it is possible for him to do so, while Y has absolutely no chance of doing so. Of course, whichever one of X or Y loses has an action on the case against the recorder for damage arising from his neglect of duty.

§ 113. Against what conveyances unrecorded deeds are valid. Unrecorded deeds are good against the grantor. Now suppose the grantor dies and his heir then conveys to a bona fide purchaser who records first. Can the grantee of the heir claim against the grantee in the unrecorded deed? When this case arose it was argued that, since the unrecorded deed was good against the grantor, the grantor's heir got nothing by descent and hence his grantee got nothing. Such reasoning, however, did not prevail, and the unrecorded deed was held not to be valid as against the purchaser from the heir (1). Such a ruling helped materially to sustain the object of the recording acts.

§ 114. Conflict between lis pendens and registration. There is a rule of the courts that when a suit in relation to land is started against a defendant, and service of summons is had upon him, the suit is constructive notice to all who may attempt to take title from that defendant. Thus suppose A conveys to B, and B obtains the conveyance by fraud. A sues B for a re-conveyance and obtains a decree in his favor. If, before any decree is rendered against B but after service of process upon him, B conveys to C, who takes without actual notice, C will nevertheless take subject to the decree afterwards entered against B and must convey to A. This is known as the application of the doctrine of lis pendens (pendency of suit). Such a

(1) Earl v. Fiske, 103 Mass. 491.

rule was necessary in order that litigation might not be prolonged indefinitely by transfers pending the suit, and so that a suit might not in the end result in a futile decree.

Now suppose A has an unrecorded claim against B by way of mortgage, and A files a suit to foreclose against B, and B is served with process. B, then, before the final decree, conveys to a purchaser for value without notice. Subsequently the decree against B to foreclose is entered. Will it bar the right of the purchaser for value without notice? Here, it will be observed, the doctrine of the recording acts comes in conflict with the rule of lis pendens. By the doctrine of lis pendens the purchaser for value had constructive notice of the suit and of A's rights. Under the rule of the recording acts he was perfectly protected in dealing with B as the owner, clear of any rights of A under A's unrecorded mortgage. Which, then, shall prevail? The courts are probably hopelessly divided upon the question. Statutes in some states have settled the point by providing for the filing of a lis pendens notice in the registry of deeds and that suits shall not be notice to purchasers by the doctrine of lis pendens unless that is done. Such is the proper solution of the difficulty.

§ 115. Estoppel: Grantor and grantee indices. Suppose (following the case stated in §§ 100-101, above) that A, having no title, conveys to B. Then X, the true owner, conveys to A, and A conveys to C, a purchaser for value, without notice of any rights of B. Can C claim against B? On the supposition that this question was not complicated with any recording of the deed from A to B, or A to C, this question was tentatively answered in the negative (§ 101 above), provided the courts followed the common holding that a legal title passed to B by way of estoppel immediately upon the acquisition by A of the title from X. Suppose, now, we inject into the above case the practical element of the recording acts. B records as soon as he receives his deed from A. A records as soon as he receives his deed from X, and C records as soon as he receives his deed from A. Now, can C claim against B? The final answer to this depends to some extent upon other considerations not yet mentioned.

If the indices to the records required by law are what are known as grantor and grantee indices, and these are the only ones in use, much may be said in favor of C's prevailing over B. Such indices simply refer to all instruments filed by the names of the grantors and grantees. Under this system a reasonably careful conveyancer in tracing a title will commence with a certain grantee and run down the column of grantors in the grantor index till he finds the name of that person. He will then make a minute of that conveyance and then run down the grantee in that conveyance again in the grantor index, and so on till he has exhausted all the conveyances. By this process it is plain that the conveyancer will run down X's name in the grantor's index until he finds his deed to A, and then he will run down A's name in the grantor's index from the date he received the title until he comes to his conveyance to C. He will never find by this process the conveyance from A to B. To cover deeds made by a grantee before he received title the searcher would have to run down each grantee in the grantor's index practically from the date of his birth. That would be an extraordinary labor. It would be a labor out of all proportion to the benefit to be derived or the danger sought to be avoided, for such cases as the one put arise with the greatest infrequency. It is believed that reasonably careful conveyancers do not attempt to make any such search. Under these circumstances a ruling by courts that the deed from A to B before A received his title, though recorded, really stands upon the footing of an unrecorded deed, since it is out of the regular chain of title, is welcomed by conveyancers and should be by the public at large. Courts have reached such a result (2). They have, however, also reached the contrary result (3).

§ 116. **Same: Tract indices, or both kinds.** Now suppose the indices required by law to be kept are what are known as tract indices, i. e., indices on which are noted on different pages the description of different parcels of property, and in the columns beneath a minute of all conveyances touching that property is noted. In that case the overlooking of the deed from A to B will be out of the question. The deed from A to B will appear in the chain of title plainly and easily. Under such circumstances the deed from A to B would be in the regular chain of title, and C, when he took his deed from A, would have constructive notice of B's interest from the records. The holding would then be in favor of B, provided always that B would prevail over C in the absence of all recording.

(2)   Calder v. Chapman, 52 Pa. 359.
(3)   White v. Patten, 24 Pick. 324.

Suppose that the only indices in fact provided for by law were grantor and grantee indices, but that as a matter of fact tract indices were kept. It would be impossible to have in such a case more than one rule for a given jurisdiction. Unless, therefore, the practice of having tract indices were universal throughout the state, it is difficult to see how it would furnish the basis for any result other than that which permits C to prevail over B.

§ 117. **Purchaser without notice from purchaser with notice.** Suppose A, having title, conveys to B, and then to C. C records first, but has notice. Then B records. C then conveys to D, who is a purchaser without actual notice of the conveyance to B. B would have had priority over C. Will B then have priority over the grantee from C?

That will depend upon whether B's deed, though recorded, will stand as an unrecorded deed so far as D is concerned, because it is out of the regular chain of title. This again may depend upon the sort of indices which are legally required to be kept. If only the grantor and grantee indices are legally required and in use, it is apparent that in making a chain of title a conveyancer having found the deed from A to C will drop A and look for conveyances from C. A rule which required the subsequent purchaser from C to take notice of deeds from A recorded after the deed to C, would require a search of all deeds from A recorded after the deed from A to C, and until such time as C might convey to D. This again would place a burden on the searcher out of all proportion to the benefits to be gained or the danger sought to be avoided, because the situation presented in the case put must arise very rarely. It has been held that in the case put D must prevail over B (4), and the contrary has also been held. When tract indices are required to be kept a different result might conceivably be reached because the above reasoning would not apply, and the recorded deed from A to B would fairly be in the chain of title.

§ 118. **A puzzle case.** Suppose X makes a first mortgage to A to secure $2,000, this not being recorded. Then X makes a second mortgage to secure $5,000 to B, which is recorded, but B has notice of the first mortgage. Then X makes a third mortgage to secure $3,000 to C, who records and has no actual notice of the first mortgage. The land sells on foreclosure for $6,000. How shall this sum be divided? Apparently A is preferred to B; B is preferred to C; and C is preferred to A. One solution of the problem would seem to be this: C is the least culpable. He has recorded properly and has no notice of the unrecorded instrument. A is in default for not recording. B, although he recorded, had notice of the prior unrecorded instrument. It is fair, then, to start with C's rights and protect them first. C then is entitled to all of the fund except $5,000, the amount he knew was ahead of his mortgage. That leaves C $1,000. The remaining $5,000 may be divided between A and B in either one of two ways: 1. It may be said that since A is preferred to B, A must have his whole $2,000 out of the fund of $5,000, leaving B $3,000; and that it is proper that B should suffer be-

---

(4) Morse v. Curtis, 140 Mass. 112. Contra: Van Rensselaer v. Clark, 17 Wend. 25.

cause he could have given C notice of A's mortgage by recording his mortgage as a *second* mortgage, and so had
C postponed and excluded from any share in the fund.
2. A juster solution, however, would give to A $1,000
and B $4,000 on the ground that if A had recorded, C
would have had nothing and B would have obtained
$4,000 of the $6,000 and A $2,000; that if you give A
$2,000 and B $3,000, you will be making B pay for the
error of A in not recording, which is a more culpable error
than B's failure to give C notice of A's unrecorded mortgage. Furthermore, it does not lie in A's mouth to say
that B has caused the trouble.

SECTION 2. REGISTRATION UNDER TORRENS SYSTEM·

§ 119. **The system of conveyancing produced by the
recording acts.** The recording system inevitably produced the abstract of title business. It was natural that
the evidence of title upon which transfers were based
should be abstracts of records made by competent professional abstract makers of known integrity and care. As
chains of title grew long and often more complicated it
became necessary that lawyers skilled in the law of titles
should give an opinion as to who had title, based upon
what the abstract showed. In many places of late, both
functions have been absorbed by corporations doing an
abstract and title business. These have added to the
business of conveyancing the feature of title insurance
backed by a guaranty surplus. This does not mean that
the title companies take any risks other than those which
the more prudent conveyancers incur. It means simply
that the opinion of conveyancing counsel and care in

making up an abstract are backed with greater financial
responsibility.

§ 120. **Defects of the system: Purchasers not completely protected.** There were some weaknesses in the
system of conveyancing built up upon the recording acts.
In the first place the recording system did not protect purchasers against the fact that a deed in the chain of title
was never delivered, or that the grantor was an infant, or
that a grantor who was declared in the deed to be a spin-
ster or a bachelor was not in fact living with a husband or
wife who could claim curtesy or dower. It did not protect purchasers in the proofs of heirship which were made
upon the death of the owner of land intestate. These difficulties, however, were not so great as seriously to interfere with the practical working of the system. General
reliance upon the good faith of transfers was justified by
the results, and it was very rare indeed that an innocent
purchaser was ever deceived or suffered loss. Furthermore, with the advent of the guaranty system by corporations, possibility of financial loss as a result of these risks
was reduced to a minimum.

§ 121. **Same: Increasing cost of transfers.** A more
serious difficulty with the recording system was the increased cost of land transfers. The chain of title must be
kept up by continuations of the abstract. In case of
foreclosures, partitions, proceedings to quiet title, or the
transfer of property by devise or intestacy, the number of
pages of abstract for a transfer may run from twenty to
fifty, at a cost of from fifty to one hundred dollars. In
cases of the foreclosure of a mortgage dealing with a sub-

division, where many different holdings have been sold to different persons and resold, the fees for the abstract have been known very materially to add to the price of each individual lot. In places where the records have been destroyed by fire and the abstract company has secured the only set of books of minutes of ante-fire records, they have been able to levy a heavy toll for ante-fire abstracts and proofs of title. Then as chains of title have grown long and more difficult, the examinations by competent counsel have become more expensive and upon each transfer a complete examination of the whole title had to be made from the beginning and paid for.

§ 122. **Benefits from title companies.** The advent of the guaranty companies did much toward ameliorating this useless waste. By well systemized records of former examinations, double examinations were avoided and each examination was made where the last left off. The cost of making abstracts for the purpose of making examinations was reduced. Thus the title company has been able to provide itself with an abstract for examination, examine it, and issue a policy representing financial responsibility, at a less cost than the independent lawyer and abstract maker could do it. The consequence is that the independent abstract maker first, and latterly the independent lawyer-conveyancer, has largely been driven from this field of work, and the title guaranty company has made itself an established place in the conveyancing business.

§ 123. **Weaknesses of title guaranty system.** But the practice of the abstract company was not without a flaw.

It still had to make abstracts, and the owner still had **a**
right to file all sorts of papers, be engaged in all sorts of
lawsuits, and die leaving a complicated will or **an in-**
solvent estate, between the date of one guaranty policy
and another, so that an expensive abstract might still be
necessary for a single transfer; and, upon examination
by the company, title might be found to be so defective
that further legal proceedings must be instituted to clear
it up.   Furthermore, the abstract and title guaranty business has tended in a given locality to become the monop-
oly of a certain corporation or corporations operating under mutual understandings, so that the complaint of excessive charges has been made.   It has also been observed
that, if the title company makes a fatal mistake, the landowner will lose his land and have a recovery for money
limited to the face of his policy, which is often allowed to
remain at the figure at which land was purchased, far below the enhanced value of the land.   The time which it
takes to close a real estate transfer through the title company is considerable.   The company has to make an abstract from the last continuation, and the title must then
be examined and passed upon.   Even in a simple case
this takes several days.   Then there is always a gap between the date of the opinion of title rendered by the company and the date of passing deeds and the purchase
price. The purchaser is obliged to take the chance that the
seller has not in the meantime made a conveyance to another or had a judgment rendered against him, or else go
to the expense of an escrow arrangement by which the
deeds and the purchase price are deposited pending the

recording of the deed and the further examination of the title.

§ 124. **Registration under the Torrens system: General aims.** To meet the difficulties enumerated above, South Australia in 1858 adopted legislation providing for a new system of registration of land titles The initiative in this movement was taken by Sir Robert Torrens, from whom it gained the name, the "Torrens system." It was generally adopted in Australia, and in varying forms is now in use in several of the United States and to a limited extent in England.

The Torrens system aims to secure three important improvements in methods of dealing with land titles: First, that the state of the title shall be once determined conclusively for all time. Second, that the sufficiency and effect of each transfer thereafter shall be determined for all time at the time it is made. Third, that the whole state of the title shall be known at any one time by a simple reference to the appropriate record of the registrar's office.

§ 125. **Methods employed.** The first object is attained by a complete judicial hearing, with service of process upon and the publication of notice to all possible adverse interests, the taking of proofs of ownership, and the settling of all disputed questions of title by a decree directing registration. The registration of the title pursuant to the decree settles the title of the real estate, whether rightly or wrongly, and, when the time for review has gone by, the title so decreed is good so long as the decrees of the court are upheld by the government. There is no such thing as taking the applicant's title away from him and giving him damages too frequently inadequate.

The second object is attained by causing the title to be transferred only by the act of registration. The deed of the party no longer passes the title—it merely directs the registrar to transfer it and places upon him the legal duty to transfer it. Title passes only as and when the registrar transfers it on his books or records. Hence, the transfer as the registrar makes it is the one that counts. So it is with incumbrances, liens and mortgages. They do not exist as incumbrances till the registrar has noted them upon his records. The registrar's certificate of title becomes the legal evidence of title, and not the act of the parties.

The third object is attained by a scientific method of bookkeeping. Each parcel of land registered has its own certificate, which is executed in duplicate. The owner has one. The other is kept on file in the office of the registrar. Whenever any lien or incumbrance is placed upon the property it is not effective until noted on the certificate. Hence, the exact state of the title is known at all times by reference to the certificate. When the title is transferred, the old certificate is cancelled and the new one made to the purchaser with such incumbrances appearing as are still liens, and the duplicate of that is again kept by the registrar.

§ 126. Indemnity fund feature. In the Torrens act as it came to us from Australia the power of the registrar in exercising a judicial discretion to determine who had title, and in whose name title should be registered, was very great. Under these circumstances the establishment of an indemnity fund, or governmental liability for the registrar's mistakes, was an essential and important feature of the act. In most of our American jurisdictions, however, a Torrens act in this original form, with such power in the registrar, would probably be held unconstitutional as vesting judicial power outside of the constitutionally established courts and depriving the landowner of his property without due process of law. Hence, our American Torrens acts necessarily include a complete judicial hearing, upon service of process, to all persons interested, before any registration is made. They may, indeed, go further and provide for a judicial hearing upon any acts of the registrar involving the exercise of any possible determination of the state of a title. The result is that the American Torrens registrar can hardly make a vital mistake as to a title which the court, on notice to all parties, has not been a party to, and inquiry into which is not precluded by an adjudication. The indemnity fund feature, or general governmental responsibility for mistakes in registration, while it exists in our American acts, is, it is believed, of much less practical importance than is usually supposed.

§ 127. **Advantages of Torrens system: Final settlement of validity of title.** The original proceeding to register is in reality (except in contested cases) only the examination of the title in the usual way by means of an abstract or other evidences of title, and the entry of a decree upon the evidence presented. This proceeding, however, has advantages over an ordinary examination of

title. It can terminate all objections to the title by means
of a judicial decree, while examinations by conveyancers
can only note the objections time after time, and conveyancing counsel can only give their opinion time after
time that certain objections may be safely disregarded.
In contested cases of registration under the Torrens acts,
legal titles and questions of incumbrances can be finally
settled.

§ 128. Same: Protection to all interested parties. Some
prejudice has been excited against the system by raising
the fear that by means of a Torrens registration a good
title in A might be taken away from him and placed in B,
and that A would have no recourse except against an indemnity fund. To this it may be replied that the same
thing may happen in any court proceeding to quiet title.
Thus, wherever anyone files a suit in court to establish
title in himself, there is usually some important adverse
interest which he is desirous of getting rid of. Suppose,
for the sake of argument, that the plaintiff has no title
whatever. He is obliged to make all persons having adverse interests parties. If they default and do not appear the plaintiff still is obliged to produce prima facie
evidence of his own title. He does so and the court scruti-
nizes his evidence to the best of its ability, and, no objection being made by anybody, renders a decree in his
favor. In such cases the true owner, who might have
been able to establish his title beyond a shadow of doubt,
may be entirely barred of his rights and without any recourse whatsoever. The same thing is true by a proceeding to establish title under the Torrens acts, but it is not

peculiar to a proceeding under the Torrens acts. The result is one common to all proceedings to establish title. As a matter of fact, the danger of a bad title being registered is less under the Torrens acts than it is under a direct court proceeding to quiet or establish title. The Torrens examiners understand from the first that they have a public duty to perform, and that they are the protectors of the Torrens indemnity fund. The result is that, from the time a petition for registration is filed, the claims and proofs of each applicant are as carefully scrutinized as in the case of a sale under the old system, where the seller submitted his abstract and proofs of title to the purchaser for examination. The Torrens examiners make a careful conveyancer's examination of the abstract of title, note all possible objections to the title, and require objections to be cleared up precisely as if no registration was to be made; and not until the objections are either waived, on grounds which a conveyancing counsel would certify as sound, or cleared up by proofs or additional deeds, will the Torrens examiners make a report to the court that a decree should be entered finding a clear title in the applicant. This represents an infinitely greater amount of care in the examination of proofs of title than is ever exercised in ordinary court proceedings where the defendants are in default and no contest is made. In such instances it is the common experience of lawyers in American jurisdictions that the court signs the decree which is handed him by counsel for the complainant, and does not pretend to go through the long and tedious process of examining proofs and evidence in support of the plaintiff's prima facie right. It cannot be too strongly insisted that under the Torrens acts there is no loophole by which an individual with no title can rush in and have himself registered as the holder of title to land which he does not in fact own.

§ 128a. **Same: State of title always a matter of record.** Under the Torrens acts title is never allowed to get away from the hands of the public officer or his assistants. The exact and authoritative state of the title is known at all times by reason of the fact that it can be changed only through the medium and by the act of the registrar. Each step in the title is scrutinized by experts when it is taken and at the very time it is made, so that any mistakes of the parties can be considered at once. Such a thing as a misdescription can hardly occur. Strange and weird clauses in deeds, made by ignorant persons, are at once brought to their attention by experts in time to have a better instrument executed and substituted. Upon the death of an owner of registered land no new certificate issues until due proof of heirship has been made or the will is presented. If any difficulties of construction occur in the will, they may be settled by a simple reference to the court which made the original registration for directions as to how the new certificate shall specify the interests.

§ 129. **Same: Facilitates rapid transfer of title.** The time required in which to close up transfers is of the briefest. The grantor makes a direction to the registrar to transfer the title to Jones and to hold the certificate till Jones pays the grantor the purchase price. The registrar makes the new certificate which shows title in Jones, and Jones makes his delivery of cash to the seller and obtains his certificate. The time necessary for the transaction can be reduced to a day.

§ 129a. Same: Reduces cost. The fees for the original registration and subsequent transfers vary, of course, in different communities. In Chicago they compare very favorably with the current rates for guaranty policies. Thirty dollars covers the cost of a registration under the Torrens act. In a simple case of valid title, no lawyer is needed. The landowner places his abstract and evidences of title in the hands of the Torrens office. The abstract is brought down to date from the public records by expert abstractors of the office. The entire title is then examined by a competent examiner, who renders an opinion upon the title with all usual conveyancer's objections noted. This is then examined and approved by the Torrens examiner, who is a competent conveyancing counsel. If the title is then found to be without any material objections the Torrens office prepares the petition making the proper persons parties thereto, files this with the clerk of the court to which the cause is assigned, sees to the securing of proper service of process upon the defendants, and, when service is complete, secures a reference by the court to the Torrens examiner, who, as a judicial officer, drafts a report based upon the evidence of title submitted, and recommends a decree in accordance with the report. This is entered, the certificate of title is thereupon issued pursuant to the decree, and the landowner receives back his evidences of title.

Now suppose the landowner desires to obtain a guaranty policy at the current rates in Chicago. He will find that these vary with the amount of the policy and this, of course, is fixed according to the value of the land. For a policy of five hundred dollars or less the rate is twenty dollars. The increase is two dollars per hundred after that until ten thousand is reached and it is three dollars per hundred for amounts over ten thousand. This, of course, means at least an equal initial cost to that of obtaining a Torrens certificate in all cases where property is worth one thousand dollars. The current charges for bringing down an abstract are as follows: Certificate, five dollars; each ordinary instrument, one dollar and a half; each judgment or tax sale or special assessment shown, one dollar and a half; each written page of chancery or probate matter, one dollar and a half; each typewritten page of chancery or probate matter, three dollars. In many cases the cost of an additional abstract without any policy would equal the fees required to secure a Torrens certificate.

Now suppose one landowner has a Torrens certificate and another a guaranty policy. What are the respective charges necessary to have a new certificate or a new policy issued to the transferee? In the case of the guaranty policy the minimum current charge is six dollars and a half, but this charge may be much increased if the title has passed by will, or by foreclosure, or in any other way involving an unusually long proceeding since the first policy was issued. In such cases the price for issuing a new policy at the same amount may approach the thirty dollar mark. If the land has increased in value by placing improvements thereon or otherwise, and it is desired to increase the face of the policy, the cost will be five dollars per thousand of increase. On the other hand, each new certificate under the Torrens act costs three dollars, and it makes no difference how difficult or complicated the step in the title may be.

§ 130. General conclusion. The Torrens system in theory is an improvement over any system of conveyancing yet put into practice. Under the guidance of an efficient registrar and an effective corps of assistants, there is no doubt that it can be made a practical success and an actual improvement over any system in force. In all jurisdictions where it has been tried it is probable that the act will need constant revision in details in the light of practical experience, in order that the best results may be obtained. Above all, the holding of office by an able registrar and the retention in their positions of able and efficient examiners and assistants, is absolutely necessary. Finally, it may be said that there would be the greatest danger in the Torrens system being made compulsory for all lands inventoried in the estates of decedents—a plan which has been agitated in at least one American jurisdiction. Such a provision would, it is believed, swamp even a large and efficiently managed office. The natural growth will be fast enough, and in the process of its development an efficient corps of men will be educated and trained to enable the work to be satisfactorily carried on upon a large scale, and the Torrens act itself improved and perfected.

CHAPTER V.

DEDICATION.

§ 130a. Conveyance by dedication. Dedication is the name for a mode of conveyance to the public of a right to use the land of the dedicator. The most usual example of this form of conveyance is the dedication of a highway for the use of the public. The conveyance by dedication is absolutely formless. In general only an intent to dedicate, expressed in any manner, and, in this country at least, an acceptance on behalf of the public, is all that is required. When the dedication is complete no title in fee to the soil passes to the public, but only a right of user. The fee of the property dedicated remains in the dedicator, subject merely to the right of user of the public for the purpose for which the dedication was made. Dedication of this character is often called a "common law dedication" to distinguish it from dedications made pursuant to statutes which prescribe the formalities for what is called "statutory dedication."

§ 131. What may be dedicated. In England public highways only may be dedicated. In this country, especially in the early part and middle of the last century, when a great territory was rapidly developing and land was extraordinarily cheap as compared with present prices, the rights that might be dedicated to the public became much enlarged. It was held that the dedication of a

190

common or park might be made. Land might be dedicated for the pious uses of a particular religious society,
or for a public burying ground (even though the right to
bury was restricted to the inhabitants of a given town),
and for public schools. Respectable jurisdictions have
permitted the dedication for a public landing-place, but
others have denied this; and a dedication for a railroad
station has and would, it is believed, be generally denied.
In some of these results the courts of the earlier period
in our history have tended to go farther than the courts
of the present would be inclined to do. The tendency today is to confine the object of dedication to such rights as
the whole world may use. That includes not much more
than highways and commons or parks. It would exclude
the gift to the public by dedication of the right to use
land for public schools, graveyards for the inhabitants of
a particular town, the pious uses of a particular religious
society, or a railroad station.

The reason for this latter-day tendency to restrict the
purposes for which a dedication may be made is the increasing value of land, and the fact that a dedication is so
far a formless mode of conveyance that there is great
danger of a dedication being forced upon an individual
unjustly. All of the considerations of policy in favor of
conveyances of real estate being permitted, only where
such formalities are complied with as to leave no doubt
of the consent of the landowner to part with his title, are
applicable in cases of dedication where the objects for
which land may be dedicated are very much enlarged.
Since such policy cannot be satisfied by the courts cre-

ating artificial formalities to evidence a dedication, the natural course is to restrict the objects for which a dedication may be made according to the formless mode of conveyance which the common law recognizes.

§ 131a. **The act of** dedication. No formal act of dedication is necessary on the part of the dedicator. All that is necessary, so far as he is concerned, is that he should express his intent to dedicate. That may be done in a hundred ways. His intent to dedicate may be expressed in words—as where a plat is made and exhibited with the strip shown for a street marked expressly as "public street" or "highway;" or the dedicator may put up a sign on the way in question declaring it to be "a public way." The intent of the dedicator to dedicate may also be expressed by interpretation from circumstantial evidence. The dedicator may have said nothing, yet his acts may speak as effectively as his words. The usual character of this circumstantial evidence of an intent to dedicate consists in the alleged dedicator opening a roadway and permitting its unobstructed use as such by the public. Such facts as these raise an inference of an intent to dedicate. Of course, this inference may be met by explanatory evidence that the alleged dedicator had no such intent in opening up the roadway, but did so for his private convenience. Careful landowners who open up roadways which they in fact desire the public to use, perhaps for the landowner's own benefit, but who do not wish to run the risk of parting with rights beyond recall, place upon the roadway a sign to this effect in substance: "Private way. No passing through." Such signs kept up continuously rebut any inference of an intent to dedicate. Much long and difficult litigation often occurs over whether the circumstantial evidence shows an intent to dedicate or not.

§ 132. **Acceptance.** In England, where only ways can be dedicated, and where land is in general valuable and the country is thickly settled, no inconvenience was felt from the rule that a dedication occurred upon the dedicator expressing his intent to dedicate, and that no acceptance on the part of the public was necessary to complete the dedication. In this country, however, a county or a township in a sparsely settled district might be ruined by the too free dedication of highways. There were two reasons for this result: First, once the highway is created, the county or township must keep it in repair or be liable for damages occurring through its being out of repair; and, second, land was so cheap that there was no brake upon the generosity of the landowner. In this country, then, acceptance is required to complete the dedication. In some states, statutes have been passed permitting acceptance to be made only by certain specified public officers. More frequently, it is believed, acceptance may be made by a municipal officer who has authority either expressed in words or arising by inference from the nature and general scope of his duties. Acceptance also may be inferred from continuous user by the public for a number of years.

§ 132a. **Effect of lapse of time.** Mere lapse of time during which the public has used the land of A for some public purpose for which land may be dedicated is important in several ways. It may aid in showing an acceptance by the public. If, however, the user by the public continues adversely to the landowner without interruption, and without concealment, for more than twenty years, it results in a dedication by operation of law without any intent on the part of the dedicator or any acceptance by the public. The highway is then said to have been created by prescription, on the same principle that easements in favor of a private owner over the land of his neighbor may be acquired by prescription, as hereinafter described (§ 119ff, below). The fact that a highway may thus be acquired by prescription necessitates a further precaution by the careful landowner who is willing, perhaps even desirous, for his own benefit that the public should use the private road, but does not wish a dedication to occur. The careful landowner has already put up the sign "Private way. No passing through," but the public keeps on passing through just the same. The user by the public is, therefore, by every just inference from the circumstances adverse to the landowner. The public continues its use in direct defiance of the notice that each and every one of them are trespassers. In spite of that sign, then, it may be that after twenty years of adverse, uninterrupted, open, and notorious user by the public, the way will become a public way in spite of the sign. What then must the landowner do? At stated periods, less than twenty years apart, he must proceed to interrupt the user by the public for an appreciable length

of time. Let him, therefore, draw chains across the way
or otherwise bar the way to the use of the public for a
day, and thereby stop the continuity of the adverse user
by the public.

PART II

TRANSFER OR ACQUISITION OF TITLE WITHOUT CONSENT OF OWNER.

CHAPTER VI.

INVOLUNTARY TRANSFER.

§ 133. **Forfeiture for crime.** At common law forfeitures of land to the state for crime were legal. In the case of treason the forfeiture was forever; in the case of lesser crimes, for a year and a day. By the Constitution of the United States forfeiture for treason is forbidden, except during the life of the person convicted (1). In most states, by statute or constitutional provision, forfeiture for crime is abolished. In some, forfeiture for a limited time still exists.

§ 134. **Forfeiture for wrongful alienation.** When a life tenant or tenant for years, by a conveyance in the form with which we are today familiar, attempts to convey more than he has, the instrument of conveyance is effective simply to transfer what the tenant may actually have. It is believed that the mere conveyance itself is not ground of forfeiture. Such ground only occurs, if at all, when the tenant unequivocally repudiates the tenancy and refuses to hold under the landlord, or wrongfully delivers possession to another.

---

(1) Const., Art III, Sec. 5, § 2.

§ **135. Execution sales.** The formalities of execution sales must be left for their description to the local statutes, which vary greatly in detail. The general subject is thoroughly treated in the article on Attachment, Garnishment and Execution in Volume X of this work.

§ **136. Bankruptcy and insolvency.** It is believed that practically all bankruptcy and insolvent acts contain provisions for transfer to the trustee in bankruptcy or the assignee in insolvency of all the land belonging to the bankrupt or insolvent. See the article on Bankruptcy, Chapter IV, in Volume X of this work.

§ **137. Marriage: Curtesy and dower.** By the common law, when a man married a woman who was then the owner in fee of real estate, the husband immediately became entitled to an estate during the life of his wife in all of his wife's real estate. This was known as the husband's estate in the right of his wife. See Domestic Relations and Persons, § 30, in Volume II of this work. If a child was born of the marriage the husband secured upon his wife's death an additional estate by the *curtesy*, as it was called, during his own life. This also was in the whole of the wife's real estate. Upon the husband's death, leaving his wife surviving, she became entitled for her life to one-third of all the real estate owned by her husband at the time of her marriage or thereafter acquired by him, whether sold by him or not unless she had joined in the transfer. This was called *dower*. No birth of issue of the marriage was required as a condition precedent to the wife's right to dower. It is this possible right of curtesy or dower which makes it imperative

in all cases for the wife or husband of one transferring
title to land to join in the deed for the purpose of releasing the right of curtesy or dower.

§ 138. Same: Statutory changes. In some jurisdictions curtesy has been abolished and husband and wife
alike have an estate of dower in one-third of the spouse's
real estate which the spouse owned at the time of the
marriage or thereafter acquired, and no birth of issue
of the marriage is required. There is some tendency
toward a legislative change by which one spouse obtains
dower only in such land of the other as he or she dies
actually the owner of. Such acts make it unnecessary
for the wife or husband to join in the deed for the purpose of releasing dower. The legislative reasons in
favor of such a reform are these: The cases where a
married woman refuses to join in a deed of her husband's
property in order to release dower, or where she asks
for separate compensation for her right of dower upon
a sale by her husband are very rare. There is no particular legislative policy in favor of the husband's right to
dower in his wife's real estate, and the instances where
he refuses to join in a deed by his wife, except for separate compensation paid to him, are likewise rare. Nevertheless, the danger that in a particular instance dower
may not have been released by the joinder of a wife or
husband is one of the principal reasons why an examination of title dating back for many years is required.
When one considers how much examination and re-exam-
ination of titles may occur during a period of seventy-
five or eighty years, when lands are sold and re-sold, all

for the purpose of catching a possible outstanding dower
or curtesy which is never found in nine hundred and
ninety-nine cases out of a thousand, it is apparent that
there is an economic waste which would be eliminated
were the law to permit dower or curtesy only in such
estates as the husband or wife actually owned at the time
of his or her death. No practical injustice would result
from such an act because of the extreme infrequency with
which, as a matter of practice, a husband or wife has
curtesy or dower in any lands other than those of which
the husband or wife dies actually the owner of.

§ 139. **Same: Community property.** In several south-
western and far western states, including Louisiana,
Texas, New Mexico, Arizona, Idaho, Nevada, California,
and Washington, property acquired by either husband or
wife after marriage except that obtained by gift, devise,
or descent, is held as "community property" of the
spouses. Generally, during the existence of the marriage,
the husband has sole power to manage and convey this
property, without even the necessity of the wife joining
in the transfer (unless his conveyance is in fraud of her
rights). Upon the death of either, the property generally, after payment of community debts, is divided equally
between the survivor and the heirs or devises of the deceased spouse. In California, Nevada, and Idaho, the
husband, as survivor, takes all the community property.

§ 140. **Attachment, judgment, and mechanics' liens.**
These are the subjects of treatment by extensive statutory provisions in all jurisdictions. Rules of practice
respecting them are to be ascertained principally by ref-

erence to the statutes of each particular state. Judgments and Attachments are also the subjects of articles
in Volume X of this work, to which the reader is referred. Contractors, workmen, and material men are in
many states given liens for a certain length of time upon
the property upon which their services or material have
been used in order to secure sums due to them therefor.
A work of this scope cannot go into the details of these
statutes.

§ 141. Partition proceedings. At common law partition of lands held jointly could be compelled only in the
case of co-parceners (§ 26, above). In the time of Henry
VIII, however, statutes were passed providing for this
in the case of other joint tenancies, and today in all states
joint owners (except tenants by the entirety) may compel
a partition or sale of the joint property. If it can be
fairly divided, it will be, and, if not, it may be sold and
the money divided. This remedy is wholly governed by
statutes or rules of courts of equity, into the details of
which there is not space here to enter.

CHAPTER VII.

ACQUISITION BY EXTINCTION OF OWNER'S TITLE.

Section 1. By Authority of the State.

§ 142. Eminent domain. When a title is obtained by the exercise of the state's power of eminent domain to take land for public purposes, the former owner's title is extinguished and a new one is created in the person or corporation or the state exercising the power. The subject of the taking of land under the power of eminent domain is treated in Constitutional Law, §§ 207-25, in Volume XII of this work.

§ 143. Tax sales. When land is sold under public authority for non-payment of taxes, the character of the resulting title is like that acquired under eminent domain proceedings (§ 142 above). Little general information can be given concerning the subject of tax titles. Its rules and regulations are fully dealt with in elaborate statutory provisions in every state. In some the tax title when acquired, is, at least after the period of redemption, a very dangerous adverse title which can only be upset with the greatest difficulty, if at all. In other jurisdictions it is well known that every tax deed can be upset by a good lawyer and a determined client who is prepared to pay the money necessary to fight the tax-buyer through to the highest court. In such jurisdictions the tax title is always noted as a serious objection to the title to the land, and some settlement with the tax-buyer, or a court proceeding to remove the tax deeds as clouds, is required before the title is regarded as merchantable.

SECTION 2.   BY STATUTE OF LIMITATIONS.

§ 144.   Statutes of limitation.   The statutes of limitation in many states provide that actions for the recovery of real estate must be brought within twenty years from the time the action first accrued.   Others reduce the time to fifteen, ten, or even less.   The precise time is a matter of great diversity in different jurisdictions.   Many states have other special statutes which protect the possession of those who have color of title in good faith, and have been in possession and paid taxes for a specified number of years, for instance, seven.   In addition it is sometimes provided that rights in land may be acquired by those who have had color of title in good faith and paid all the taxes on lands for a period of years, say seven, during all of which time said lands have remained vacant and unoccupied, and then have taken possession.   The requirement that there must be color of title in good faith is satisfied by any deed, good in form, such as a tax deed.   Color of title "in good faith" is self-explanatory.

§ 145.   Operation of statutes of limitation.   The most widely known form of statute of limitation in respect to actions for the possession of real estate is that which bars a true owner's right of action when he has failed to assert it for a specified number of years.   In this form it will be observed that the act merely bars the true owner's right of action.   Of course, when the true owner is attempting to recover the possession from the adverse holder, the defendant need rely only upon the literal language of the statute which bars the plaintiff's remedy. Suppose, however, the adverse holder voluntarily goes out of possession and the owner who has been dispossessed for over twenty years takes possession again. If the statute only bars the true owner's remedy, that bar has been waived, and the adverse holder could not now sue to recover possession from the true owner in possession. If, however, the adverse holder has acquired a good title by virtue of the adverse holding for the prescribed time, then the true owner has lost his title; and the adverse holder for twenty years has gained a new and original title under the statute, and can recover possession from any one. This is the result which the courts reach even upon statutes which purport only to bar the owner's remedy (1). It is now generally assumed that all statutes of limitation with respect to real estate operate to raise a new and original title in the adverse holder who has held adversely for a sufficient length of time.

§ 146. **Adverse holding after unlawfully taking possession.** The important question to determine frequently is, when does the statute begin to run—or, as it is often put, when was the true owner disseised, or when did the adverse possession begin? In the ordinary case where the true owner entitled to possession in fee is dispossessed at a given time, and the adverse holder takes possession by a trespass at that time, there is not so much difficulty.

_____

(1)   School Dist. No. 4 v. Benson, 31 Me. 381.

It is all a question of when the adverse holder becomes a hostile stranger to the owner's possession.

§ 147. **Adverse holding after lawfully taking possession: By tenant.** The difficult problem arises when the one claiming to be an adverse holder has originally come into possession by the act and with the consent of the true owner. When does the possession of such a one become adverse?

Suppose, for instance, a tenant in possession repudiates the tenancy and declares that he holds the title in fee and refuses to pay rent or acknowledge the landlord. It is clear that such an oral disclaimer in this country generally would be a ground of forfeiture of the tenancy, but it should not be regarded as terminating the tenancy automatically and at once—being no more than a ground for forfeiture. There is no termination of the tenancy till the landlord elects to forfeit. Until then the tenant is still a tenant, and cannot be an adverse holder. Respectable courts, however, have intimated views to the contrary (2).

Suppose that a tenant for the life of another holds over after the life estate terminates. It is submitted that the possession of the former life tenant at once becomes adverse. But here again it cannot be said that the authorities are precisely agreed. If the tenancy were a tenancy for years, then, upon holding over with the assent of the landlord, a new tenancy arises for a new period—usually for a year—and thereafter a tenancy from year to year

---

(2) Sherman v. Champlain Trans. Co., 31 Vt. 162, 177; 2 Taylor, Landlord and Tenant (9th ed.), § 522.

may arise. The holding over, therefore, by a tenant for years would not be an adverse possession, unless at the same time the landlord refused to recognize him as a tenant.

§ 148. **Same: By licensee.** So, where a licensee holds possession, there is no disseisin or adverse possession on his part, even after the license has terminated by operation of law by the conveyance of the land or the death of the licensor, unless the occupant ceases to claim under the license and begins to claim in his own right (3). Suppose one enters under a parol conveyance or gift of the fee, which of course is ineffective to pass the title, is his possession adverse at once? Why may it not be urged that he is in possession by the license of the owner, so that his possession is not adverse? The answer is, because such is not the fact. The donee enters *as the owner in fee,* and holds claiming a fee and not under any license (4).

§ 149. **Must adverse possessor have wrongful intent.** There was formerly an interesting division of judicial opinion in regard to whether a positive wrongful intent to deprive another was necessary to an adverse possession. This arose in regard to the common case where a neighbor built or placed his fence over the line by mistake, thinking he was within the true line of his own property. Clearly in such a case the person in possession, although by mistake, is actually trespassing and is liable for his trespass. Furthermore, he is claiming the

---

(3) Bond v. O'Gara, 177 Mass. 139.
(4) Sumner v. Stevens, 6 Metc. (Mass.) 337.

land actually occupied over the line which does not belong
to him as his own. If any one were to ask him where his
line was and what actual physical space he was claiming
as his own, he would point to the edge of his house or to
the fence as it actually stood. He would be claiming up
to the point to which his actual occupation ran in the
lands even though his claim was founded upon a mistake.
It is now clear to most courts that such possession by a
neighbor occupying over the line, is an adverse possession
(5). Some courts which formerly thought it was not
have changed their minds (6). But some respectable
jurisdictions still maintain that such a possession is **not**
adverse (7). They protect the adverse holder with the
wrongful intent; but the man who acts on a mistaken idea
of his rights and perhaps makes expensive improvements
relying thereon, is, by reason of his pure motives, penalized.

§ 150. **Adverse possession by one where others claim
under the same instrument.** Suppose A, having no title
to Blackacre, devises it to B for life and then to C in fee.
B enters and occupies the premises adversely for twenty
years. B then obtains, as between himself and C, only a
life estate, and upon B's death C becomes entitled in fee.
The reason for this is that, as against the true owner, B
can claim to be entitled to possession and an estate in
fee simple, if you will; but as between B and C, B cannot deny the terms of the instrument under which he

---

(5) French v. Pearce, 8 Conn. 439.
(6) Taylor v. Fomby, 116 Ala. 621, 626.
(7) Grube v. Wells, 34 Ia. 148.

took possession, and, being by that instrument a life tenant only as respects C, cannot maintain any adverse possession as against C nor deny that C is next entitled (8).

§ 151. Adverse possession against future interests. When a tenant in possession for life or years is disseised, when does the adverse possession begin against the one next entitled to possession? Of course, the adverse possession against the one next entitled to possession will begin when the tenancy expires in the ordinary course—that is, in case it is a life tenancy, at the death of the life tenant. Suppose, however, that the tenant in possession is a life tenant, who is disseised and remains out of possession twenty years, so that all his right to possession is barred. The adverse holder then obtains the fee as against the life tenant. It would seem logically proper to say that, when the life tenant was barred, adverse possession would begin to run against the one entitled after the life tenant. Very respectable courts, however, can be found which refuse so to hold, and assert, instead, that, while as soon as the life tenant is barred the holder of the future interest can elect to enter and claim possession (9), yet in the absence of such a move on his part no adverse possession begins against him till the life tenant actually dies (10). Hence, where B has a life estate and C a fee afterwards, D may hold adversely for sixty years, and, unless B dies more than

(8)   Board v. Board, L. R. 9 Q. B. 48.

(9)   Field v. Peeples, 180 Ill. 376.

(10)   Dawson v. Edwards, 189 Ill. 60.

twenty years before the sixty years expire, C can still claim. The law seems here unnecessarily tender to the person in C's position.

§ 152. Interruption of adverse possession. When the true owner finds that his land has been in the possession of another adversely, he has two courses open to him: (1) To bring suit for possession; or (2) to interrupt the continuity of the adverse possession by making an entry upon it. Whether an entry upon the adverse possession has been accomplished is a question of fact. No rule can be given for precisely what amounts to an entry. It is necessary that the true owner or his agent actually go upon the land physically and invade the possession of the one in adverse possession. Surveyors who find a line improperly run and a fence placed to the disadvantage of their clients sometimes begin slashing up the shrubbery and cutting small trees and undergrowth upon what they deem the land belonging to their client. The rational ground for such seeming vandalism is that their client's rights may be at once protected by the making of a distinct entry upon the possession of the neighbor in adverse possession. Such in fact is its operation. In one case the running of the twenty year statute of limitations was prevented by such action of a surveyor by a margin of only fifteen days.

§ 153. Constructive adverse possession: Size of holding. The rule which defines and makes equal to adverse possession a constructive or fictitious adverse possession is peculiar to this country. It had its origin in the early part of the last century, when the amount of land to be

taken up and improved in this country must have seemed
to be without limit, and when it was as desirable that
titles to large tracts which it was difficult for the claimant
to have actual possession of should be quieted, as it was
in England in the case of tracts of which the actual
possession might at all times be had. To meet this end
the rule was put forth by the courts that a constructive
adverse possession was as good for the purpose of acquiring title under the statute of limitations as an actual
adverse possession.

Constructive possession was held to exist when there
was actual occupation of part of a tract, with a paper
title to the whole. This paper title must have been a
deed or instrument of conveyance, at least perfect in form
for the transfer of title to land (11). Furthermore, the
actual occupation of part, with this paper title to the
whole, could only be constructive possession of so much
as might be deemed "a reasonable appendage to the part
actually occupied." What was such reasonable appendage must depend upon the state of the country and character of the improvements and settlement. One might
well believe that "a reasonable appendage" would be a
very different thing in New York state today from what
it was a century ago, or a different thing in Massachusetts
and in Texas today.

§ 154. Same: Notoriety. Another requirement of a
good constructive possession was that the actual occupation of the land must be such as to give the real owner
notice that his land was being occupied adversely. Thus

(11)   Jackson d. Gilliland v. Woodruff, 1 Cow. (N. Y.) 276.

if there is paper title to a house-lot and also to a lot across
the street, and there is actual occupation of the house-lot
only, there can hardly be any constructive possession of
the lot across the street (12). Suppose there is a paper
title to a house-lot and to an adjoining lot separated by
a fence, and suppose there is actual occupation of the
house-lot only, can there be a constructive possession of
the lot adjoining? This question must be determined
by the application of the rule above mentioned to the
particular facts in each case. Courts have apparently
obtained different results in respect to this problem, but
it is very difficult to say that two cases are exactly alike
with reference to the fact whether the actual occupation
of the house-lot was such as to give the true owner notice
that the adjoining lot was claimed with it.

§ 155. **Same: Conflicting** holdings **and tacking.** In
case a good constructive possession is made out, it should
be observed: (1) that of two conflicting adverse possessions the prior prevails, and, (2) that while there is a
difference of judicial opinion as to whether the terms of
successive adverse holders can be tacked together to
make up the required period of adverse possession; yet,
in the case of constructive adverse possession, it is in-
variably the rule that to tack successive constructive
adverse possessions by different holders in order to make
the statutory period there must be a chain of title valid in
form between the successive constructive adverse
holders (13).

---

(12)   Bailey v. Carleton, 12 N. H. 9.
(13)   Simpson v. Downing, 23 Wend. (N. Y.) 316.

§ 156. **Disabilities.** The usual twenty year statute of limitations provides for the disabilities on the part of the true owner of minority, marriage, insanity, and absence from the country. Where the true owner suffers from any one or more of these disabilities the time within which the true owner may sue for possession is ordinarily extended to ten years after the removal of the disability. Observe, however, that the regular period of limitation— let us say twenty years—does not cease to run in the case of the existence of disabilities. The statute merely operates to extend the time within which the true owner may bring the action. It should be observed also that the only disabilities which can be counted are those which exist at the time when the adverse possession begins (14). The true owner is not allowed to tack disabilities accruing later: that is to say, if, at the time the adverse possession begins, the true owner is an infant, and afterwards before coming of age marries, the disability arising from the marriage cannot be added to the disability of infancy, and the action brought for the recovery of possession ten years after the disability of marriage is terminated. The infant will be allowed ten years only from the time of the termination of the disability of infancy.

The one under a disability is always entitled to at least twenty years from the time the adverse possession begins in which to bring an action for possession. The allowance of ten years from the time the disability ceases will, therefore, only be taken advantage of when it results in

---

(14) Griswold v. Butler, 3 Conn. 227.

requiring a period of adverse possession longer than twenty years. Thus, if at the time the adverse possession begins the true owner is an infant of the age of thirteen years, ten years from the time the infant came of age would only result in eighteen years of adverse possession. In such a case, therefore, the true owner can claim the full twenty years from the time adverse possession begins. If at the time the adverse possession begins the true owner is an infant under the age of eleven years, he will naturally claim the full period of ten years from the time the disability of infancy is removed.

§ 157. Tacking adverse possessions: Questions concerning. It frequently happens that one adverse holder does not have possession for the full period required by the statute, but that the adverse possession of two or three together is necessary to make up the statutory period. The questions then arise: (1) When may such adverse possessions be tacked together to bar the true owner? and, (2) what is the effect of the successive adverse holdings upon the title as between the successive adverse holders?

§ 158. Tacking to bar the true owner. It is clear that where A disseises the true owner and dies and A's heir or devisee continues the adverse possession, such heir or devisee can tack his adverse possession to that of his ancestor for the purpose of defeating the action of the true owner. When A disseises the true owner and conveys to B by a conveyance sufficient in form to pass title to real estate, and B continues the adverse possession of A, B can tack his adverse possession to that of A in order to bar the action of the true owner. If, however, the transfer of possession from A to B is by word of mouth only and not by any instrument of conveyance sufficient to pass title to real estate, many jurisdictions refuse to allow B to tack even for the purpose of barring the true owner. Perhaps an equal number of jurisdictions will be found holding the contrary (15). These, it is submitted, have adopted the result based upon the sounder reasoning, for, when the question is whether the true owner shall be barred of his action, the material fact is how long has he been out of possession—how long has he failed to bring the suit for possession which he had a right to assert. Now suppose that A disseises the true owner and is in turn disseised by B, who continues without a break the adverse possession, can B tack his adverse possession to that of A? The English cases have adopted the view that B can tack to bar the true owner's remedy (16). This it is submitted is sound, upon the same reasoning as is applicable where A transfers to B by word of mouth only. It cannot, however, be asserted with confidence that any American jurisdictions follow the English rule.

§ 159. Same: Special illustration. In American jurisdictions which allow tacking to bar the true owner where A disseises the latter and then conveys orally to B, a very nice question of fact sometimes arises as to whether there has been a transfer of possession from A to B by word of mouth in the following case: A, being the owner of

---

(15)   Overfield v. Christie, 7 S. & R. 173.
(16)   Doe d. Goody v. Carter, 9 Q. B. 863.

lot one, occupies it together with five feet of lot two, which he does not own. The fence includes all of lot one and the five feet of lot two. The possession of the five feet of lot two is adverse. A then conveys lot one by deed to B, and B takes possession of five feet of lot two according to the fence. Is there any parol transfer by A to B of the five feet of lot two? It is believed that in the typical case put there is. A actually hands over all that is embraced within his fences and that includes five feet of lot two. The fact that in his deed he only describes lot one, and perhaps did not know that he was in possession of more than lot one, does not impugn the fact that A did physically and intentionally hand over to B all that was within his fence line (17). At least one respectable court, however, has refused so to hold (18).

§ 160. **Tacking to obtain title.** Now suppose the question is, what is the state of the title between the successive holders after the true owner is barred? Take, for instance, the case where A disseises the true owner for five years, and is in turn disseised by B, who holds possession for ten years, and is in turn disseised by C, who holds possession for six years. Assuming that the true owner is barred according to the view of the English cases, who has the title as between A, B, and C? Surely not C, for he has only occupied six years, and, since he disseissed B, B can sue him for possession. Surely not B, for he has not occupied twenty years, and, since he

(17) Webber v. Anderson, 73 Ill. 439; Wishart v. McKnight, 178 Mass. 356. But see Ely v. Brown, 183 Ill. 575.

(18) Erck v. Church, 87 Tenn. 575.

disseised A, A can sue him for possession. A's possession, however, can be assailed by no one. Hence, if any one does, A must obtain the legal title and can recover from B or C. The English cases so hold (19).

Now suppose A disseises the true owner, occupies for five years, then conveys to B by parol, and B occupies for sixteen years. The true owner is barred under the rule recognized in some American jurisdictions. Does A or B obtain the title? Logically why does not A obtain the title as between A and B? Can A recover from B at any time until the statute of limitations has run in favor of B and against A? A's transfer by parol is invalid as a conveyance of land, and A can elect to treat B as a trespasser at any time. Hence, A is the only one with an unassailable right to possession, and so must have title. It is not believed that this problem has been settled by any jurisdiction in this country, though lawyers and laymen alike are apt to assume that B will obtain title. Of course, in all cases where A disseises the true owner and then transfers to B by a conveyance valid in form to pass title, as by devise or deed, B, when the true owner is barred, will obtain the title as against A.

SECTION 3. BY PRESCRIPTION.

§ 161. **Origin of doctrine.** The statute of limitations provides only for the acquisition of title by reason of adverse possession for a given length of time. It does not in the usual case provide for the acquisition of mere rights in the land of another by adverse user for a par-

---

(19) Doe d. Carter v. Barnard, 13 Q. B. 945.

ticular period—say twenty years. Yet a mode of acquiring easements or rights in the land of another by lapse of time is almost as desirable from the point of view of public policy as the acquisition of title by adverse possession. The courts have managed, therefore, to find ways—in their earlier stages full of legal fictions—of making a rule by which easements and rights in the lands of another may be acquired by reason of long continued user, very much as title is acquired by virtue of the statute of limitations. This method of acquiring rights in the lands of another is called "prescription."

§ 162. **Usual statement of rule of prescription.** Most courts are now committed to the proposition that an easement may be acquired by prescription when there has been a user and enjoyment of the right in question in the land of another, which has been continuous, uninterrupted, open and obvious, and adverse, for the period required for the acquisition of title to real estate by adverse possession under the statute of limitations in force in the particular jurisdiction. The difficulties which arise concern the determination of when a given user is (1) "continuous," (2) "uninterrupted," (3) "open and obvious," and (4) "adverse."

§ 163. **User must be continuous.** A series of disconnected trespasses will not do. Now where the user is of a right of way which is necessarily not used continuously, as that word is ordinarily employed, how can the user be continuous and not a mere series of disconnected trespasses? The answer to this is simple. If the acts of user are in fact related one to another in a series—if they are similar in character and object, occur with a certain periodical regularity in connection with the same estate, and are appropriate to an actual easement—then they are related and make a continuous user within the proper meaning of "continuous," though the specific acts occur at very considerable intervals of time. Thus, it has been held that a user only once a year of a way to a woodland lot for twenty years was a continuous user (20).

§ 164. **User must be uninterrupted.** The adverse user is interrupted when suit is brought questioning the right, or when there has been a physical interference with the exercise of the user. Mere oral declarations of protest, however, are not, it is believed, generally sufficient to make an interruption (21), though it is occasionally held that they are (22).

§ 165. **User must be open and obvious.** Of course, the user must be open and obvious as opposed to secret. How far, however, must the servient owner who suffers the adverse user of his land have actual notice of the user? When the servient owner is in possession of the servient estate at the time the adverse user begins, it seems that it is not necessary to bring home to him actual knowledge. It is enough if the user was open and obvious so that he had reasonable means of knowledge. If, however, the servient owner was out of possession and his tenant was actually in possession at the time the adverse user began, the time during which the tenant's possession

---

(20)   Bodfish v. Bodfish, 105 Mass. 317.

(21)   Lehigh Valley R. R. Co. v. McFarlan, 43 N. J. L. 605.

(22)   Chicago & N. W. Ry. Co. v. Hoag, 90 Ill. 339.

continues cannot count as an adverse user against the
landlord unless he has actual notice of the user (23). But
if, on the termination of the tenancy, the landlord comes
into possession long enough to have reasonable means of
knowledge of the user, then that will take the place of
actual notice; and a prescriptive right may be acquired
against him, though he had no actual knowledge, and
though he shortly afterwards let to another tenant who
holds for more than twenty years (24).

§ 166. **User must be adverse: What amounts to a license?** The user is adverse when it results in a trespass
giving rise to a cause of action on the part of the servient
owner. The use is adverse entirely with reference to the
way it affects the servient owner. The clearest case,
therefore, where the use is not adverse, is where it is
under some express license or permit of the servient
owner. In a number of cases therefore the prescription
failed because the user was actually and expressly permitted by the servient owner. The special difficulty in
determining what user is adverse arises in attempting to
ascertain how far the court will find, by circumstantial
evidence surrounding the user, a user by express permission of the servient owner. It is believed that a license,
expressed by interpretation from all the evidence, can be
found only when the following two elements concur:
(a) where there is an acquiescence in the user by the
dominant owner; and (b) where the user by the dominant
owner is in conscious subordination to the title of the

---

(23)   Daniel v. North, 11 East. 372.

(24)   Cross v. Lewis, 2 B. & C. 686.

servient owner. Clearly the mere acquiescence of the servient owner alone, however good-natured and neighborly, cannot prevent an adverse user, or make out a user by permission; for, if it did, then non-acquiescence would mean interruption and acquiescence would mean license, and, between the two, rights by prescription could not be acquired at all. If, however, there be added to acquiescence by the servient owner a conscious submission to the servient owner's title by the dominant owner, there is a fair and proper ground for finding a license by interpretation from the surrounding circumstances, and the user may, in the language of the cases, fairly be called "permissive."

§ 167. **Same: Fictitious** licenses. No attempt will be made here to generalize as to what evidence will show an acquiescence of the servient owner together with the conscious subordination of the dominant owner, so that an express license by interpretation from circumstantial evidence may be found. It is sufficient to say that courts have reached all manner of results in cases which appear on the surface somewhat similar. Courts have displayed various attitudes in handling the evidence—some appearing to do all that they could to prevent the acquisition of the easement and going to great lengths in finding a permissive user and others apparently tending to support the acquisition of the easement by refusing to find a permissive user unless it actually and clearly existed. In some instances a rule of law has sprung up which declares that a fictitious permission exists under certain circumstances. For instance, in some jurisdictions, if land is left open and uninclosed a user is taken as at least prima facie permissive as a matter of law (25). A species of legal presumption arises that the user is permissive. The permission is a judicial fiction. There is no permission and no proof of permission. The law ought to say that, when land is open and uninclosed, a right of way cannot be acquired by prescription unless there is affirmatively proven a user by the servient owner under an affirmative claim of right. It is unfortunate that courts express such a rule, not directly, so that all may clearly know what the rule is and its dogmatic character, but indirectly, by way of the affirmation of a fictitious circumstance which does not exist.

§ 168. **Same: Abuse of doctrine of implied license.** It is apparent that the whole doctrine that a license may be found by interpretation from the surrounding circumstances is subject to great abuse. In fact, the cases where a permissive use was found in this manner strongly suggest a soft spot in the doctrine of prescription where the court relieves against hard individual cases in its discretion. It is very apparent that in many cases where the court, upon no evidence at all, calls the user permissive, it is, under the guise of a sound rule, simply doing what it regards as justice in a particular case, where the servient owner allowed the user good-naturedly as a neighborly act, and that the dominant owner knew he had no actual right. This species of ''officious kindness,'' should be frowned upon and courts should con-

---

(25) Donnell v. Clark, 19 Me. 183; McKey v. Garrett, 1 Bailey (S. C.) 341.

scientiously set their faces against the loose finding of a permissive user which is largely fictitious.

§ 169. **What rights may** be **acquired** by prescription? Presumably all sorts of *rights of user* of the land of another—such as most commonly the easement of a right of way—may be acquired by prescription. Some particular easements cannot be acquired by prescription. For instance, in practically all jurisdictions of the United States, no easement of light can be acquired by prescription. This is in reality in accordance with principle, for it is impossible that there should be any adverse user by one claiming an easement of light in the land of his neighbor. Thus, suppose A opened windows in the wall of his house overlooking B's vacant land adjoining. How can it be said that A's windows are an adverse user of B's land? Can B sue A for looking out over his land? Certainly not. Does B have to build a blank wall to prevent A from overlooking his land? The thing is absurd. The same is true of the right of adjacent support from B's land. Suppose the downward and side thrust resulting from A's building is met by the pressure of B's solid vacant lot adjoining. How can it be that this is an adverse use of B's land? Can B sue A because of the existence of the thrust? Certainly not. Does B have to dig his land out so as to assert his right not to have this thrust against his land? Certainly not. The same is true of the claim to a right to have the free and unobstructed flow of a current of air across B's land to A's windmill. A can obtain no right to such an unobstructed flow by long user, because such user cannot be adverse. It is a purely historical accident that the English courts became committed to the rule that the right to light and air (but not to a free current of air to run a windmill) and to adjacent support, could be acquired by prescription. Sound policy as well as logical reasoning upon principle has saved the courts of this country from becoming committed in a general way to any similar position (26).

§ 170. **Disabilities.** The analogy to the rule laid down by the statute of limitations in regard to disabilities is strictly followed by some courts. Only disabilities existing at the time the adverse user begins can be counted. As, however, there is no provision like that of the statute of limitations for extending the time within which suit may be brought for ten years from the time the disability is terminated, the courts can only say that where a right is attempted to be acquired by prescription, there must be the full period of user after the disability ceases. Other courts have allowed the deduction of all periods of disability which occur during the period of adverse user. This makes it necessary that there should be twenty years adverse user exclusive of disabilities. When, after one disability, a period of non-disability less than twenty years intervenes and then another disability starts up, what shall be done? Must there be a continuous period of twenty years adverse user without disability, or may the twenty year period of adverse user be made up from snatches of user occurring between disabilities? The an-

(26)   Parker v. Foote, 19 Wend. (N. Y.) 309.

swer to this question, as a matter of policy and logic, depends upon considerations that cannot be discussed in the space here at command.

§ 171. **Tacking.** It is believed that the rules respecting tacking of adverse possessions in applying the statute of limitations would obtain in respect to tacking adverse users so as to make up the period of prescription. Usually the easement sought to be acquired is known as an easement appurtenant. That is, it is a right over the land of a servient owner in favor of a particular dominant property. Whenever the dominant property is validly transferred and the transferee continues the adverse user, of course his adverse user could be tacked to that of his predecessor in the title of the dominant estate. Whether one who receives the dominant estate by a transfer by word of mouth only, and continues the adverse user, can tack his adverse user to that of his predecessor, must depend upon whether it is recognized as law in a particular jurisdiction that where A disseises the true owner and conveys by word of mouth only to B and B continues the adverse possession, B can tack his adverse possession to that of A.

CHAPTER VIII.

ORIGINAL ACQUISITION: ACCRETIONS.

§ 172. Accretions defined. Accretions are the imperceptible increase in land where it borders upon the sea, a lake, or a river.

§ 173. Ownership of accretions: Unintentionally produced. Where that part of the earth's surface which is covered with water is owned by the state, or by some person other than the owner of the land bordering upon the water, the question naturally arises who becomes the owner of these accretions—the owner of the land covered with water, or the owner of the riparian property? It is now clear that, as between different private individuals, and as between the private individual and the state, the accretions belong to the riparian owner. The reason for this now given is one of public policy. The right of access for the riparian proprietor to the water is of great value to him. It is an essential part of the value of his land, whether for commercial purposes or mere esthetic enjoyment. The proprietorship of an infinitesimal width of imperceptible accretions which form upon the water's edge at a given time is of no practical value to the one who owns the title to the land under the water. To let him have the title to such accretions would be to begin the process of depriving the riparian owner of a great advantage, and confer no corresponding benefit on anybody else. Hence, the sensible rule that the accretions go to the riparian proprietor. There is perhaps still a slight question as to whether the accretions go to the riparian owner when the actual boundary between the land and the water is marked with fixed monuments, or otherwise definitely known. But sound opinion seems to be against making any exception even in such a case.

§ 174. **Same: Intentionally produced by artificial means.** In some places the question becomes acute as to what rule shall be adopted where the accretions are formed by artificial structures. The late Professor Shaler of Harvard, in one of his lectures upon the action of streams, used to tell the story of the crafty riparian proprietor who, by the protection of his bank at one point, managed to cause the stream to eat away the land of his neighbor opposite and then deposit that land in the shape of imperceptible accretions upon the crafty one's meadow below. The direct intent to take away the opposite riparian owner's land and add it to his own may be well concealed in the ostensible purpose of protecting the crafty one's own bank. But suppose the intent be clearly proved to deprive the neighbor, should the crafty one lose the land added to his meadow below and thereby lose his riparian frontage? It is submitted that he should not. Admitting that the crafty one has done wrong in damaging his neighbor's land, the law seeks only to compensate the one injured for the damage which he has suffered, and that damage is to be estimated in money damages. To give the injured party a small or large strip of land, as the case may be, between the wrongdoer's land and the river lower down would be a very crude way of measuring damages. It would be also an extremely unjust way of doing it, for in some cases it might be wholly inadequate and in others grossly excessive. The injured neighbor should sue the crafty one for damages for causing the stream to wash away his land and receive compensation for the damage done—no more and no less.

§ 175. **Same: Against the state.** On the shore of a lake, where a great city and its suburbs have grown up and land has become very valuable, there is a great temptation on the part of the riparian proprietor to put out a breakwater for the ostensible purpose of protecting his beach, but in reality to build up a little more land by accretions. Again let us suppose that the riparian proprietor's intent to cause the accretions by artificial structures jutting out into the lake is clear. Let us assume also, what would be the probable fact, that the state owns the bed of the lake. Can the state then sue the riparian proprietor in ejectment for the made land? The same reasoning that was set out with reference to the case put by Professor Shaler would cause us to reply in the negative. It is true the riparian proprietor acted illegally when he put out the breakwater, no matter how innocent his motive in so doing may have been. It is true that his motive was improper. It is true that the state has suffered no pecuniary damage, so that none can be recovered. But the state, if it desired to move in the matter, could have required the removal of the piers from the beginning, and no statute of limitations runs against the state. The state, therefore, was not without remedy.

But to take away the riparian proprietor's access to the water, because of his wrongdoing, and to insert between him and the lake a small and perhaps growing strip of land owned by another, who can make in many cases no use of it except to annoy the former riparian proprietor, is retribution out of all proportion to the wrong done. The views just expressed are not, as far as the writer knows, sustained by authority. Neither has there been any such contradiction of their soundness as would make their appearance here improper.

Finally, it should be observed that the views above expressed have no application at all to the case of artificial filling in, and by this means making land where the fee of the land covered by the water is in the state or in another individual. In such a case the made land belongs to the individual or the state owning the land beneath the water.

§ 176. **Division of accretions: Two rules.** So far as there are any mechanical rules on this subject, two may be singled out for mention. One rule is that each proprietor owns upon the new shore line in the same proportion that he owned upon the old shore line (1). According to this rule the old shore line should be measured and the respective proportions of ownership of the riparian owners determined. Then the new shore line should be measured and the same proportions laid off upon it. Then lines should be drawn from the termination of the division lines upon the old shore line to the

---

(1)   Deerfield v. Arms, 17 Pick. (Mass.) 41.

points upon the new shore line which represent its division.

The other rule is that you shall first find the middle thread of the stream as it exists after the accretions have been formed. Then extend the old boundary lines perpendicular to it (2). In favor of the latter rule it may be said that it takes account of the fact, in very many cases true, that the riparian proprietors own the bed of the stream to the center, while the former rule ignores that fact. In favor of the former rule, however, it may be said that it can be applied by the riparian proprietors themselves upon the bank of the stream, while the division of the accretions by the latter rule will require the expert services of a surveyor. Only a consideration of the condition of a particular community can determine whether the greatest good to the greatest number will follow from the adoption of the first or the second rule.

---

(2)   Miller v. Hepburn, 8 Bush. (Ky.) 326.

MORTGAGES.

JAMES WIGGINS SIMONTON,
A. B. (Indiana University)
J. D. (University of Chicago)

Chicago Bar.

CHAPTER I.

REAL ESTATE MORTGAGES.

SECTION 1. NATURE AND ESSENTIAL ELEMENTS.

§ 1. **Mortgages under the early common law.** A real estate mortgage is a lien or interest in land created by agreement between the parties, or by a transfer of such interest, for the purpose of securing the performance of an obligation. The party who makes the mortgage is the *mortgagor* and the one to whom it is made is the *mortgagee*. The early form of mortgage of land consisted of an absolute conveyance of the land by the owner or mortgagor to the mortgagee subject to a condition, or defeasance, as it was called. This condition or defeasance provided that, on the payment of the debt or performance of the obligation which the mortgage was given to secure at a certain date, by the mortgagor, he could re-enter on the land and have full ownership again. The mortgagee got an absolute right to the land, and could take possession and collect the rents and profits. The only right the mortgagor had was to get his land back again on performance of the obligation strictly according to his agreement. If he failed to perform the obligation on or before the day set, the "law day," as it was called, the property was forfeited to the mortgagee. Strict performance of the condition was required to prevent the loss of the property. The law courts disregarded the fact that the real purpose of the transaction was to make a kind of pledge of the land to secure the payment of a debt. Under this harsh doctrine a land owner who had given a mortgage often lost valuable land because he was unable to repay a small loan at the time and in the manner agreed upon.

§ 2. **Growth of the equitable doctrine.** Courts of equity began to give the mortgagor relief from the injustice of the common law and began to allow the mortgagor to redeem his land after he had made default. About the time of Charles I (1625-49) it became a well settled doctrine that a mortgagor could redeem his property after default by paying the money which was actually due. This right of the mortgagor was called his "equity of redemption." When this right of redemption was first allowed there was no limit to the time within which the redemption might be made, so that a mortgagee could never get the property free from a possibility of redemption, and, if the land years after the default became very valuable, naturally the mortgagor would try to redeem it. In order to obviate this difficulty equity allowed the mortgagee to bring a bill to foreclose the mortgage and cut off the right of redemption. In such a proceeding a decree would be entered requiring the mortgagor to exercise his right to redeem by a certain day, fixed in the decree, or his right would be cut off forever. On his failure to redeem at the time fixed the property became the absolute property of the mortgagee. It must be remembered that, from the date of the execution of the mortgage until payment of the debt or redemption, the mortgagee had an absolute right to take possession of the property and secure the income from it, so that he could get the entire income during the existence of the mortgage, in addition to the full payment of his debt and the right to forfeit on default by the mortgagor. On account of these unjust advantages courts of equity took the view that since the whole transaction was intended by the parties as a transfer of the land, merely to secure the payment of a debt, this intention ought to be carried out. Hence the mortgagor was regarded as the real owner of the land and had the right to exercise all the powers of an owner, so far as consistent with the purpose of the mortgage, and the mortgagee was regarded as having merely a lien on the land to secure his debt.

§ 3. Legal and equitable theories of mortgages. "Title theory." "Lien theory." As explained in the preceding subsection, courts of law and courts of equity had different views as to mortgages—the former regarding the mortgagee as the owner, subject to the right of the mortgagor to perform his condition and re-enter; the latter regarding the mortgagee as having only a lien on the land as security. In England and many of our states the law courts still hold to the old legal theory and regard the title and right of possession as passing to the mortgagee, though the strict legal doctrine has become much modified. For convenience, we may call this theory the "title theory" of mortgages, since the title passes to the mortgagee. In these "title theory" jurisdictions are courts of equity which enforce the equitable theory of mortgages, so that, while the law courts will give the mortgagee the right to take possession of the property at any time, the mortgagor can go into a court of equity and force the mortgagee to account for any income from the property he gets while in possession. This equitable accounting is enforced so strictly that there is little or no advantage to the mortgagee in taking the possession from the mortgagor, even though he has the right to do so. But even in the law courts of "title theory" states the mortgagor today is regarded as the real owner as to everyone except the owner of the mortgage (1).

---

(1) The states in which this view prevails are Alabama, Arkansas, Connecticut, Illinois, Maine, Maryland, Massachusetts, New Hampshire, New Jersey, North Carolina, Pennsylvania, Rhode Island, Tennessee, Vermont, Vir inia and West Vir inia

In the majority of our states the law courts have adopted the equitable theory of mortgages, and in these states the title remains in the mortgagor, who is the owner of the property, and the mortgagee has only a lien on it. This view we shall, for convenience, call the "lien theory" of mortgages. In the "title theory" states the law is tending towards the "lien theory," and probably in the future the old legal theory of mortgages will disappear entirely (2).

§ 4. **Once a mortgage, always a mortgage.** After equity began to allow a mortgagor in default to redeem the property, persons with money to lend could no longer obtain such a great advantage over needy debtors as formerly, and so they sought to cut off the right of redemption by getting the mortgagor to contract not to exercise it, or to transfer it to the mortgagee, if default was made, or to make some other agreement which would make the exercise of this right difficult or impossible. Courts frequently, however, thought that the mortgagor ought to be protected from such unjust contracts which he might be forced to make because of his necessity. Consequently it was held that the right of redemption was an integral part of every mortgage and could not be waived or limited by any agreement, in the mortgage

---

(2)   The states in which this view prevails are California, Colorado, Florida, Georgia, Idaho, Indiana, Iowa, Kansas, Kentucky, Louisiana, Michigan, Minnesota, Montana, Nebraska, Nevada, New York, North Dakota, Oklahoma, Oregon, South Carolina, South Dakota, Texas, Wisconsin, Utah and Washington.

In Delaware, Mississippi and Missouri there is a combination of the two theories. Before default the mortgagee has only a lien, after default he has the legal title.

or separate from it, made before or at the time the mortgage was executed. This principle is often expressed by the phrase "once a mortgage, always a mortgage." In other words, the mortgagor could not be bound by an agreement that there was to be a mortgage for a certain time and then it was to become something else.

In an old English case there is an illustration of an attempt to limit the right to redeem. It was agreed that only the mortgagor and the heirs of his body should have a right to redeem after default. The question which arose in the case was whether one to whom the mortgaged land had been transferred could redeem. The court held such an agreement was not binding on the mortgagor, and his assignee could redeem the property. In this case then an attempt to limit the redemption merely to certain persons was held invalid, and this is well settled law (3). Any attempt to destroy it entirely is, of course, invalid.

§ 5. **Contract for** future sale of **equity of redemption to mortgagee.** Not only is a contract which limits or cuts off the equity of redemption, if made when the mortgage is executed, invalid as to the mortgagor, but a contract made subsequent to the mortgage, by which the mortgagee is to have the equity of redemption transferred to him at some future time, is invalid, no matter how much is to be paid for the equity. The mortgagee can buy the equity of redemption outright—that is, if it is to be transferred to him immediately; but, even if he does this, equity will set the transaction aside at the re-

(3)   Howard v. Harris, 1 Vernon, 33.

quest of the mortgagor, unless it appears that it is perfectly fair and just. A case of this sort arose in California. The mortgagor made a present sale of his equity to the mortgagee, who paid about what it was worth. Then the mortgagor tried to get the court to set aside the sale and allow him to redeem, probably because the property had greatly increased in value in the meantime. The court declared the sale should stand, for it was fair and above board and the price paid was reasonable; but the court said that such transactions would be carefully examined and set aside unless they were reasonable and free from unfair dealing (4).

§ 6. **What** property can be mortgaged? In general any interest in land which can be sold, granted, or assigned may be mortgaged. Equitable as well as legal interests may be mortgaged. Some of the common interests subject to mortgage are fee simple estates, estates for life, estates for years or leaseholds, dower interests of a widow or the curtesy of a husband, a mortgagee's interest, and a mortgagor's interest. Land may be mortgaged separately from the improvements, or the improvement separately from the land. A landowner may mortgage crops growing on the land. It is needless to enumerate all of the various interests that may be mortgaged.

§ 7. **Same: Future** acquisitions. Property which one does not own, but expects to acquire in the future, is not subject to present sale and hence cannot be mortgaged. But if an attempt is made to mortgage property to be acquired, and such property is acquired subsequently, while there is no legal mortgage, equity creates a lien as soon as the property is acquired, which is good as to all persons who subsequently acquire rights in the property and are not bona fide purchasers for value without notice. The rule that a legal mortgage cannot be made of property to be acquired in the future has an apparent exception. When there is a mortgage on real estate, and a building or other improvement is attached to the land, the mortgage covers such building or improvement. This is because when the building is attached to the land it becomes a part of it and consequently is covered by the mortgage, which is on all the land. A mortgagee of real estate gets a legal interest in it and is a purchaser within the recording acts. If he takes his mortgage for value and puts it on record, he gets a prior right as to all unrecorded deeds of which he had no notice.

§ 8. **Forms of mortgage: Ordinary form.** The common form of mortgage which is still much used in "title theory" states is a deed which conveys property to the mortgagee, subject to a condition. It is an instrument which must be in writing and executed with all the formalities of a deed conveying land, for this is what it purports to be. The condition or defeasance need not be incorporated in the deed of conveyance, but may be in the form of a separate deed. If separate, it must be executed at the same time as the other deed, or as a part of the same transaction. At common law a separate defeasance must be executed with the same formalities as the conveyance, or there was no legal mortgage. In equity, however, the transaction is enforced as a mortgage, even though the defeasance is not formal. It is enough if it shows the parties intended the conveyance to secure a debt. In "lien theory" states short forms of mortgages are usually authorized by statute, and a mortgage is usually not such a formal, technical instrument as in "title" states. Mortgages are, in all states, required to be recorded if the mortgagee desires to be protected against subsequent purchasers of the land for value without notice of the mortgage. When recorded, the record of the mortgage is constructive notice of the mortgagee's right as to all subsequent purchasers.

§ 9. **Same: Absolute conveyance.** As was stated above, if a separate defeasance is not formally executed, no legal mortgage results; but equity will declare the transaction a mortgage and enforce it as such. Furthermore, if an absolute deed is made to a person to secure a debt, if it can be shown by parol or extrinsic evidence what the real nature of the transaction is, equity will declare it a mortgage. This is allowed in spite of the rule of evidence that a written instrument cannot be varied by evidence outside of the writing itself—that is, by extrinsic evidence. But before an absolute deed will be declared a mortgage, equity requires the mortgagor to show by clear and convincing evidence that it was really so intended. Thus, in a Pennsylvania case, the plaintiff in a bill to redeem had made a conveyance to the defendant. Twenty years later, a bill to redeem was brought, the plaintiff claiming that the defendant had in fact agreed orally to reconvey, as soon as he was paid back the money due, and that the transaction was really a mortgage and not an absolute conveyance. The court held that parol evidence to show the deed a mortgage was admissible, but that here the plaintiff's claim was not sustained by such clear, precise, and indubitable evidence as to induce equity to declare an absolute deed a mortgage, and hence the deed would not be declared a mortgage (5).

§ 10. **Same: Sale with right to repurchase.** A land owner may sell his land and have an agreement that he is to have the right to repurchase it for a certain price within a certain time. Such a sale on condition is not invalid. But advantage may be taken of this by a person with money to loan, and such a conditional sale may be made when the real purpose is to secure a debt. In this way the one who loans the money can in effect avoid the right to redeem which is a part of every mortgage. Courts of equity, in pursuit of the policy of preventing oppression of the mortgagor, allow extrinsic evidence to be admitted to show whether the transaction is what it purports to be, or whether it was intended to secure a debt. If the latter, it is declared to be a mortgage. The presumption in such a case is that a conditional sale is a mortgage, and the vendee must show by clear evidence that it was really intended as a sale with right to repurchase, the rule being the opposite of what it is when an absolute deed is shown to be a mortgage. In determining whether a transaction is a conditional sale or a mortgage,

---

(5)   Wallace v. Smith, 155 Pa. State 78.

the fact there was an indebtedness existing or created at the time of the conveyance is almost conclusive in favor of a mortgage, as is also the fact the grantor remained in possession of the property, while the fact that a reasonable price was paid for the land indicates a conditional sale.

A man conveyed his farm, worth $15,000, by absolute deed, for a consideration of $5,000. A separate informal instrument gave him the right to repurchase the farm within four months from date, on payment of $5,000. He did not repurchase. Later he brought a bill in equity to redeem, and introduced testimony to show that the transaction, a conditional sale in form, was really a mortgage. The court held that the transaction was clearly shown by the evidence introduced to be a mortgage, and decreed that the grantor be allowed to redeem. It said that the court would look behind the forms with which the contrivance of the buyer had enveloped the transaction (6). This case shows that a conditional sale may be shown to be a mortgage. It also shows that the defeasance may be informal in equity, for the separate writing here was not a formal deed.

§ 11. Same: Deed of trust. Trust deeds are often used in the place of ordinary mortgages for the purpose of securing debts. The property is conveyed to a trustee to hold in trust, and, if the payment is made, the trustee is to reconvey to the grantor. If there is default in payment, the trustee sells the property and applies the proceeds to the payment of the debt secured. Thus in effect

---

(6)   Russell v. Southard, 12 Howard, 139.

there is a mortgage.   Such an instrument is particularly
convenient where the debt is owned by a large number of
persons.   When it is desired to issue bonds secured by a
mortgage on a railroad, for instance, a trust deed may be
made to secure the whole issue.   The bonds are then
sold to whomsoever wishes to buy.   If default is made,
the trustee can sell the road and pay the various bond-
holders.   It would be impracticable in such cases to give
each bondholder a separate mortgage.

§ 12.   **The obligation.   Description of** debt.   The debt
secured is usually in the form of a note or bond separate from the mortgage.   The debt need not be explicitly
described in the mortgage, in order to make it valid as
against subsequent purchasers and creditors.   It is
enough if sufficient is stated so that the amount of the
debt can be ascertained.   A mortgage provided that it
was given to secure all debts of the mortgagor for which
the mortgagee was already liable as surety for the mortgagor, and all debts for which he might become so liable
in the future.   At the time it was executed, the mortgagee had paid some debts for the mortgagor, and was
surety for others not yet due.   The mortgage was properly recorded.   Certain creditors of the mortgagor
claimed that the mortgage did not give a lien prior to
their claims, so as to secure debts which came due after
the execution of the mortgage and were paid by the mortgagee, because the description of the debt in the mortgage was so vague and uncertain.   The court held the
description was sufficient.   The mortgage was recorded
and they could have ascertained the amount of the debt.

(7) It is therefore sufficient if a general description is given.

§ 13. **Same: Future advances.** A mortgage, which by its terms states it is to secure a definite debt, cannot be extended by an agreement between the parties to cover money subsequently advanced, so as to make it a valid lien for such advances as to third persons, though such an extension is good between the parties to the mortgage. But when a mortgage states that it is to secure future advances, it is valid even as against subsequent purchasers and creditors, and, by the weight of authority, it need only state that future advances are secured without stating the amount to be advanced (8). Under such a mortgage the mortgagee has a prior lien for all advances he makes without knowledge of the rights under subsequent mortgages or liens, but not as to subsequent mortgages or liens of which he has notice. However, he does not have to make any attempt to discover such mortgages and liens, even though they are recorded. If such subsequent liens are recorded, some states hold that each advance is in effect a separate mortgage, and the records are constructive notice to him, the prior mortgagee (9), while others hold he is not charged with notice by the records (10).

§ 14. **Personal liability of mortgagor.** The mortgagor is usually personally liable for the mortgage debt, not because he makes a mortgage, but because he made some

(7)   Youngs v. Wilson, 27 New York, 351.
(8)   Allen v. Lathrop, 46 Ga. 133.
(9)   Spades v. Lawler, 17 Ohio 371.
(10)   Frye v. Bank of Illinois, 11 Ill. 367.

note, bond, covenant, or other contract by which he agreed to pay the debt. The mortgage is held valid in most states, though there is no debt which can be enforced personally against the mortgagor, as where the debt is barred by the statute of limitations. A mortgage may also be made to secure the performance of obligations other than debts.

§ 15. **Effect** of illegal purpose. The courts try to deal with illegality in the way they think will tend to discourage it. Therefore, when a mortgage is given for an illegal purpose, if both parties are considered equally culpable, or in pari delicto, as it is called, the law leaves them where it finds them—it refuses to give aid to either party. Accordingly, the courts have refused to enforce a mortgage given to obtain the suppression of a criminal prosecution (11), or to secure a gambling debt (12), or a debt for liquor illegally sold (13). When the mortgagor is not considered in pari delicto, the courts will aid him if he applies to them, but if he comes into a court of equity asking aid, equity requires him to pay whatever sums he justly owes, for he that comes into equity must do equity. Cases of this sort often arise under usury statutes. Where the mortgage provides for a rate of interest which is above the legal rate, the mortgagor, being regarded as having been forced into the agreement by his necessity, is not in pari delicto with the mortgagee in the eyes of the law. If he comes into

---

(11)   Atwood v. Fisk, 101 Mass. 363.
(12)   Barnard v. Backhaus, 52 Wis. 593.
(13)   Baker v. Collins, 9 Allen 253.

a court of equity for relief, however, he must in most states pay the principal and legal interest due, and only the usurious interest is forfeited.

SECTION 2.   RIGHTS AND LIABILITIES INCIDENT TO MORT-
GAGE RELATION.

§ 16.   Mortgagor's interest.   The mortgagor, even in "title theory" states, is regarded as the owner of the land.   He has the same right to control the property as before making the mortgage, except as against the mortgagee.   He may sell the land, or lease it, or make any number of subsequent mortgages.   When he dies his interest passes as real estate to his heirs, if he leaves no will, and his widow gets dower rights in it.   His interest may be sold by a judgment creditor under execution, but in most states the mortgagee himself cannot get a judgment for the mortgage debt against the mortgagor and levy on the mortgaged property, though he can levy on any other property belonging to the mortgagor.

§ 17.   Mortgagee's interest.   In "title theory" states the mortgagee has the legal title and right of possession of the mortgaged property, but can exercise the rights of an owner only when desirable to protect his security. In order to protect his security he can bring actions at law against the mortgagor or third persons, as if he were the owner of the property.   He may eject the mortgagor or any trespasser on the land, or may sue anyone who wrongfully removes timber or fixtures from the property, or commits waste thereon.   Thus, in an Illinois case, a man who was assignee of a mortgage debt undertook to exercise rights of ownership, and tried to eject a person wrongfully in possession of the land. The court held he could not eject the party in possession, because, being assignee of the debt only and not of the mortgage, he had no legal title; but if he had had the legal title ejectment would have been allowed (14). In "lien theory" states the interest of the mortgagee is, as was stated before, a mere lien on the land, and he is in no sense the owner and has no rights of ownership. His remedies for preventing injury to his security will be discussed later.

§ 18. **Right to possession of mortgaged property.** In "title theory" states the mortgagee is entitled to possession of the property, and can eject the mortgagor and take possession at any time, unless there is an agreement that the mortgagor is to retain possession. That the mortgagor is to have possession may also be implied from the terms of the mortgage, as when the mortgage provides that the mortgagor is to cultivate the land. As a rule, the mortgagee does not exercise his right to possession, because if he takes possession he is required to account for all the rents and profits he receives from the land; and equity holds him so strictly in such an accounting that there is nothing to be gained by taking possession of the property. In states where the "lien theory" of mortgages prevails the mortgagee is not entitled to possession; but in some of these states it is held that if he gets possession of the property after default by the mortgagor, he can retain possession till the land

---

(14)   Barrett v. Hinckley, 124 Ill. 32.

is redeemed. Aside from this, in ''lien theory'' states the mortgagor is entitled to possession till judicial sale on foreclosure.

§ 19. **Rents and profits: Mortgagor in possession.** While the mortgagor is in possession of the property he is entitled to all the rents and profits from the land. In a ''lien theory'' state this is clear. In a ''title theory'' state he is in the position of a tenant at will, for his possession can be taken away by the mortgagee, but he is a tenant so long as allowed to remain. In a case decided by the United States Supreme Court, the mortgagee brought suit against the mortgagor to recover rents and profits which the latter had collected while holding the mortgaged land. The Supreme Court held that, as mortgagee, he was not entitled to the rents and profits of the land until he took actual possession. He may get possession by ejectment, or, if there are tenants on the land, he may give them notice to pay the rent to him; but, if he suffers the mortgagor to retain possession personally, or to collect rents from the tenants, he cannot recover the rents and profits which the mortgagor has actually received. A mortgagor in possession is liable for interest on the debt, and not for rents and profits (15). This case is law, even when the mortgaged property is not adequate security for the debt; but in such a case the mortgagee can have a receiver appointed to take charge of the property and collect the rents and profits for the benefit of the mortgagee.

§ 20. **Same: Mortgagee in possession.** If the mort-

---

(15)   Teal v. Walker, 111 U. S. 242.

gagee takes possession he can collect the rents and profits, but if the mortgagor redeems, such rents and profits must be accounted for. However, the mortgagee can keep all the income he gets from the property until an accounting is required of him. Such an accounting may be required if the mortgagor redeems the property, or if the mortgagee forecloses his mortgage. On accounting, any income the mortgagee has received from the land is applied to the payment of the mortgage debt. The mortgagee is required to account for all he got from the land, whether much or little. If he does not get as much for the land as a man by reasonable care and diligence should have gotten, he must account for what he ought to have gotten. To illustrate, a mortgagee took possession of a farm and allowed the house to remain vacant and the land untilled part of the time. He also cut a lot of timber and sold it. The mortgagor redeemed the land, and in accounting the court required the mortgagee to pay over what he ought to have gotten as rent for the premises, and also to account for the money he received for the timber he sold from the land. The court said it would not do for a mortgagee in possession to fold his arms and use no means to procure a tenant. At least, if the house was not rented, he ought to have the land properly tilled (16). The above case shows pretty clearly why it is of no advantage to a mortgagee to take possession of the property, for, if he does so, he will have to account some day, and may be held liable for more than the income he actually got out of the land.

(16)   Schaeffer v. Chambers, 6 New Jersey Equity 548.

§ **21.** **Effect of** lease **of** mortgaged land: **Before the** mortgage. When a lease of the land is made before it is mortgaged, the lessee gets a good lease, for he got his lease at a time when his lessor had full right and title to the land. The mortgagee takes subject to such lease and cannot take the possession from the lessee. He can, however, serve the lessee with notice that he, as mortgagee, has title to the property and that rents must be paid to him. Thereupon, the tenant, if he holds his lease, must pay to the mortgagee all rents which have accrued since the mortgage was executed and are still unpaid and rents which accrue in the future. A case on this point arose in Connecticut. A company, which we will call the A Company, owned a railroad and leased it to a second company, which we will call the B Company. Then the A Company mortgaged its railroad to a third company, the C Company. After a time default was made in the payment of the interest on the mortgage debt, and the C Company gave notice to the B Company to pay all rents then due, and all which thereafter should become due under the lease, to it. Some rent was due at the time and a creditor of the A Company attached this rent which was due under the lease. The court held the creditor had acquired no right to the rent, for, as soon as notice was served on the B Company to pay rent to the mortgagee, the B Company became liable to pay to the mortgagee instead of to the mortgagor, and thus did not owe the mortgagor anything (17).

§ **22.** **Same:** **After the** mortgage. After the mort-

---

(17) **King** v. Housatonic Railroad Company, 45 Conn. 226.

gage is made, the mortgagor cannot make a lease which will in any way affect the rights of the mortgagee. The lessee must take subject to any existing mortgage. In "title theory" states, the mortgagor being only a tenant at will, the lessee who takes his lease after the mortgage cannot get any better right than the mortgagor has, consequently the mortgagee can eject him and put an end to the lease, or he can demand rent of the lessee; and the lessee must recognize him as landlord if he wishes to remain on the property. If the lessee recognizes the mortgagee as his landlord and pays rent to him, what is in effect a new tenancy is created, the tenant thereafter holding under the mortgagee. In a certain New York case a landowner made a mortgage of his land and then leased it to a tenant. The mortgagor defaulted in the payment of the mortgage debt, and the mortgagee thereupon demanded the rent of the tenant, who agreed to pay his rent to the mortgagee. The mortgagor sued the tenant for the rent under the lease. The court held that he could not recover, for the tenant was forced either to pay rent to the mortgagee or lose his lease. He had a right then to recognize the superior right of the mortgagee (18). When the tenant agrees to pay rent to the mortgagee it amounts to an eviction of the mortgagor from possession, and the mortgagee thereafter has possession of the property.

§ 23. **Mortgagee's expenditures to protect property: Taxes and incumbrances.** A mortgagee can pay off or redeem from a superior incumbrance in order to protect

---

(18)   Jones v. Clark, 20 Johnson's Reports 51.

his security, and can charge the amount so paid up to the mortgagor. In the same way he may pay taxes or special assessments which are a lien on the land, or defend suits which threaten the title of the mortgagor, and recover sums so expended. In general, he may make any reasonable expenditures which are necessary to protect the title to the property. If not allowed to do this, his security might be sold and thus lost to him. The mortgagor should make all such expenditures, and if he does not, the mortgagee is allowed to make them for him.

§ 24. Same: Repairs and improvements. A mortgagee in possession may make all necessary repairs, and, on foreclosure or redemption, charge them against the mortgagor. He may make such improvements as are necessary for the proper enjoyment of the premises, and recover their value, but cannot recover for improvements which are desirable, but not necessary. Thus, a mortgagee in possession repaired the house on certain mortgaged premises, and paid for insurance on the buildings. He also built some new fences and a new house. The mortgagor redeemed the property, and, in the accounting between the parties, the court held the mortgagee should have credit for the repairs to the old house, for the new fences he put up, which were badly needed, and for the insurance premium he had paid. All these were held necessary and proper expenses. But he was not allowed credit for the new house, because that was not a necessary improvement (19). The reason why the mortgagee is not allowed for any improvements except

(19) McCumber v. Gilman, 15 Ill. 381.

what are necessary is that if he could recover for all improvements he would often prevent redemption. Suppose, for instance, that the mortgagor was poor, and the improvements put on the property amounted to more than the value of the land when mortgaged. The mortgagor would not be able to raise the money necessary to redeem from the mortgagee in many cases, for, when he goes into equity to redeem, he has to pay the sum due in cash. There is one exception to the above rule as to improvements. When a mortgagee takes possession and makes improvements innocently, thinking that he is owner of the land, as where he purchased at a judicial sale which was later declared void on an appeal to a higher court, he is allowed credit from the mortgagor, in case of redemption, to the extent of the increased value of the land due to such improvements.

§ 25. Insurance by mortgagor and mortgagee. The mortgagor, being regarded as owner of the mortgaged property, has an insurable interest in the property, and can insure it for full value, regardless of the amount for which it is mortgaged. By the terms of the mortgage he is often required to insure for the benefit of the mortgagee, and if he fails to keep up the insurance, the mortgagee can insure and charge the cost up against him. This insurable interest of the mortgagor continues until his right to redeem is barred. The mortgagee has an insurable interest in the property, which continues until the mortgage is extinguished. When he insures for the benefit of, or at the expense of, the mortgagor, in case of loss the proceeds of the insurance must be applied to the reduction of the mortgage debt. When he insures for his own benefit and at his own expense, if he collects insurance money it belongs to him and the mortgagor has no right to any benefit from it. But the insurance company which paid the money is entitled to be subrogated to the mortgagee's right against the mortgagor to the extent of the insurance it paid, so that the mortgagee is not really entitled to collect and keep both the insurance money from the company and the mortgage debt from the mortgagor (20). The interests of both the mortgagee and of the mortgagor may be insured at the same time. See Insurance, in Volume VII.

§ 26. **Remedies of mortgagee for injury to property.** The owner of land subject to a mortgage has a right to a reasonable use of the land for the purposes for which such land is ordinarily used. He may improve it, cut timber from it, or do any act which can fairly be regarded as done in the exercise of good husbandry. His rights are similar to those of an ordinary tenant, though perhaps somewhat greater. He is not allowed to do acts on the land which will substantially impair its value as security for the mortgage debt. Thus, he may not cut large amounts of timber, or tear down the buildings, or cut shade trees, fruit trees and the like, if the act tends to lessen the safety of the security. The mortgagee can restrain such acts by injunction. If the damage is already done, and the timber or lumber already severed from the land, he can, in "title theory" states, replevy the property wrongfully severed, sue the mortgagor in trespass, or sue him for its conversion. The reason he has these actions is

(20)   Norwich Fire Ins. Co. v. Boomer, 52 Ill. 442.

that the title to the land is in the mortgagee, and, as soon as a tree is cut, though it becomes a chattel, the title of this chattel is in the mortgagee, so he can sue anyone wrongfully removing it or who wrongfully obtains it. In the ''lien theory'' states these actions will not lie, for the thing when severed belongs to the mortgagor—he has the title to it. In such states the mortgagee can enjoin anyone who is committing waste, and can sue the party who wrongfully severs an article for doing the wrongful act.

The mortgagor is not liable for depreciation in the value of the land due to the ravages of time. The mortgagee in possession owes a duty not to commit waste, and can be restrained by injunction from doing so, and must account for any loss due to injury to the premises by him. He is bound to make certain necessary repairs, but is not liable for failure to repair unless he has been grossly negligent in this respect.

SECTION 3. TRANSFER OF MORTGAGED PROPERTY.

§ 27. **Effect of transfer in general.** The mortgagor can give, sell, or will the mortgaged property, and if he dies intestate it passes to his heirs if he has a freehold interest, and to his personal representative if he has less than a freehold. Any person who derives his right to the property through the mortgagor, as an assignee or an heir, stands in the same position as the mortgagor and may have the same but no greater rights than the mortgagor had. A transferee of the mortgagor's interest may redeem the land, and may require a mortgagee in possession to account for rents and profits, or he may enforce any other rights which the mortgagor had.

§ 28. **Liability of transferee.** One who takes a conveyance of mortgaged property is not personally liable for the mortgage debt because of the conveyance. The land is liable, not the transferee. He is not personally liable unless he agrees expressly or impliedly that he will assume or pay the mortgage debt. His agreement to assume the debt may be implied, however, from the terms of the transfer of the land to him. For instance, when it appears that a certain sum, say $5,000, was to be paid for land subject to a $3,000 mortgage, and the transferee paid $2,000 and took a conveyance of the land subject to the mortgage, it has been held that there was an implied agreement by the transferee that he would assume the mortgage debt (21). The transferee is personally liable directly to the mortgagee, where he assumes the mortgage debt, but there are two theories on which he is so held liable. One theory is that the contract with the mortgagor, by which the transferee assumes the debt, is a contract for the benefit of a third person who can sue the obligor on a contract made for his benefit (22). The other theory is that the transferee is the principal debtor and the mortgagor the surety. In equity, a creditor is entitled to be subrogated to any right the surety has against the principal for his indemnity, and therefore the mortgagee is subrogated to the mortgagor's rights against his transferee (23).

---

(21)   Townsend v. Ward, 27 Conn. 610.
(22)   Burr v. Beers, 24 N. Y. 178. See Contracts, §§ 92-100, Volume I.
(23)   Keller v. Ashford, 133 U. S. 610.

§ 29. **Liability of mortgagor after transfer.** When
the transferee of mortgaged land assumes the debt, he
becomes the person who is primarily liable to pay it, as
between him and the mortgagor, for he has promised the
mortgagor he will pay it. The mortgagor then becomes
a surety for the payment of the debt, and the transferee
is the principal. This has no effect on the right of the
mortgagee against the mortgagor personally, unless he in
some way consents to hold the mortgagor as a mere
surety. After such a transfer the mortgagee is in many
states bound to recognize the relation of principal and
surety, and if he extends time of payment to the principal,
here the transferee, the mortgagor is thereby released
from liability. Thus, where the mortgagor had conveyed
the land to another person, and this one in turn to a second party, each party in turn assuming the debt, the supreme court of Illinois said that each subsequent purchaser became an original promisor for the payment of the
mortgage debt, and the original mortgagor became a
surety for its payment to the creditors (24).

§ 30. **Transfer of part of property only.** Several portions of the mortgaged property may be conveyed, by
similar conveyances made at the same time, to a number
of different persons, none of whom assumes the mortgage
debt. In such a case each portion of the land so conveyed
is security for its proportional share of the entire debt.
But the mortgagee can foreclose and sell any part he
pleases, and may proceed to enforce his lien against one
part. If the owner of this part, to save his land, pays the

---

(24) Flagg v. Geltmacher, 98 Ill. 293.

entire debt, he can force the owners of the other portions to pay their proportion based on the value that the portion each man owns bears to the value of the whole property. If, then, the party who paid the debt held one-fourth of the land, he would recover three-fourths of the amount he paid from the other owners. If the mortgagor of land transfers several portions to parties who do not assume the debt, and retains part of the land himself, clearly the part he holds ought to be liable for the whole debt, for, after all, the mortgagor is the person who owes the debt and he ought to pay it. Accordingly, in equity, while the mortgagee has the right to enforce his mortgage against any or all parts of the land, as between the mortgagor and his transferee, the land held by the mortgagor is liable for the whole debt (25).

§ 31. **Same: Successive transfers.** We have assumed so far that the portions of the land conveyed away at first were all conveyed at the same time. Suppose that the land was conveyed in four portions, the conveyances being several weeks apart, and that none of the transferees assumed the debt. The part conveyed last would, as to the other three parts, be the one primarily liable for the whole debt, it being the last part owned by the mortgagor. Now, the same principle applies to all the four conveyances. When the first part is conveyed, then the rest of the land is primarily liable before this first part and remains so. All the three subsequent parts should be sold and applied to the debt before the part first conveyed. The third and fourth parts would like-

---

(25)   Inglehart v. Crane et al, 42 Ill. 261.

wise be liable before the second part, and the fourth part before the third. To state the principle in the form often used, the land so conveyed in portions at different times is liable in "the inverse order of alienation" (26). A different rule applies where any grantee of a portion of the mortgaged land assumes the debt, for the one who assumes the debt becomes by his contract personally bound to pay it. If, then, other grantees have to pay the debt to save their land, such grantees would be subrogated to and entitled to enforce the mortgagee's right against the grantee who assumed the debt.

Section 4. Transfer of Debt or Mortgage.

§ 32. **Express transfer.** In "title theory" states, since the mortgagee has the legal title to the land, in order to make a complete legal transfer of the mortgage there must be a conveyance sufficient to pass title to land. Some of these states have provided by statutes simple forms of transfer. In any event, the transfer ought to be in writing, and should be recorded in order to protect the assignee against subsequent bona fide purchasers.

§ 33. **Transfer of mortgage debt without mortgage.** In equity, since the making of the mortgage is regarded as a transaction for the purpose of securing a debt, the debt is the principal thing and the mortgage a mere incident to the debt. The mortgage is not enforceable except by the owner of the debt. If the debt is assigned, the assignee has the benefit of the mortgage, and, in many states, all the rights and remedies of the mortgagee are

---

(26) Clowes v. Dickenson, 5 Johnson's Chancery 235.

conferred on him. Where the mortgagee has the legal title and assigns the debt alone, he holds the mortgage in trust, after assignment, for his assignee. In equity, a mere oral assignment of the debt is enough to pass the right to the debt to the assignee, and this carries the right to enforce the mortgage with it. In an Illinois case the mortgagee's debt was evidenced by a note. The mortgagee died and his administrator assigned the note to the plaintiff. The defendant was in possession of the land and the plaintiff sought to eject him. The court held that the plaintiff had only an assignment of the note, and that the legal title to the land was in the heirs of the mortgagee. The plaintiff could enforce the mortgage in equity, because the heirs held as trustees for him, but he had no legal title and hence could not eject the defendant. Had he taken a conveyance of the mortgage and thus got title, he could have maintained eject-ment (27).

§ 34. **Assignment of part of mortgage debt.** If a part of the mortgage debt is assigned, the assignee is entitled to the benefit of the mortgage security. The debt is frequently evidenced by several promissory notes or bonds, so that one or more of these may be assigned and the rest retained. The assignee of one of the mort-gage notes or bonds, being owner of a part of the mort-gage debt, is entitled to share in the benefit of the mort-gage security. In a New Hampshire case, the mortgage debt was in the form of five promissory notes. One of these notes the mortgagee assigned to the plaintiff in

---

(27) Barrett v. Hinckley, 124 Ill. 32.

the case.   The mortgagor then paid the other four notes, and the mortgagee released the mortgage.   The plaintiff brought a bill to foreclose the mortgage, claiming the release was not binding on him.   The mortgagor, who defended, pleaded the release of the mortgage.   The court held that a mortgage was a mere attendant of the debt, and, if the debt were assigned in parts to different persons, in the absence of an agreement to the contrary, the mortgage would follow and secure the fragments. Therefore, even though the other notes were paid, the plaintiff could have the benefit of the entire mortgage and could proceed to foreclose (28).

§ 35.   **Transfer of mortgage without debt.**   In "title" states the transfer of the mortgage without the debt gives the transferee only the bare legal title, which he holds in trust for the owner of the mortgage debt.   In "lien" states a transfer of the mortgage without the debt is of no effect at all—it is a nullity, for the legal title is in the mortgagor and the right to the mortgage security is in the owner of the debt.   Such a case arose in New York, a "lien theory" state.   The mortgagee assigned the mortgage alone to the plaintiff in the case, who brought an action against the defendant in possession to recover the land.   The court held the mortgagee had a mere chattel interest in the land and the mortgagor had the freehold.   The mortgage was only security for the debt, and an assignment of it alone could pass nothing to the assignee and was a mere nullity (29).

(28)   Page v. Pierce, 26 N. H. 317.

(29)   Jackson v. Bronson, 19 Johnson 325.

§ 36. **Effect** of **transfer** upon equities against mortgagee. The mortgage debt is a chose in action. See Personal Property, § 9, in Volume IV of this work. Where
a chose in action is not in the form of a negotiable instrument, an assignee takes it subject to all defenses
that can be made against the assignor, but, if a negotiable
instrument is transferred, by the law of negotiable instruments a transferee for value without notice takes
free from defenses against the transferor. These rules
apply to debts secured by mortgages as well as to other
debts. Thus, if a debt is in form of a non-negotiable
note for $1,000 and is assigned, the assignee gets no
greater rights than the assignor had. If only $500 is
actually due, the assignee can enforce it for only $500,
regardless of whether he knew this fact when he took
the assignment of the debt or not. If the note is negotiable, however, and the assignee takes it for value, before maturity, without notice that only $500 is actually
due, he takes it free from defenses against the assignor
and can enforce it for the full amount. In most states,
where the mortgage debt is negotiable in form, the assignee before maturity and for value without notice can
not only enforce the note personally against the mortgagor in full, but can likewise enforce the mortgage which
secures it. To illustrate, in a certain case the plaintiff
took a negotiable note secured by a mortgage, for value
before maturity, without notice of any defense which
the mortgagor had against the mortgagee, and brought
a bill to foreclose the mortgage. The mortgagor claimed
he had given the mortgagee a lot of flour to sell and apply the proceeds to the payment of the note, and that

the value of this flour should be deducted from the mortgage debt. The court held that, since the plaintiff had no notice of this arrangement, he could enforce the mortgage for the full amount of the note (30).

§ 36a. **Same: Contrary view.** A few states hold, however, that though the *note* is subject to the law of negotiable instruments, the *mortgage* is not; and while the note can be enforced free from defenses of which the assignee had no notice, the mortgage, if enforced, is subject to all defenses against the mortgagee. In an Ohio case a negotiable note secured by a mortgage was transferred to the plaintiff, who was a bona fide purchaser for value without notice. The action was a bill to foreclose the mortgage. The note had been given in payment for a patent, but the transaction was so fraudulent that it could not be enforced by anyone who had notice of such fraud. The court held the plaintiff could not enforce the mortgage where this fraud was set up as a defense, for the negotiable character of the note did not extend to the mortgage which secured it (31).

§ 37. **Record of assignment.** Assignments of mortgages should be recorded in order to charge subsequent purchasers with notice of the rights of the assignee. Otherwise, assignments will not be good as to persons who subsequently deal with the mortgagee, thinking he is still owner of the mortgage. The record of the assignment, however, is not notice to the mortgagor, for his right is prior to the assignment; and he can safely

(30)   Carpenter v. Longan, 16 Wall. 271.
(31)   Bailey v. Smith, 14 Ohio State, 396.

go on dealing with the mortgagee as owner, making payments, etc., until he has actual notice of the assignment. Therefore, an assignee of a mortgage should always notify the mortgagor or his successors of the assignment.

SECTION 5. PAYMENT, REDEMPTION, AND DISCHARGE.

§ 38. **Payment or tender of payment: Before default by mortgagor.** At common law payment of the mortgage debt, at or before the time it was due, the "law day," as it was called, terminated the mortgage and revested the title to the land in the mortgagor, upon entry by him, without any further formality. A tender of the money when due, according to the condition in the mortgage, also terminated the mortgage, and it could not thereafter be enforced, though the mortgagee could still enforce the debt personally against the mortgagor. This is still the law in "title theory" states. However, the mortgage, if recorded, will remain a cloud on the title to the land until the record shows it is released. Such a cloud on title has no effect on the owner's actual rights, but it makes the title apparently defective. A case arose in Massachusetts which illustrates the above principle. A creditor of the mortgagor made a levy and sold the equity of redemption on execution. This sale, being of an equity, was not valid if instead of an equity the debtor had the full title to the land. The mortgagor had, in fact, paid the mortgage debt and gotten a release of the mortgage, just before the levy was made, but the release was not recorded. The mortgagor claimed the levy was invalid because he had at the time the full legal title. The court held this was correct, for, as soon as payment

was made, the title revested in him, regardless of whether
a release was given or not. The release not being necessary, its record was immaterial to the case. The levy
was not properly made and was invalid (32). In equity,
and in states where the "lien theory" prevails, tender
or payment of the debt at maturity extinguishes the lien;
but, if there is only a tender, the mortgagee can enforce
the debt personally against the mortgagor, just in the
"title theory" states.

§ 39. Same: After default. At common law if the
debt was paid after default, a reconveyance was necessary to revest title in the mortgagor. This is true in
most "title theory" states to-day. Tender of payment
has no greater effect than payment. After tender of
payment, the mortgagee cannot enforce the mortgage
or eject the mortgagor from the property. Where the
"lien theory" prevails, payment completely extinguishes
the mortgage lien and tender has the same effect, except
that it must be kept good—that is, the mortgagor must
be ready to pay at any time if payment is demanded.
In such states there is no legal title to be conveyed, for
the mortgagor retains the title. If the mortgage is recorded, the record will constitute a cloud on the title,
if it does not show a discharge; so a formal discharge
should be obtained and the mortgage released of record.
In any state, if the mortgagee refuses to give a release
voluntarily, he can be compelled to do so by a bill in
equity to remove the cloud on the title, or by proceedings
provided by statute for this purpose.

. (32) Grover v. Flye, 5 Allen 543.

§ 40. **Enforcement** of **right** of redemption. At any time after default and before the mortgage has been foreclosed, the mortgagor may exercise his right to redeem from the mortgagee, unless his right has been barred by lapse of time. If the mortgagee refuses to consent to redemption, as where he is in possession claiming he has an absolute deed to the land, the mortgagor has to file a bill in equity to redeem. In such bill he must allege he is ready and willing to pay whatever the court finds due, and must, in fact, pay when ordered to do so by the court. If he does this, the court will compel the mortgagee to give up the property. This right to redeem we have seen (§ 2, above) may be cut off by a foreclosure, but even when the mortgagee does not foreclose it does not continue forever. The right to redeem may be barred by the failure to exercise it, for the law requires a man to be diligent in enforcing his rights. Equity will usually hold the right barred after the lapse of the period during which suits at law may be brought to recover land. This period is twenty years in most states, but less than that in some. There may be circumstances under which equity will declare the right barred in a shorter period. The above principle, as to barring the right by lapse of time, applies only when the mortgagee is in possession, holding the land adversely to the mortgagor. If the mortgagor retains possession his right cannot be barred by lapse of time.

§ 41. **Same: Parties** entitled to redeem. All persons who acquire interests in the mortgaged land, or legal or equitable liens thereon, which are inferior to the mort-

gage thereon, are entitled to redeem from such mortgage.
These parties are those who acquire rights subsequent
to the mortgage, or those whose rights, though prior in
time, are inferior to the mortgage; as when the mortgagee is a bona fide purchaser without notice of an
equitable lien, or when he recorded his mortgage firs˙ and
thus got priority over former unrecorded mortg;·ges.
Thus, the right to redeem may be exercised by purcʰas-
ers of all or part of the land from the mortgagor or his
assignee, by heirs or devisees of the mortgagor, by subsequent mortgagees or judgment creditors, or by a wife
or husband having dower rights in the land. One whose
right is prior to the mortgage, as a prior mortgagee, or
one with no interest at all, cannot redeem.

§ 42. **Amount required to be paid for redemption.**
Any person who redeems from a mortgage must pay the
entire mortgage debt, with interest, and all other sums
to which the mortgagee may be entitled by reason of the
mortgage. All this must be paid, no matter how small
the interest of the one redeeming, for the mortgage secures the whole debt and the mortgagee cannot be required to release his lien until he gets all that is due
him. Thus, where the widow of the mortgagor, having
a dower interest amounting to the use of one-third of
the land for life, filed a bill to redeem, the court held
she could redeem only on payment of all sums due under
the mortgage (33).

§ 43. **Contribution and indemnity between parties redeeming.** The doctrine of contribution is an equitable

(33) Gibson v. Crehore, 5 Pickering (Mass.) 146.

doctrine to the effect that, when there are two or more persons equally liable for a debt and one pays it all, he is entitled to have each of the others contribute his share of the debt. See Guaranty and Suretyship in Volume VII of this work. This right he can enforce in equity. Where there are several persons entitled to redeem from a mortgage and one pays the debt and secures the release of the mortgage, since this benefits the others by removing the lien from land in which they have interests, they can be forced to contribute to the one who redeemed. In the case of Gibson v. Crehore, stated in § 42, above, the widow, who redeemed, paid the whole debt. Her interest perhaps amounted to one-eighth the value of the land, and she was no more bound to pay than the others. Therefore, the other owners should contribute to her seven-eighths of the amount she paid to redeem. Indemnity applies when one has to pay a debt who is not primarily liable for it, as where payment is made by a surety. See Guaranty and Suretyship, as above. Such person is entitled to indemnity—that is, to repayment from the one primarily liable to pay. We have seen that, where a mortgagor transfers the land to one who assumes the mortgage, the latter is primarily liable (§ 29, above), so, if the mortgagor had to pay the debt, he would be entitled to repayment from his assignee.

§ 44. **Enforcement** of contribution **and** indemnity: **Subrogation.** Subrogation is an equitable doctrine by which one, who is compelled to pay a debt for which he is not primarily liable in order to protect his interests, is entitled to stand in the place of the original creditor

with all the creditor's rights against the one primarily
liable for the debt, and especially with a right to the securities which the creditor may have for the debt. See
Guaranty and Suretyship in Volume VII of this work.
The rights of contribution and indemnity explained in
the preceding subsection are usually enforced by applying the doctrine of subrogation. Take the case where
the widow having a dower interest redeemed from a
mortgage (34). The court said she was entitled to contribution from the other owners. She had no way of
enforcing this right directly, for there was no contract
relation between the parties. All of them apparently
had gotten their interests through the death of the mortgagor. Hence, the only way to enforce contribution
would be by allowing the widow the rights which the
owner of the mortgage had against the land. He had
a mortgage on the land, so the court said the widow could
enforce this against the land to the extent of the money
rightfully due her. In general, any person entitled to
redeem, who redeems, may be subrogated to the rights
of the mortgagee against land and against other owners
of interests in the land, provided he is not primarily
liable for the debt (35). Also, anyone who pays off the
mortgage at request of the one primarily liable, with
the understanding he is to have the benefit of the mortgage, has the right of subrogation; but if a stranger voluntarily pays the debt he has no such right.

§ 45. **Marshalling securities.** Suppose a debtor has
two tracts of land. One man has a mortgage on both

(34)   Gibson v. Crehore, §§ 42-43, above.
(35)   Bergein v. Brehm, 123 Ind. 160.

tracts to secure a debt, and another man has a second mortgage on one of the tracts. If the first mortgagee enforces his right against the land covered by the second mortgage, and exhausts the security, the second mortgagee will have nothing. Ordinarily, the first mortgagee has the right to enforce his lien as to any portion of the land. But there is a principle in equity that one who has two funds, out of which he can secure satisfaction of his debt, shall not by his election disappoint one who has only one of the funds to proceed against. This applies to the first and second mortgagees in such a case. While the first mortgagee may enforce against the land covered by the second mortgage, if there is not enough left to pay the second mortgagee's debt, the latter is entitled to be subrogated to the first mortgagee's right against the other tract of land, provided it will not prejudice the mortgagor or any third person (36).

§ 46. **Merger of mortgage and equity of redemption.** If the mortgagee of land acquires the equity of redemption, the two interests merge and the mortgage is extinguished, for the mortgagee owns both the mortgage and the equity of redemption and cannot have a mortgage on his own land. In equity the two interests are not regarded as merging when it would prejudice the rights of any person interested, or when the contrary is necessary for purposes of justice.

SECTION 6. MORTGAGE FORECLOSURES.

§ 47. **In general.** As has been previously stated (§ 2, above), foreclosure was allowed in order that the mort-

(36) Andreas v. Hubbard, 50 Conn. 351.

gagee might have a means of putting an end to the equity of redemption, and on foreclosure the right to redeem was cut off and the mortgagee got the land. This was called strict foreclosure. Now the decree for foreclosure usually orders a sale of the property and a payment of the debt out of the proceeds. Any surplus is turned over to the mortgagor. The mortgagee cannot get the land, unless he buys it at the sale. Strict foreclosure is not allowed except in special cases, because the land may be worth far more than the mortgage debt and the mortgagee is only entitled to the money due him.

§ 48. **When right to foreclose arises?** The owner of a mortgage has a right to foreclose as soon as the mortgagor fails to perform the obligation secured by the mortgage, usually when he fails to pay the debt when due. The mortgage, however, often provides that, if the interest on the debt is not paid when due, the whole debt shall immediately be due and payable and foreclosure may be had, or, it may provide that the right to foreclose shall accrue on failure of the mortgagor to pay taxes, keep up insurance on the premises, or on default of some other obligation calculated to affect the security for the debt.

§ 49. **When right to foreclose is barred by lapse of time?** We saw in a preceding subsection (§ 40) that when the mortgagee is in possession of the land the right to redeem may be barred by lapse of time. Likewise, if the mortgagee fails to exercise his right to foreclose his mortgage within a certain time, his right will be barred. When there is no express statute of limitations, equity usually declares the right barred after the lapse of the period within which action for recovery of land may be brought. After the lapse of this period, it is presumed that, since no effort has been made to enforce the mortgage, it must have been satisfied. This presumption that the mortgage was satisfied may be overthrown, however, by showing that within the period the mortgagor has acknowledged that the debt is unpaid, by making a payment or by some other act. The other right of the mortgagee—the personal right against the mortgagor—comes within various other statutes of limitations, and the action on it will be barred within the period provided for in the statute which applies. These statutes vary as to different kinds of obligations, and vary in different states. The time within which the personal action is barred is almost always less than that within which the right to foreclose will be barred. In most states the mortgage can be foreclosed after the right to sue the mortgagor personally is barred. In a New York case a mortgage had been given to secure a promissory note, and in that state the action on a note is barred six years after the right to sue arises, if there has been no acknowledgment of the debt meanwhile. A bill to foreclose the mortgage was started nineteen years after the note was due. Foreclosure was not barred in New York until after twenty years. There had been no partial payment or other act acknowledging the debt since it became due. The court held that, though the right to sue on the note had long been barred, the right to foreclose might be exercised at any time within twenty years and that foreclosure should be allowed (37). In a few states the mortgage is regarded as so much an incident of the debt that it cannot be enforced after the right to enforce the debt is gone. In an Illinois case, the debt was in the form of a promissory note, and actions on such notes are barred after ten years. A bill to foreclose the mortgage was filed more than ten years after the debt was due, and the court held that the mortgage, being a mere incident to the debt, could not be enforced after action on the note was barred (38).

§ 50. **Strict foreclosure.** Strict foreclosure is a foreclosure by which the mortgagee gets the land free from the right of redemption. The decree provides that if the debt is not paid by a certain date the right to redeem shall be gone forever. Strict foreclosure is not allowed when the land is worth more than the amount of the debt, for it would result in the mortgagee getting more than he is entitled to. It is allowed in many states when the rights of the mortgagor will not be prejudiced. When the land is not sufficient to satisfy the mortgage debt, strict foreclosure may be had without injustice to anyone. By it the rights of the mortgagor and of persons who have junior liens can be cut off. A strict foreclosure satisfies the mortgage to the extent of the value of the land and the mortgagee can sue the debtor personally for any unsatisfied part of the debt.

§ 51. **Foreclosure by entry and by writ of entry.** Foreclosure by entry and by writ of entry are forms of fore-

---

(37)   Pratt v. Huggins, 29 Barb. 277.
(38)   Harris v. Mills, 28 Ill. 44.

closure provided for in some of the New England states. The effect is similar to that of strict foreclosure, the mortgagee getting the land and the debt being satisfied to the extent of the value of the land.

§ 52. **Equitable proceeding for sale of mortgaged premises.** The usual method of foreclosing a mortgage is by a proceeding in equity, or a proceeding under some statute provided for the purpose, to sell the land and pay the debt out of the proceeds. The sale is made by a master in chancery or some other officer of the court, who gives the purchaser a deed to the land, pays the mortgagee the sum due him, applies the surplus, after deducting the costs, to any junior lien which may be on the land, and pays any remainder, after all claims are satisfied, to the mortgagor. A purchaser at a foreclosure sale in a "title theory" state gets whatever record title the mortgagor had when he made the mortgage. His title is good as to all persons whose rights were inferior to the mortgage. He takes subject to all rights superior to the mortgage which was foreclosed. Hence, when a second mortgage is foreclosed, the purchaser at the sale takes subject to the first mortgage and the first mortgagee may foreclose at any time. The purchaser knows this or can easily find it out, so of course he will bid only what he is willing to pay for the land subject to the first mortgage. In many states the statute gives a short period—from six months to two years usually—within which persons entitled to redeem may redeem after foreclosure sale, the purchaser getting his deed after this time has expired. This is a purely statutory right and did not exist at common law.

§ 53. **Mortgage with power of sale.** It is often provided in a mortgage that, on default by the mortgagor, the mortgagee may sell the land without judicial proceedings. Such a "power of sale" is valid in most states, though there are a few states which refuse to allow a sale except by judicial proceedings. The power of sale makes the mortgagee the agent of the mortgagor to sell the land, and therefore the principles of the laws of agency apply. Death of the principal terminates an agency, unless it is what is called an "agency coupled with an interest." See Agency, §§ 46-47, in Volume I of this work. In "title theory" states the mortgagee has an agency coupled with an interest, so, if there is a power of sale in the mortgage, the death of the mortgagor does not revoke the power to sell the land. The beneficial interest of the mortgagee, even in "lien theory" states, is generally held sufficient to satisfy this doctrine, though in a few states the power is terminated by the death of the mortgagor. All agree that there is such an interest that the mortgagor cannot revoke the power of sale during his lifetime. Statutes usually provide that the sale must be public, after proper notice of it has been given. In the absence of statute the sale may be private. Since a mortgagee selling under a power of sale is acting as agent of the mortgagor, he is not allowed to purchase at the sale, unless the mortgagor gives him permission; for an agent cannot himself purchase what the principal has given him power to sell, unless the principal consents. The purchaser, at a sale made under the power given in the mortgage, gets, in a "title theory" state, the title which the mortgagor had when he made the mortgage, because that title is in the mortgagee who makes the sale. Therefore, a purchaser takes free from all subsequent liens and is in as good a position as if he had bought at a foreclosure sale. The same result is reached in "lien theory" states, since the exercise of the power conveys the title as it was when the lien became effective.

§ 54. Sale under trust deed. When a trust deed is given to secure the payment of a debt it is regarded as a mortgage. The trustee is given power to sell the land and apply the proceeds to the mortgage debt, if default is made in payment of the debt. A sale by such a trustee passes to the purchaser the title which the trustee has. A trustee, like a mortgagee, selling under a power of sale, is not permitted to purchase the property himself. On sale, either by a trustee under a trust deed, or by mortgagee under a power of sale, the surplus proceeds after the debt is paid belong to the mortgagor.

§ 55. Effect of mortgage providing for attorneys' fees. An agreement in the mortgage that, in the event of foreclosure, a certain sum shall be allowed for attorneys' fees is found in many mortgages. But if the courts consider the amount named in the mortgage too large, they will allow only what they consider reasonable.

§ 56. Parties entitled to foreclose: Mortgagee and assignees. The mortgagee is the proper person to foreclose, if he still owns the mortgage debt. If he has assigned the mortgage debt, even without the mortgage, the assignee is the one who then has the right to enforce the mortgage. A mortgagee who has assigned the debt no longer has any right to foreclose, for, even though he has not transferred the mortgage and still has the legal title to the land, he only holds this in trust for the benefit of the owner of the debt; but, as the holder of the legal title, he should be made a party to the suit so that the court can, at the sale, pass this title to the purchaser. Any person who owns a portion of the debt has the benefit of the security, and hence may foreclose the mortgage. If he cannot get the other owners to join him as parties plaintiff, he must in his bill to foreclose make them parties defendant, in order to pass a clear title to the purchaser at the sale, for, whatever rights they have in the land, will persist unless they are made parties to the suit. Rights of those interested, either in the debt secured or in the land, cannot be cut off unless they are made parties to the suit; but, if made parties, they may assert such rights and will be bound by the decree of the court.

§ 57. **Same: Personal representatives of mortgagee or assignees.** On death of the owner of the mortgage, the debt, being personal property, passes to his personal representatives, and with it the right to foreclose. If he had the legal title, this passes as real estate to his heirs or devisees, who hold it in trust for the benefit of the owner, just as the mortgagee would hold it after he assigned the debt. There is a conflict of authority as to whether such persons should be made parties to a bill to foreclose, or not. Strictly, they seem proper parties.

§ 58. **All parties interested in land should be joined in foreclosure.** The purpose of forclosure is to cut off all rights to the land inferior to the mortgage. It is therefore necessary that all persons, who have interests which would entitle them to redeem, should be made parties to the suit, so that the decree of the court will be binding on them. Those not made parties will not have their rights cut off by the decree. Persons who assert adverse claims to the land, paramount to the mortgage, need not be made parties. Their rights, if valid, are superior. The foreclosure only cuts off inferior rights and the land is sold subject to all superior liens.

§ 59. **Deficiency decrees in foreclosure proceedings.** We have seen that the mortgagor is personally liable for the mortgage debt. A mortgagee can sue him at law and foreclose the mortgage at the same time. The fact he has started one proceeding does not bar the other, but he can pursue both remedies until the debt is satisfied. Formerly, if he foreclosed and sold the land and the proceeds were not sufficient to satisfy the debt, he had then to sue at law to recover the deficiency. In most states today, statutes provide that the court, in a foreclosure proceeding, may provide for a deficiency decree. If the proceeds of the sale pay only part of the debt, the court will then enter a decree for the remainder of the money due, and the mortgagee can levy execution against other property of the mortgagor. Thus the mortgagee gets the sale of the land and a judgment for the part of the debt unsatisfied, in the one proceeding.

CHAPTER II.

CHATTEL MORTGAGES.

Section 1. Nature, Form, and Validity.

§ **60. Historical development.** At common law a mortgage of personal property was a sale or transfer of the title on condition that, if the debt secured was paid when due, the sale should become void and the title revert to the mortgagor, but otherwise to remain in full force. If the debt was not paid, the title of the mortgagee became absolute, and the mortgagor lost all right to the mortgaged property; so, in fact, a chattel mortgage amounted to a conditional sale, and it still is so regarded in the courts of law. As in the case of real mortgages, there was no way by which the mortgagor could pay his debt and get back the property, however valuable it might be, after he had once made default in payment; and it made no difference that he failed to make payment by reason of some fraud or mistake. Equity, considering that the real nature of the transaction was a transfer of the property to the mortgagee to secure the payment of a debt, allowed the mortgagor to recover his property on payment of the amount due, thus regarding the mortgagee as having a mere lien on the property as security for his debt. This right to redeem allowed in courts of equity was, and still is, called the "equity of redemption." To enable the mortgagee to cut off this equity of redemption, after default, equity allowed him to foreclose his mortgage just as in case of real estate mortgages. Up to this point the law of chattel and of real estate mortgages developed in the same way (see §§ 1-3, above). For some reason, perhaps because chattel mortgages were formerly less common than real estate mortgages, chattel mortgages never came to be regarded by the law courts as anything more than conditional sales, and, after default, the mortgagor even today can get no relief in a court of law. In almost all states the "title theory" of mortgages prevails as to chattel mortgages, and the right to redeem is not a legal right and can only be enforced by resorting to a court of equity.

§ 61. **Chattel mortgage distinguished from sale with right to repurchase.** A chattel mortgage is often hard to distinguish from a sale with the right to repurchase, because they are both in form conditional sales and in courts of law are treated the same. But in equity, if the transaction was to secure a debt, it is a mortgage, so the important fact whether it was so intended has to be determined. Where it is clear there is a debt secured, the transaction is a mortgage, of course; and, if it is merely shown there is a debt between the parties, the presumption is that the transaction is a mortgage, though this presumption may be overcome by clear evidence that a conditional sale was really intended. Inadequacy of price also indicates a mortgage. Whenever the evidence is such that the court is doubtful what was intended, it always presumes the transaction is a mortgage. In an early Alabama case there was an instrument in the form of an absolute transfer of the property to the defendant. Another instrument, made two months later, gave the plaintiff the right to repurchase the property at a certain date. At the time the first instrument was executed, there was a debt due the defendant from the plaintiff. The plaintiff was to retain the possession of the property. After failing to repurchase, the plaintiff brought a bill to redeem. The defendant claimed the transaction was a sale with right to repurchase. The court said it had doubt as to whether an absolute sale was intended, but that it was a practice of courts of equity, when in doubt as to whether there was a conditional sale or mortgage, to declare it a mortgage. Accordingly the plaintiff was allowed to redeem (1).

§ 62. **Chattel mortgage distinguished from pledge.** There are two important distinctions between a chattel mortgage and a pledge. The first of these is that in a chattel mortgage the legal title passes to the mortgagee, while the pledgor retains the title, a pledge being a mere giving of the possession of the property to hold as security. The second distinction is that the pledge from its nature cannot exist, unless possession is given to the pledgee, while the fact the possession is retained by a mortgagor has no effect whatever on the validity of the mortgage. In fact, chattel mortgagors commonly keep possession of the mortgaged property. When the transaction is oral and possession is delivered over, whether it is a pledge or a mortgage is a question of intention of the parties, the presumption being in favor of a pledge. When there is an instrument in the form of a mortgage,

---

(1)   Locke v. Palmer, 26 Ala. 312.

however, the transaction cannot be shown to be a pledge. A case arising in New York illustrates the difference between a mortgage and a pledge. A plaintiff sued in trover, claiming he had pledged three horses to the defendant and the defendant had wrongfully refused to receive payment of the debt and return them. The defendant produced an absolute bill of sale of the horses for a certain sum, and a separate writing of the same date binding him to return them if the sum was repaid by a certain date. The court held the plaintiff could not recover, as this was a mortgage and not a pledge. It said, "A mortgage is an absolute pledge to become an absolute interest if not redeemed within a specified time. After the condition is forfeited the mortgagee has an absolute interest in the thing mortgaged, whereas the pawnee has but a special property in the goods to detain them for his security" (2). This case also illustrates the view law courts take of chattel mortgages, for the transaction here was clearly a chattel mortgage and the mortgagee was declared to have absolute title to the horses, since the mortgagor had not paid the debt when it was due.

§ 63. **Form of chattel mortgages.** At common law a parol contract of sale of personal property is just as valid as a written agreement. A chattel mortgage is but a conditional sale, and therefore is perfectly valid though made orally. In many states, however, a parol mortgage is not enforceable because a section of the statute of frauds requires all contracts for the sale of goods, wares, and

(2) Brown v. Bennett, 8 Johnson 75.

merchandise, when amounting to more than a certain sum in value, to be in writing. Where such a statute is in force a chattel mortgage must be in writing if for a sum within the statute. Another difficulty about a parol mortgage is that it cannot be recorded, and recording is required by statute in most states to protect the mortgagee from subsequent purchasers who have no notice of the mortgage, if possession of the property is retained by the mortgagor. A chattel mortgage usually consists of a bill of sale of the goods, with a condition attached. No particular form of words is required, it being enough if the language is sufficient to pass title to personal property. Many states, in order to prevent clandestine bills of sale, made to defraud creditors of the mortgagor, require that the mortgagor attach his affidavit to the effect that the mortgage was made in good faith, in order to make it valid except as between the parties.

§ 64. **Same: Absolute conveyance.** The defeasance or condition may be in a separate instrument, just as in the case of real estate mortgages. Such instrument, however, must be intended as a part of the original transaction; though, if so intended, it need not be made at the same time. Such defeasance is sufficient if it is shown that the bill of sale, absolute in form, was intended to secure the payment of a debt. This was shown in the case of Brown v. Bennett in the preceding subsection. There the bill of sale and defeasance were separate, but, although they were made two months apart, they were considered as part of one transaction. In a court of equity it can be shown by extrinsic evidence that an absolute bill of sale was intended as a mortgage, or that there was a purely oral defeasance (3). In a court of law, however, extrinsic evidence cannot be admitted to vary the terms of the writing, though if the sale, too, is oral, there may be an oral defeasance. The only difficulty where the bill of sale is written and the defeasance oral is the rule of evidence by which parol evidence cannot be used to vary the terms of the written instrument.

§ 65. **Property subject to chattel mortgage: Fixtures.** The general rule is that any personal property, which is subject to present sale, is subject to chattel mortgage; for a chattel mortgage is in form a conditional sale. There arises a great deal of difficulty as to chattel mortgages on fixtures. Fixtures include a vast variety of articles which are more or less firmly attached to land, or to buildings on land, and in law, by such attachment, cease to be chattels and become a part of the real estate. (See Landlord and Tenant, Chapter VI, in Volume IV of this work.) A chattel mortgage may be given before attaching the chattel to the land, but, after attaching, the title cannot be in the chattel mortgagee because he has a chattel mortgage only and the articles covered have changed their character and become real estate. The chattel mortgage does not amount to, nor was it intended as, a mortgage on real estate, and therefore, when the fixture is attached to the land, the title to it is in the land owner. But such a chattel mortgage is good in equity between the parties. Suppose, however, the land to which the mortgaged chattels are attached is mortgaged. Here a conflict arises between the two mortgagees. Where the

(3) Parks v. Hall, 2 Pickering (Mass.) 206.

real estate mortgage was in existence at the time the chattels were attached to the land, the rule is that the chattel mortgagee has a right in equity to a lien to the extent to which the attachment of the chattels or fixtures increases the value of the land, for the real mortgagee did not rely on this additional value when he took his mortgage. There are some courts, however, which hold that when the fixtures are attached they become a part of the realty, subject to the mortgage on the land; and, even though the parties to the chattel mortgage agree that they shall remain chattels, this agreement does not affect the right of the real mortgagee.

§ 66. Conflict between real and chattel mortgages: Illustrations. The rule as first stated is illustrated by a leading Michigan case. In this case an owner of timber land, which was subject to a mortgage, purchased an engine for a saw mill he wished to build, and gave the vendor a chattel mortgage for part of the price, the parties agreeing the engine should remain a chattel. It was set upon the land. The chattel mortgage was properly executed and recorded. The real mortgagee foreclosed his mortgage, sold the property, and the purchaser at the foreclosure sale took possession of the property, including the engine. On his refusal to give up the engine to the chattel mortgagee, the latter sued him in trover. The court held he should recover, for the engine was erected subject to an agreement that it should remain a chattel, and the real mortgagee was in no way misled by the transaction between the chattel mortgagee and mortgagor (4).

----

(4)   Crippen v. Morrison, 13 Michigan 23.

Where the mortgaged chattel is attached before the real mortgage is executed, the better view is that the real mortgagee gets a prior right to all that is a part of the realty when he gets his mortgage, and consequently he has a prior right to the fixtures. In an Ohio case an engine, on which a chattel mortgage had been given and an agreement made that it was to remain a chattel, was set up in a saw mill. Then a mortgage was given on the land. The land was sold on foreclosure of the real mortgage, and the chattel mortgagee sued the purchasers at the foreclosure sale for conversion of the engine. The court held the engine when attached became a part of the land, and was conveyed to the real mortgagee by his mortgage. The chattel mortgagee had no title to the engine after it was attached, and his right would not prevail unless the real mortgagee had notice of it when he took his mortgage (5). In the above case the chattel mortgage was recorded, but, as a rule, a chattel mortgage record is not constructive notice to one who acquires rights in real estate, so this did not aid the chattel mortgagee. While the above case represents the logical view, there is a conflict on this point and many courts hold that when the parties agree a chattel shall remain a chattel it does not, by attachment to realty, become part of such realty; and therefore the chattel mortgage is superior to any real estate mortgage whether made before or after the attachment of the mortgaged chattel to the land.

§ 67. **Chattel mortgage of future property.** A chattel mortgage, being in form a sale on condition, cannot cover

---

(5) Brennan v. Whitaker, 15 Ohio State 446.

property to be acquired in the future; for, as a general rule, one cannot make a present sale of an article he does not own. (See Sales, §§ 29-32, in Volume III of this work.) To illustrate, one cannot give a legal mortgage on a stock of goods in a store where goods are being constantly sold and replaced with new purchases, so as to cover the goods purchased after the mortgage was given. The attempt to make such a mortgage is sufficient to give a lien in equity on the after-acquired goods, but, this being only an equitable right, is not good against subsequent purchasers for value, without notice of such right (6). Some courts of equity hold an attempted mortgage of after-acquired property amounts to a contract to give a mortgage on the property, and can be specifically enforced in equity, a contract to give a mortgage being specifically enforceable.

§ 68. **Description of property.** The property covered by a chattel mortgage should be described so particularly that it can be identified. If this description is indefinite, extrinsic evidence cannot be used to show what property is really covered. But the description need not be so careful that a stranger without any aid could, by referring to the mortgage, select the goods covered by it. Evidence can be admitted to identify the mortgaged goods by showing they come within the description. Thus such descriptions as: "two horses belonging to the mortgagor" (7), or "all my goods or tools in my shop" (8), or, "my entire

(6) Holroyd v. Marshall, 10 House of Lords Cases 191.
(7) Harding v. Coburn, 12 Met. 333.
(8) Brooks v. Aldrich, 17 N. H. 443.

crop of cotton and corn for the present year'' (9), are sufficiently definite. It is best, however, to describe the property covered by the mortgage so definitely that there can be no question as to the identity of the mortgaged property.

§ 69. **Description of** mortgage debt. The obligation secured by a mortgage may be pre-existing, contemporaneous, or one to arise in the future. The debt must be so definitely described and limited in the mortgage, that it may be recognized and distinguished from other debts. A general description is sufficient, and it is not necessary to state the exact amount of the debt, or the time of payment, if means are provided so that, by reference to other papers, it can be ascertained what debt was intended to be secured by the mortgage, and when it falls due. Descriptions such as: "what I may owe on my books," and, "all sums that the mortgagee may become liable to pay" have been held good (10). A chattel mortgage to secure advances to be made in the future is valid, and secures all advances made in good faith, without actual notice of the rights of third parties which were acquired subsequent to the mortgage. The mortgage need not even state the amounts intended to be advanced, but, if a definite amount is stated in a mortgage made for future advances, the mortgage cannot be enforced, as against subsequent purchasers, for a larger sum. If given for a larger sum than is advanced it can be enforced only for the sum which is actually due.

(9) Ellis v. Martin, 60 Ala. 394.
(10) Lawrence v. Tucker, 21 Howard (U. S.) 14.

§ 70. Execution and delivery of chattel mortgage.
The statute of frauds requires written instruments to be
signed by the party to be charged, and this statute applies
to chattel mortgages. Consequently, the instrument
should be signed by the mortgagor. It is not necessary to
seal a chattel mortgage, however, unless a specific statute
requires it, for it is a conditional sale in form and may be
valid though made orally. It is quite common, however, to
seal chattel mortgages. After execution of a sealed chattel mortgage it must be delivered by the mortgagor to the
mortgagee and accepted by the latter, before it is valid;
the law in this respect being the same as in respect to
other common law or mercantile specialties, such as deeds
or promissory notes.

**§ 71. Formalities required as against innocent pur-
chasers of mortgaged property: Change of possession.**
By agreement or permission of the mortgagee, the mortgagor is usually allowed to remain in possession of the
mortgaged property. Assuming that this retention of
possession is not actually fraudulent, the rights of innocent purchasers of the property from the mortgagor depend upon considerations similar to those governing the
rights of such purchasers from a vendor of chattels who
remains in possession, concerning which there is a conflict
of judicial opinion. (See Sales, §§ 77-78, in Volume III of
this work.) In many states there is in such cases
a presumption of fraud, which must be explained in order
to protect the mortgagee. In some the presumption of
fraud is conclusive. The mortgagee is, of course, protected where he actually takes and continues in the pos-

session of the mortgaged property. In most or all states this question is now obsolete, on account of the existence of recording statutes, described below.

§ 72. Same: Recording acts. In order to enable a party to make a valid chattel mortgage and retain possession of the mortgaged property, recording laws are in force in most of the states which provide that, if a chattel mortgage is not recorded or filed according to the requirements of the statute, it shall not be valid as against subsequent purchasers and creditors if the mortgagee does not take possession. Anyone interested, by searching the chattel mortgage records, can find out whether personal property is mortgaged, and, if no mortgage appears on record, can safely proceed to purchase or take a mortgage on such property in the owner's possession. A mortgagee, on the other hand, by recording or filing his mortgage, can protect himself against subsequent bona fide purchasers and creditors, for the chattel mortgage record is constructive notice of his mortgage as to all third parties. If the mortgagor resides in the state, the mortgage must be recorded in the county where he resided when it was executed, or, by some statutes, in the county where the property is located; if he lives outside the state, it must be recorded where the mortgaged property was located when the mortgage was executed. The statute usually provides that when there are several mortgagors, some residents of the state and some non-residents, the mortgage must be recorded in the county or counties where the resident mortgagors reside, and also in the county where the property is located when the mortgage was executed (11). When a mortgage covers both real and personal property it should be recorded both in the real mortgage records and in the chattel mortgage records.

§ 73. **Same: Delivery after failure to record.** When a chattel mortgage is not recorded, it is generally made valid, under the recording laws, if the property is delivered to the mortgagee before any third parties have acquired adverse rights in it. Delivery of the mortgaged property to the mortgagee not only makes an unrecorded chattel mortgage valid as to third parties, but also covers any indefiniteness in the description of the goods in the instrument, for, after delivery to the mortgagee, there is no doubt as to the goods intended to be covered by the mortgage (12).

SECTION 2.   OPERATION AND EFFECT.

§ 74. **Right to possession of mortgaged chattel: At common law.** Under the common law a chattel mortgagee, like a real mortgagee, was entitled to possession of the mortgaged property (§ 18, above). Being thus entitled, he can demand the property, and, if it is withheld either by the mortgagor or by any third person, the mortgagee may bring an action either in replevin to recover the property itself or in trover to recover its value. In Frisbee v. Longworthy (13), an officer seized the entire property subject to a chattel mortgage, under an execution against the mortgagor, and sold it. The mortgage provided that the mortgagee might take possession of the

---

(11)   Stewart v. Platt, 101 U. S. 731.
(12)   Morrow v. Reed, 30 Wis. 81.
(13)   11 Wis. 393.

property and sell it at any time he deemed his debt inse-cure. The mortgagee brought an action for conversion against the officer who sold the property. The court held that, since the plaintiff could by the terms of the mortgage take possession and sell at any time, he had a right to maintain trover against the officer, who wrongfully sold the entire property instead of the mortgagor's interest in it, and thus was guilty of a trespass as to the plaintiff. Here the action was against a third person, i. e., the officer who seized the goods.

§ 75. **Same: By agreement or permission.** Often it is expressly agreed in the mortgage that the mortgagor shall retain the possession, and, in the absence of such an agreement, he is often permitted to do so. When there is a provision for retention of possession by the mortgagor, the conditions and circumstances under which the mortgagee can take possession are usually fully provided for. If there are no such conditions expressed in the mortgage, the presumption is that the mortgagee can take possession of the property on default in payment of the mortgage debt. The right of the mortgagor to keep possession need not be express, but may be implied from other provisions in the instrument, such as provisions as to the time when the mortgagee shall take possession, or that the mortgagor shall care for the property, or keep it in repair.

§ 76. **Same: After forfeiture.** The mortgagee has the right to take possession of the mortgaged property after default, and may retain such possession until the amount due him is actually paid. He can force the mortgagor to bring an action to redeem, and need not give up the goods then, until the money is actually paid into court. As soon as the mortgagee takes possession after default he may sell the property and bar the right of redemption, independently of any decree of court or express power of sale (14). He has a power of sale in such case similar to that of a pledgee, who may sell after default in payment, after giving due notice to the pledgor. In Patchin v. Pierce (15), a New York case, a chattel mortgage had been given on two horses and default made in payment. After default the mortgagor paid part of the debt, and then brought an action at law in trespass against the mortgagee, for refusal to give up the horses. The court held this action at law would not lie because, on forfeiture, the title became absolute in the mortgagee, and the receipt of a part of the debt was not a waiver of the forfeiture. The entire debt must be accepted to constitute such a waiver (§ 81, below). It must be remembered that this was a court of law. The mortgagor here could still go into equity and redeem, but could not secure relief except by resorting to a court of equity.

§ 77. **Right to profits from mortgaged property.** The law regarding right to the profits of mortgaged chattels is the same as in respect to mortgaged realty (§§ 19-20, above). If the mortgagor is in possession of the mortgaged property, he is entitled to the income from it as his own.

Thus, in Stewart v. Frye (16) there was even a provi-

---

(14)   Wilson v. Brannan, 27 Cal. 258.

(15)   12 Wend. (N. Y.) 61.

(16)   3 Ala. 573.

sion in the mortgage that profits received by the mortgagor from the mortgaged property should be applied on the debt, and the mortgagee sued the administrator of the mortgagor to recover such profits collected by the mortgagor. The court held that, when the mortgagee permitted the mortgagor to collect the profits from the mortgaged property, such profits belonged to the mortgagor, and the mortgagee was not entitled to an accounting for them.

If the mortgagee is in possession he is entitled to collect the profits, but if he undertakes to foreclose his mortgage, or if a bill is brought to redeem the property, he is required to account for such income, and it is applied first to the liquidation of the debt and interest, and the surplus, if there be any, must be paid to the mortgagor.

§ 78. **Mortgagor's right to sell or transfer mortgaged property.** Whatever right the mortgagor has in the mortgaged property he may transfer or sell, subject, of course, to the mortgage. Even after he has made default in payment of the debt and has no legal estate in the property, he still has his rights to redeem in equity, and this he may sell to anyone, even to the mortgagee. But, as in case of real mortgages, when the equity of redemption is sold to the mortgagee, the transaction can be set aside in a court of equity unless it appears to be fair and proper (§ 5, above). Since the mortgagor can sell his interest in the mortgaged property, it follows that he may give a subsequent mortgage on it. When a chattel mortgage is given by a merchant or shopkeeper on a stock of goods in his store, there is usually an understanding that the mortgagor is to continue the business. He must then have the power to sell goods free from the lien of the mortgage. Such mortgagee usually expressly gives the mortgagor power to sell goods. A parol agreement that he may sell goods is sufficient, or power to sell may be implied from other terms of the mortgage. If the mortgagee, when there is no such power to sell, express or implied, knows the mortgagor is selling goods and does not try to prevent such sales, he will be estopped from denying their validity (17).

§ 79. **Assignment of mortgage by mortgagee.** The mortgagee may assign the mortgage. Such assignment, to be legal, should be in writing or by a transfer of the instrument itself. But an assignment of the mortgage, without an assignment of the debt also, is a nullity, for the mortgage is a mere incident of the debt (§ 35, above). On the other hand, the assignment of the debt, without formal assignment of the mortgage securing it, gives the assignee an equitable title to the mortgage, and he can enforce such mortgage in his own name in a court of equity (18). Such assignee of the debt, not having legal title to the mortgage, cannot maintain legal actions, such as trespass, trover, and replevin, except in the name of the mortgagee. The mortgagee, who has assigned the debt alone, holds the mortgage in trust for the benefit of the owner of the debt secured by it. The assignment of a part of the mortgage debt operates pro tanto as an equitable assignment of the mortgage, and the assignee is

---

(17)   Brooks v. Record, 47 Ill. 30.
(18)   Langdon v. Buel, 9 Wendell 89.

entitled to share proportionately in the benefit of the mortgage security. Such a partial assignee, however, having only an equitable right, would lose it should the mortgagee make a legal transfer for value of the whole debt and mortgage to one who had no notice of the prior partial asignment.

§ 80. **Same: Effect upon equities against mortgagee.** When the mortgage debt is evidenced by a negotiable instrument, such as a bond or promissory note, and such instrument, together with the mortgage, is duly assigned before the debt is due, the assignee, by the law of most states, can enforce both the note and the mortgage free from equities existing between the mortgagor and mortgagee (19). (See § 36, above.) A few states, however, hold that, while the assignee takes the note subject to the law as to negotiable instruments (i. e., free from equities of which he had no notice), this negotiable cl aracter does not extend to the mortgage; and, if he enforces the mortgage, the mortgagor may take advantage of any equitable defense he may have against the mortgagee (20). If the mortgage debt is not in the form of a negotiable instrument, an assignee of it must take it subject to any defense which the mortgagor may have against the mortgagee (§ 36, above).

§ 81. **Effect of tender or payment.** A tender of payment or a payment of the mortgage debt, when the debt falls due, extinguishes the mortgage and terminates the mortgagee's right and title to the mortgaged goods; for

(19) Carpenter v. Longan, 16 Wallace 271.
(20) Olds v. Cummings, 31 Ill. 188.

this amounts to a performance of the condition of the mortgage so that it terminates by its very terms. After default in payment of the debt the mortgagee can refuse a tender of payment, because at law the title on default becomes absolute in the mortgagee. The mortgagor has simply an equity of redemption which he can enforce only in a court of equity. If the mortgagee accepts payment after default, he waives the forfeiture of the goods for default and the title to them passes back to the mortgagor, who can at once sue for their recovery if they are not given to him. When a horse was mortgaged and default made in payment, the mortgagor offered the entire amount due to the mortgagee, who accepted the payment but refused to give up the horse. The mortgagor sued him in trover and recovered, the court holding that the acceptance of the money was a waiver of the forfeiture and title revested in the mortgagor, who therefore could sue for wrongful detention (21).

Two or three states hold a theory of chattel mortgages similar to the "lien theory" as to real mortgages (§§ 3, 39, above), regarding the title as in the mortgagor and the mortgagee as having a lien on the goods to secure his debt. In such states a mere tender of payment after default will extinguish the lien of the mortgage (22).

§ 82. **Mortgagor's right of redemption.** After default in payment of the mortgage debt, courts of equity, in order to prevent the injustice to the mortgagor resulting from forfeiture of his title to the goods when the value of the goods was greater than the amount of the debt due,

(21)   Leighton v. Shapley, 8 New Hampshire 359.
(22)   This view prevails in Michigan and Oregon.

decreed that if the mortgagor would pay into court the full amount due within a reasonable time, he should have the right to recover his property. This right of redemption became an incident of every mortgage, and if the mortgagor makes any agreement or contract with the mortgagee, at the time of the execution of the mortgage, which bars or limits his right to redeem, such agreement is not binding on him and he may redeem just as if it never existed (§§ 4-5, above). In order to redeem his goods, the mortgagor must make a tender of the full amount due to the owner of the debt, before bringing his bill to redeem. His action then must be brought within a reasonable time. What is a reasonable time depends on the circumstances of each case, but ordinarily the statute of limitations in reference to actions to recover personal property is applied by analogy by the courts of equity. Sometimes the time within which redemption must be made is fixed by a special statute. Thus, in Bryd v. McDaniel (23), an Alabama case where some slaves were mortgaged, the court held that, by analogy to the statute of limitations applicable to actions for recovery of personal property, equity would not entertain a bill to redeem after the expiration of six years from the law day of the mortgage.

§ 83. **Foreclosure of equity of** redemption. The proceeding to foreclose a chattel mortgage does not differ essentially from that to foreclose real mortgages, but is seldom resorted to, because chattel mortgages usually contain an express power of sale, the exercise of which is

----

(23)   33 Ala. 18.

quicker, simpler and less expensive than a bill to foreclose. A discussion of foreclosure will be found in §§ 47-
59, above.

§ 84. **Foreclosure of a chattel mortgage under power of
sale.** As stated in the preceding subsection, chattel mortgages usually contain an express power of sale, which
may be exercised by the mortgagee after default. This
power is essentially like the implied power of sale which
a pledgee has, as an incident to his pledge. In most
states, statutes provide that such sales shall be public
after due notice has been given by publication of the time
and place of sale. Such statutes must be strictly followed.
In the absence of statute the only requirement as to a
sale, under a power in a chattel mortgage, is that the sale
be made with good faith and fairness as to the mortgagor (24). The sale may be public or private, and notice
to the mortgagor that such sale is to take place, though
usually required, is not everywhere necessary. The mortgaged goods may be sold in a lump, or in parcels; but, if
sold in parcels, the sale must be ended as soon as enough
is realized to satisfy the mortgagee's claim, for its continuation would amount to an unlawful conversion of the
remaining goods. Thus in the case of Charter v. Stevens
(25) the mortgage contained a power of sale, and under
this power the mortgagee of some horses sold a part of
them for enough to satisfy the entire debt. This sale was
after default in payment. Later the mortgagee sold the
rest of the horses, and the mortgagor sued him for con-

(24) Robinson v. Bliss, 121 Mass. 428.
(25) 3 Denio (N. Y.) 33.

version, claiming the first sale extinguished the mortgage and the remaining horses belonged to him, so that this sale by the mortgagee was therefore wrongful. The court held that, while a tender of the amount due after default would not reinvest the mortgagor with his title to the property, if full payment were accepted, all right of the mortgagee would be extinguished and title would revest. What was done here—the sale under the mortgage of the first horses for enough to satisfy the debt—amounted to full payment of the claim, title to the remaining horses reverted to the mortgagor, and a subsequent sale of them by the mortgagee was clearly a conversion for which he is liable in damages.

MINING LAW

GEORGE PURCELL COSTIGAN, JR.,

A. B., A. M. (Harvard University)
LL. B. (Harvard University)

———

Professor of Law, Northwestern University.

———

CHAPTER I.
INTRODUCTION.

§ 1. **Scope of article.** In this article will be considered only the law of mining peculiarly applicable to the precious metal mining states and territories of the United States, with a brief note on coal, stone, and timber entries. By permission of the West Publishing Company such use has been made as seemed desirable for an article of this kind of the matter contained in Costigan's American Mining Law, to which reference is made for a fuller treatment of the various topics.

§ 2. **Origin of American mining law.** The mining law of the United States had its beginning with the discovery of gold in California and the rush there of the "forty-niners." The thousands of miners and adventurers who sought for gold took advantage of the small and scattered force at the command of the military governor of California and claimed by virtue of discovery and occupation the tracts of United States lands shown to be of value for mining. They insisted upon their right to take the gold from the federal domain free from rentals or fees, and the military governor of California for prudential reasons did not interfere, but contented himself with preventing as far as he could "broils and crimes." As there was no federal mining legislation until the act of 1866, and as the various federal authorities followed the precedent of non-intervention set by the military governor, the miners and adventurers proceeded to hold miner's meetings and to organize mining districts governed by regulations adopted at such meetings. The regulations so adopted covered some matters about which the miners had no business to legislate in such a way, but so far as they related to mining matters they were in general valid and have furnished the model for all subsequent legislation on the subject of mining.

§ 3. **Mining districts and miners' rules.** Mining districts have been well described as "quasi municipal organizations," having a territorial extent to meet the needs and notions of their organizers and having full power to legislate reasonably in regard to the size of claims, their method of location and relocation, the amount, character, and frequency of work on them necessary to keep them valid claims, etc., except so far as that power has been restricted by federal legislation and by state legislation authorized by Congress. Prior to the federal act of 1866 there was no restriction on that power except the fundamental requirement that a mining rule or regulation must be reasonable, but under the federal act of 1872 such rules and regulations must be consistent, not only with congressional legislation, but also with the supplemental state legislation. In § 2324 of the Revised Statutes of the United States it is enacted that "the miners of each mining district may make regulations, not in conflict with the laws of the United States or with the laws of the state or territory in which the district is situated, governing the location, manner of recording, and amount of work necessary to hold possession of a mining claim, subject to the following requirements: The location must be distinctly marked on the ground so that its boundaries can be readily traced. All records of mining claims hereafter made shall contain the name or names of the locators, the date of the location, and such a description of the claim or claims located, by reference to some natural object or permanent monument, as will identify the claim." Then follows the annual labor requirement with the provision for relocation prior to resumption of work and the provision under which one co-owner may forfeit the interest of another co-owner who fails to contribute his share of the annual labor expenditure. All of these matters will engage our attention later, but just here we are interested in the limitations they impose on the power of the miners to legislate.

§ 4. **Importance of district rules.** Because state legislation has greatly narrowed the field for mining district rules, there is a tendency on the part of mining law writers to slight such rules, but when it is remembered that in Utah and Wyoming something, and in Arkansas and Alaska still more, is left to mining district rules, that in California practically everything that the state legislature could require is so left, that under some of the mining codes considerable room still exists for district rules as to placer claims, and that other states may some day follow California by repealing their mining statutes, these district rules are seen to have such an actual and potential value, in addition to their historical significance, that it is only right to give them careful attention.

A mining claim need not be in a mining district to be valid, but if it is in a mining district then it is bound by and should comply with all mining rules and customs of the district that are shown actually to exist, to be acquiesced in, to be reasonable, and not to conflict with state or federal laws. Every owner of an unpatented mining claim should therefore find out whether his claim is in a mining district, and, if it is, then proceed to get acquainted with the rules and customs of the district and to obtain competent legal advice as to the validity of those rules and customs which he desires to disregard.

§ 5. **Effect of violation of district rules.** There is a difference of opinion as to the effect of a non-compliance with a district rule. If the rule is legal and expressly provides that non-compliance with it shall work a forfeiture, no one doubts its effect. The controversy is as to rules which do not contain express clauses of forfeiture. In California and Arizona the courts hold that unless a miner's rule itself provides that forfeiture shall follow non-compliance with it there is no forfeiture (1). In Montana and Nevada, on the other hand, the violation of a mining district rule has been held to work a forfeiture in the absence of an express clause of forfeiture (2). The Supreme Court of the United States has recently refused to go out of its way to pass on the question (3).

§ 6. **State legislation on mining.** From what has already been said, it is apparent that in many states the legislatures have adopted mining codes that have superseded in great measure, if not entirely, the miner's rules and regulations. In fact, all of the mining law states except California have mining codes. So long as state legislation on mining does not conflict with any federal legislation or with any constitutional provision, it will be upheld. The right of Congress to authorize, as it has, supplemental state legislation has been sustained by the Supreme Court of the United States, the final arbiter. In the case of Butte City Water Co. v. Baker (4) that court upheld state legislation which made a mining location invalid unless, among other things, the recorded

---

(1)   Emerson v. McWhirter, 133 Cal. 510; Johnson v. McLaughlin, 1 Ariz. 493, 4 Pac. 130.

(2)   King v. Edwards, 1 Mont. 235; Sisson v. Sommers, 24 Nev. 379.

(3)   Yosemite Gold Mining & Milling Co. v. Emerson, 208 U. S. 25.

(4)   196 U. S. 119, especially p. 126.

location certificate (then called in Montana "the declaratory statement") contained the dimensions and location of the discovery shaft, or its equivalent, and the location and description of each corner with the markings thereon. The court pointed out that in disposing of the public mineral lands Congress acts as the agent of the nation as owner rather than as a legislative body proper. "While the disposition of these lands is provided for by congressional legislation," says the court, "such legislation savors somewhat of mere rules prescribed by an owner of property for its disposal. It is not of a legislative character in the highest sense of the term, and as an owner may delegate to his principal agent the right to employ subordinates, giving to them a limited discretion, so it would seem that Congress might rightfully entrust to the local legislature the determination of minor matters respecting the disposal of these lands."

§ 7. **Federal legislation on mining.** As has already been indicated, the validity of miner's rules and regulations and of state legislation on mining on the public lands of the United States rests on federal legislation approving those rules and authorizing such legislation. The federal legislation consists of the act of July 26, 1866, the act of July 9, 1870, and the act of May 10, 1872, as embodied in the United States Revised Statutes and amended from time to time. The act of 1866 authorized the location of mining claims and provided for the patenting of lode claims. The act of 1870 provided for the patenting of placer claims. The act of 1872 amended in material ways the act of 1866 (not the least important

being that while under the act of 1866 the miner located
a lode, under the act of 1872 he locates a surface with the
lodes apexing in it) (5), embraced the matters covered
by the act of 1870, and added new features. The act of
1872 was in its turn embodied in the Revised Statutes of
the United States and it is to the sections of that revision,
and to the amendments to those sections, rather than to
the original acts that one looks for the federal legislation on mining; for it is settled that when the meaning
of any section of the revised statutes is plain, the section
of the revision controls, although the original statute may
have had a larger or a smaller application than the section in the revision has (6). The acts of 1866, 1870 and
1872 are to be examined only in case of doubt as to the
meaning of the revised statutes.

---

(5)   Gleeson v. Martin White Min. Co., 13 Nev. 442, 457.
(6)   Deffeback v. Hawke, 115 U. S. 392, 402.

CHAPTER II.

DISCOVERY AND LOCATION.

§ 8. **Lodes and placers.** Mining claims are divided into two classes—lode claims and placers. Lode claims are those located "upon veins or lodes of quartz or other rock in place, bearing gold, silver, cinnabar, lead, tin, copper, or other valuable deposits" (1). Placers include "all forms of deposits excepting veins of quartz or other rock in place" (2).

SECTION 1. LODE CLAIMS.

§ 9. **Discovery.** The first essential of every location, whether it be a lode claim or a placer, is a discovery. In lode mining, discovery is the finding of a vein or lode which may be located. A genuine vein or lode must be found. In Waterloo Min. Co. v. Doe (3) the testimony showed that at the time the Oregon No. 3 claim was located there was no discovery of a vein or lode; that it was located in the hope of finding some ore in it at some time; that subsequently under a lease of the ground one Stevens took out about three tons of silver-bearing ore which yielded him $600; and that other mineral-bearing ore existed in the claim. But as the ore taken out did not come from any defined vein or lode, the court held that there was no discovery to support the location.

---

(1) U. S. R. S., § 2320.
(2) Ibid, § 2329.
(3) 56 Fed. 685.

"It is a very curious notion among prospectors in this country that if they sink a shaft, which they call a discovery shaft, to a depth of more than ten feet and put up their stakes, they acquire thereby some sort of an interest in the public domain, although within the limits of their shaft or cut there may be no indications whatsoever of a vein or mineral deposit and work has ceased. Whatever may be the comity in respect to this matter among miners and prospectors, as a matter of law such a location is absolutely worthless for any purpose" (4).

§ 10. Valuable mineral deposits. While a vein or lode must be found, the value of the ore in it is relatively immaterial. The federal statute throws open to exploration and purchase "all valuable mineral deposits in lands belonging to the United States" (5), but the courts have been liberal in their interpretation of those words. Under the decisions, lands are mineral if they contain recognized minerals in such quantities that they are more valuable for mining purposes than for agricultural; and the mining deposits in such lands are deemed valuable within the meaning of the federal statute, if, when taken up first for mining, they have such value that the locator cannot be called irrational in locating and working them, or if, when taken up first for agriculture, they can be mined at a profit (6). As the statement just made shows, the presumption is in favor of the first claimant. If such claimant takes up the land as mineral, then he need show only a value sufficient to justify him as a

(4)   McLaughlin v. Thompson, 2 Colo. App. 135.
(5)   U. S. R. S., § 2319.

reasonable mining man in prospecting the ground. In the case of a lode claim, his discovery must disclose a vein, but its value may be slight so long as under all the circumstances it cannot be said that he is not warranted in going ahead with its development. As Judge Hallett once said in charging a jury: "A lode cannot exist without valuable ore; but if there is value, the form in which it appears is of no importance. Whether it be of iron, or manganese, or carbonate of lead, or something else yielding silver, the result is the same. The law will not distinguish between different kinds and classes of ore, if they have appreciable value in the metal for which the location was made. Nor is it necessary that the ore shall be of economical value for treatment. It is enough if it is something ascertainable, something beyond a mere trace, which can be positively and certainly verified as existing in the ore. In the case of silver ore the value must be recognized by ounces—one or more in the ton of ore; and if it comes to that it is enough, other conditions being satisfied, to establish the existence of the lode" (7). But if the first claimant seeks to hold the land as agricultural, then it can be wrested from him as mineral only if it will pay to work. The good faith of the prior claimant helps him to keep what he has unless it is demonstrably wrong for him to do so.

§ 11. Vein or lode defined. Since in the case of a lode claim the valuable mineral deposit to be discovered must

---

(6) Costigan, American Mining Law, 111.

(7) Stevens v. Gill, 1 Morr. Min. Rep. 576, 579; Fed. Cas. No 13,398.

be in the form of a vein or lode, a word is necessary in regard to what is a vein or lode. It is impossible to give a satisfactory definition of a vein or lode as meant in the federal statute. That statute meant to embody the miners' conception of a vein rather than the geologists', but that conception varies considerably according to the formation and peculiar characteristics of the particular districts in which the given mineral deposit is found. While a vein or lode, within the meaning of the federal statute, is incapable of a hard and fast legal definition, it may be said in general that it is a reasonably continuous body o᷄ mineral-bearing rock in the general mass of the mountain and of greater value than the surrounding country rock. After a very full discussion of the words vein and lode, the supreme court of Utah concludes as follows: "It would seem, from these considerations, that any deposit of mineral matter, or indication of a vein or lode, found in a mineralized zone or belt within defined boundaries, which a person is willing to spend his time and money to follow in expectation of finding ore, is the subject of a valid location, and that, when metallic vein matter appears at the surface, a valid location of a ledge deep in the ground, to which such vein matter leads, may be made" (8).

§ 12. "Unappropriated land of the United States." Not only must a vein or lode be discovered before there can be a valid lode location, but that vein must be discovered in unappropriated land of the United States. A discovery on the dip of a vein, the apex or top of which

---

(8)   Hayes v. Lavagnino, 17 Utah 194, 197.

has already been located, will not support a location of
the dip belonging to such located apex (9). So a location
based on a discovery in a prior located claim is void, until
such time as it is validated by a discovery on unappropriated ground. Whether it will be validated by the mere
abandonment by the senior locator of the ground containing the discovery is a debatable question, but in the
state of the authorities no prudent locator will take any
chances (10). The wise locator will always see that his
discovery is made on unappropriated land, or, if he has
been so unfortunate as to make a location on a discovery
within a senior claim, he will take the first opportunity
afforded by the senior locator's abandonment of his claim
or failure to do the annual labor, to make a complete relocation of the ground. Unless the discovery is made
originally on unappropriated ground or by relocation or
relation becomes one on such ground, the location will be
invalid. In this connection it is important to remember
that noting and claiming a vein or lode, discovered and
disclosed to view by a previous prospector who has aban-
doued or forfeited it, and adopting the discovery as one's
own, is making a discovery (11).

§ 13. **Pedis possessio.** While discovery is essential to
a valid location, it must be borne in mind that, pending a
discovery by anybody, the actual possession of the prior
prospector—his pedis possessio—will be protected to the

<hr>

(9)   Bunker Hill, etc., Co. v. Shoshone Min. Co., 33 Land Dec.
(Dep. Int.) 142.

(10)   See Costigan, American Mining Law, 151-154, 311-313, 388-390.

(11)   Hayes v. Lavagnino, 17 Utah 185.

extent needed to give him working room and to prevent probable breaches of the peace. Just how much ground he may hold in this way pending a discovery by anybody has never been decided, but it would seem clear that it can be only a reasonable amount for the purpose of prospecting. It has been stated that it cannot be deemed the full extent of the claim located (12). And while this pedis possessio of the first prospector is thus protected, it must yield to an actual location on a valid discovery made by one who has located peaceably and neither clandestinely nor through fraudulent purpose. As was pointed out by the court in Thallman v. Thomas: ''A valid claim to unappropriated public land cannot be instituted while it is in the possession of another who has the right to its possession under an earlier lawful location. Nor can such a claim be initiated by forcible or fraudulent entry upon land in possession of one who has no right either to the possession or to the title. But every competent locator has the right to initiate a lawful claim to unappropriated public land by a peaceable adverse entry upon it while it is in the possession of those who have no superior right to acquire the title or to hold the possession. Any other rule would make the wrongful occupation of public land by a trespasser superior in right to a lawful entry of it under the acts of Congress by a competent locator'' (13). While the case of Erhardt v. Boaro (14) has been deemed by some to give greater

(12)   Bonner v. Meikle, 82 Fed. 697, 703.
(13)   Thallman v. Thomas, 111 Fed. 277, 278-9.
(14)   113 U. S. 535.

rights to a prospector who has discovered "float" and with reasonable diligence, but after a subsequent discoverer's discovery, uncovers the vein, it is believed that the case did not go further than to permit a jury to find that the first prospector actually made the prior discovery. Permitting the jury to predicate a discovery by the first and diligent prospector on very slight evidence is a very different thing from giving the first prospector priority where there is no evidence of a discovery by him. In any event, despite conflict and confusion in the cases, it would seem that a pedis possessio, unsupported by a valid discovery, must yield to an actual location, based on a valid discovery, and made peaceably and openly.

§ 14. **Who may discover and locate mining claims?** By § 2319 of the Rev. St. U. S., mineral lands are thrown open to exploration, occupation, and purchase by citizens of the United States and those who have declared their intention to be such. No age requirement is set by the statute, so minors may discover and locate claims as effectually as adults (15). The statute does not require that the discovery and location be made by the locator in person, so one may locate a mining claim by his agent. So mining locations may legally be made by corporations created under the laws of the United States or of a state or territory of the United States (16), though it would seem that a corporation is only one person, and not "an association of persons" so far as the placer mining laws are concerned and therefore can locate and

---

(15)   Thompson v. Spray, 72 Cal. 531.
(16)   McKinley v. Wheeler, 130 U. S. 630.

hold as one placer location only 20 instead of 160 acres of ground (17).

§ 15. Aliens. While the right to locate is given only to citizens and to those declaring their intention to become such, an alien's location is not void. The reason is that no one can object to his location except the government. That objection must be raised in a suit brought by the government direct, or be urged for the government by a party in an adverse suit in patent proceedings, to which the government is regarded as being in a sense a party. Moreover, the objection is ineffective if the alien has transferred the land before the objection is made, or if after it is made he takes out his first naturalization papers (18).

§ 16. Land office employees. Under a special statute land office employes are prohibited from purchasing, or becoming interested in the purchase of, public lands (19). The question of the effect of a location of a claim by a deputy mineral surveyor of the United States has arisen under that statute. It has been held in a Utah case that the location is void and that the deputy mineral surveyor can convey no rights in the claim to another (20). On the other hand, a Nevada case holds that deputy United States mineral surveyors are not covered by the statute at all (21). The land department agrees with the Utah

---

(17) See Costigan, American Mining Law, 172-173.
(18) Manuel v. Wulff, 152 U. S. 557.
(19) U. S. R. S., § 452.
(20) Lavagnino v. Uhlig, 26 Utah 1.
(21) Hand v. Cook (Nev.), 92 Pac. 3.

court that they are covered by the statute (22), and that would seem to be sound; though it would also seem that nobody but the government could possibly object to a location by a deputy mineral surveyor and that, in the absence of further legislation, a rule like that applicable to aliens (§ 15) should be applied.

§ **17. Location of lode claims.** The word "location" is given by mining lawyers and miners two distinct meanings. "The location of a mining claim is the act of appropriating a parcel of public mineral land in accordance with the provisions of the mining law. The term is also applied to the parcel of land so appropriated" (23).

Lode mining claims are appropriated or located by a series of acts required by the state statutes and district rules, where such exist, and by the federal statutes. The first thing for an intending locator to do is to consult the statutes of the state in which he intends to take up a claim and find out if there are any local rules, regulations, and customs with which he must comply. He will find in most states that it is either desirable or necessary to perform the following acts to perfect a lode mining location, namely: 1. Post a discovery notice. 2. Sink a discovery shaft or perform the equivalent work specified by statute. 3. Mark the location on the ground. 4. Post a notice of location. 5. Record a certificate of location in the proper recording office or offices. A word must be said about each of these acts of location.

(22)   Philip v. Contzen, 37 Land Dec. 497.
(23)   Tomera Placer Claim, 33 Land Dec. 560.

§ **18.** **Discovery or prospector's notice.** While in most states a discovery notice is not required by statute, it is desirable to post such a notice. The purpose of a discovery notice is to show that the locator is the first one on the ground and that he abandons no rights. Such a notice would seem to be absolutely essential to the determination of priority of right where one is seeking to locate a vein which outcrops so fully that all who go by may see it with the naked eye, unless, indeed, the prospector is there visibly in possession and completing the acts of location. In Idaho the statute specifies what such a discovery notice should contain, but in most states a simple statement above the locator's signature giving the date of discovery and claiming the statutory time to complete location would suffice.

§ **19.** **Discovery shaft or its** equivalent. In Alaska, in California, and in Utah the discovery work is not prescribed by statute, but in the other mining law states and territories a discovery shaft must be sunk on the claim or equivalent work done to perfect the location. In some states the size of the opening is prescribed by statute and in all discovery shaft statutes the depth of the shaft is fixed at 10 feet at least. In those states in which the size of the opening is not specified, the opening must be of such size that ordinary miners would reasonably regard it as a shaft. The depth of the shaft is estimated from the lowest part of the surface rim. To make the shaft a discovery shaft the vein should be disclose1 by the shaft, though the shaft nee1 not be sunk at the precise point where the prospector first discovers the lode.

Nearly all mining codes permit certain other development work to be substituted for a discovery shaft. The Colorado statute is typical and provides that "any open cut, cross cut, or tunnel which shall cut a lode at a depth of ten feet below the surface shall hold such lode the same as if a discovery shaft were sunk thereon, or an adit of at least ten feet in, along the lode from the point where the lode may be in any manner discovered, shall be equivalent to a discovery shaft" (24). The Colorado decisions have confused all the distinctions between an adit and an open cut, but "no prospector should consider his discovery complete until he has ten feet in depth at the breast of his cut, or a covered adit at least ten feet in along the vein" (25). The Montana statute wisely avoids the words "adit" and "open cut" and makes the equivalent of a discovery shaft any cut or tunnel which discloses the vein at a vertical depth of at least ten feet below the natural surface of the ground and which constitutes at least 150 cubic feet of excavation (26).

The time for sinking a discovery shaft or doing the equivalent work is controlled by statute, or else is a reasonable time. The local statutes should be consulted. As in the case of the other acts of location, any time prior to the attaching of adverse rights will do; but if the work is not done in the time allotted or before relocation, a peaceable location by others will be upheld (27).

---

(24)   Mills Ann. Stats. Colo., § 3154.
(25)   Morrison's Mining Rights (13th ed.) 43.
(26)   Mont. Laws, 1907, p. 20.
(27)   Walsh v. Henry, 38 Colo. 393.

§ 20. **Marking** the location upon the ground. Under § 2324 Rev. Stats. U. S.: "The location must be distinctly marked on the ground so that its boundaries can be readily traced." It is to be noticed that the requirement is not that the boundaries are to be marked, but that the *location* is to be marked upon the ground so that the boundaries can readily be traced. That distinction has become of importance in the case of placer claims in states where the federal statute has not been supplemented by specific state legislation, but, in the case of lode claims where by uniform custom boundaries always are marked, it has been relatively unimportant. In many states the statute prescribes boundary markings, and these must be complied with.

§ 21. **Same: Size of claim.** In marking the location the first thing of importance is to determine its size. By Rev. Stats. U. S., § 2320, a claim may equal, but not exceed 1,500 feet in length, and shall not extend more than 300 feet on each side of the middle of the vein at the surface. In all the states and territories the full 1,500 feet in length is allowed and in most the full 600 feet in width. In Colorado, 300 feet in width is fixed, save for a few counties where only 150 feet in width can be taken (28). In North Dakota 300 feet in width is fixed for all lode locations (29). A claim may be smaller than the size fixed, but not larger (30).

§ 22. **Same: Posts.** When it comes to marking the

---

(28)   Mills Ann. St. Colo., § 3149.

(29)   Rev. Codes, N. D. 1899, § 1427.

(30)   For a discussion of excessive locations, see Costigan, American Mining Law, 196-204.

location, the state statutes as to the number, size and
placing of posts should be strictly complied with. The
state statutes usually require at least six posts—one at
each of the four corners and one in the center of each
side or of each end line. Where there is no state statute,
fewer than four posts have at times sufficed, though no
prudent miner would use less than six. Preferably for a
perfectly rectangular claim the locator should provide
at least eight posts, and for other claims he should provide an additional post for each additional angle.

"These posts should be set, one at each of the four
corners, one at the center of each side, and one at the
center of each end line, and they should be so placed that
the end lines will be parallel. The latter point will be
emphasized when we consider extralateral rights. If
there are angles in the side lines, an extra post should
be placed at each angle. No angles should be allowed
in the end lines, which should be parallel.

"The center posts, as well as the corner ones, should
be numbered. Each stake should be blazed on the side
toward the discovery, and on the blazed part should be
written the number of the stake, the name of the claim,
and the date of location. Though the latter date seems to
be required only in Washington, it is well to comply with
the strictest tests in all cases. If one does more than the
state statute requires, no harm is done; but one must not
do less. If under the local statute still more needs to
be done, as, for instance, to blaze trees, cut away brush,
etc., so as to enable an intelligent searcher for the claim
to find it, that should be done. Then the locator should

measure the distance from his discovery shaft, and ascertain the direction therefrom of the natural objects or permanent monuments selected'' (31).

§ 23. **Same: Monuments.** **Time for marking claim.** The reason why the distance and direction of natural objects and permanent monuments is to be noted is that in the mining law states and territories, the recording of some kind of a location certificate is required, and § 2324 Rev. Stat. U. S., which provides that the records when required shall contain among other things, ''such a description of the claim or claims located by reference to some natural objects or permanent monuments as will identify the claim,'' therefore applies. This requirement is in furtherance of the purpose of requiring the location to be marked on the ground, namely, to give full notice to subsequent prospectors of the situs and extent of the claim. The business of the locator is, of course. to select the most prominent and reasonably near natural objects or permanent monuments possible under the circumstances, so as to facilitate the identification of the claim by subsequent prospectors.

The local statutes usually fix the time for marking the boundaries of the claim. Where no time is fixed, a reasonable time is the proper rule (32), though in California the marking must follow the discovery ''immediately'' (33). In any case the location is marked in time if the

---

(32) See Doe v. Waterloo Min Co. 55 Fed. 11; 70 Fed. 455.

(33) Newhill v. Thurston, 65 Cal. 419.

(34) Crown Point Min. Co. v. Crisman, 39 Ore. 364.

(31) Costigan, American Mining Law, 193.

boundaries are marked before a location by third parties is attempted (34).

§ 24. **Posting notices of location.** While the federal statute does not require the posting of a notice of location on the claim, nearly all the mining law states and territories require it. Some states require more information in such notices than do others, and an intending locator should consult the latest local statute on the matter and use a form of notice which complies with that statute. The fundamental need of a posted notice is to assist subsequent prospectors to find and identify the claim. Whether a given notice answers that purpose satisfactorily is a question of fact, and in determining that question the marked boundaries are important. In those states where a literal or a substantial copy of the posted notice is to be recorded, the posted notice must comply with the federal requirements for record, and must contain, therefore, "the name or names of the locators, the date of location, and such a description of the claim or claims located by reference to some natural object or permanent monument as will identify the claim" (§ 23, above), in addition to anything else prescribed by the state statutes.

In some states the time within which notices must be posted is fixed by statute. Where it is not fixed, the rule in regard to marking boundaries would doubtless be followed, the question being whether a reasonable time should be allowed or whether the posting must take place immediately (§ 23, above). A reasonable time should properly be the same time as that allowed for marking boundaries.

§ 25. Recording. While the federal statute does not require a record, it prescribes, as we have just seen, the minimum contents of a recorded certificate if one is called for by the local rules and statutes. All of the mining states and territories seem to require a record with the mining district recorder or with the county recorder, and some require it with both. The form and contents of the paper to be recorded are prescribed with minuteness in some of the states and an intending locator should acquaint himself with the state statute on the point and use a form which complies with it. Under the federal statute the description of the claim by reference to some natural object or permanent monument is essential.

The time within which record must take place varies in the different states and territories. A failure to record within the proper time will not make the location invalid, if it is otherwise valid, and if adverse rights of third parties do not intervene before record is had. If, however, after a first locator's time for record has expired and no record has taken place, a second locator comes in and peaceably makes a location over the first locator's ground, the second locator is properly entitled to priority (35), though there are cases to the contrary.

§ 26. Same: Amendments of record. A locator may desire to amend his location certificate for various reasons, and he may do this by complying with the local statute, if there is one, or, if there is none, by proceeding

---

(35) Brown v. Oregon King Min. Co., 110 Fed. 728; Copper Globe Min. Co. v. Allman, 23 Utah 410. Contra: Ford v. Campbell (Nev.), 92 Pac. 206; Sturtevant v. Vogel, 167 Fed. 448.

in the same way that he did to record. The amended location certificate should contain a statement that it is an amendment, though that is not strictly necessary. The usual situation calling for an amendment is where the boundaries of the claim are to be changed for any reason, though the amendment may be made to supply some defect in the certificate itself. If the defective record sought to be cured was so defective that third parties were entitled to disregard it and make locations for themselves, and they actually did so before the amendment, the intervening rights of such parties will not be cut out by the amendment; but in other cases the amendment will take effect by relation back to the record of the original certificate and cut out any intervening rights (36).

SECTION 2. PLACER CLAIMS AND LODES WITHIN PLACERS.

§ 27. **Discovery.** In the case of placers, as in the case of lodes, there must be a discovery. Mere indications of mineral will not do in the one case any more than in the other. Contrary to the popular notion, a discovery sufficient to support an oil placer location is not shown by establishing slight drippings of oil and the presence of oil-bearing sand rock. The oil deposit must be disclosed. As the Oklahoma supreme court has said: "It is the common experience of persons of ordinary intelligence that petroleum in valuable quantities is not found on the surface of the ground, nor is it found in paying quantities seeping from the earth. Valuable oil is found by drilling or boring into the interior of the earth, and either

---

(36) Beals v. Cone, 27 Colo. 493.

flows or is pumped to the surface; and until some body or vein has been discovered from which the oil can be brought to the surface, it cannot be considered of sufficient importance to warrant a location under the mineral laws" (37). And the California court also has said: "While perhaps it would be stating it too broadly to say that no case can be imagined where a surface discovery may be made of oil sufficient to fill the requirements of the statute, yet it is certainly true that no such case has ever been presented to our attention, and that in the nature of things such a case will seldom, if ever, occur" (38). But if a discovery actually is made on unappropriated land of the United States, it is not necessary to its validity that it should be shown with reasonable clearness that the placer will pay to work. It is enough that it has a present or prospective commercial value (39).

§ 28. **Pedis possessio.** The same rule as to pedis possessio governs in the case of placers that does in the case of lode claims (§ 13, above), though the placer claimant, because of the greater labor and expense in making a discovery, should be dealt with even more liberally than the lode claimant on the question of when a discovery has been made.

§ 29. **Number of acres for one discovery.** There must be a discovery for each placer claim, but where, under the statute, a location of 160 acres as a placer is made by "an association of persons," it is now held that one

---

(37)   Bay v. Oklahoma, etc., Co., **13** Okl. 425.

(38)   Miller v. Crissman, 140 Cal. 440, 446.

(39)   Madison v. Octave Oil Co. (Cal.), 90 Pac. 176.

discovery is enough for the 160-acre location. The land department still insists, however, that "while a single discovery is sufficient to authorize the location of a placer claim, and may, in the absence of any claim or evidence to the contrary, be treated as sufficiently establishing the mineral character of the entire claim to justify the patenting thereof, such single discovery does not conclusively establish the mineral character of all the land included in the claim, so as to preclude further inquiry in respect thereto" (40).

§ 30. **Location of placers.** The acts of location for placers are generally fixed by the local statutes and are in the main the same as those for lodes (§ 17, above), though only a few states require discovery work on placers.

§ 31. **Discovery notice and discovery work.** What has been said as to discovery notices in the case of lode claims (§ 18, above) applies to placers. The discovery notice required is just like that for lodes except, of course, that instead of the distance along the vein being stated, the number of acres claimed should be given. In a few jurisdictions, discovery work is required to perfect placer claims. The local statutes should be consulted.

§ 32. **Marking the location on the ground.** The federal requirement that a mining location must be marked on the ground so that its boundaries can readily be traced (§ 20, above), applies to placers. It is complicated in the case of placers by the further requirement of the federal statute that placer claims upon surveyed ground

---

(40)   Ferrell v. Hoge (on review), 29 Land Dec. 12, 15.

"shall conform as near as practicable with the United States system of public land surveys and the rectangular subdivisions of such surveys" (41). In consequence where a placer claim is laid out according to the subdivisions of the public surveys, the federal statute about marking the location is seemingly complied with if a notice is posted on the placer, claiming it by the proper survey subdivision description (42). In some states the local statutes require much more than this in the way of marking and those statutes must of course be complied with. So the time for marking under the local statutes and decisions must be observed.

§ 33. **Location notice and record.** The location notice requirements in the case of placers vary in the different jurisdictions, but are much like those in the case of lode claims (§ 24, above). The local statutes must be complied with in the case of both. Recording requirements for placer claims vary in the different jurisdictions, but are much like those governing the case of lode claims (§ 25- § 26, above). Prudence dictates the making of a record, even where the local rules and statutes do not require it. Where a record is required or furnished, the federal provisions as to its contents should be met, in addition to complying with the local statutory requirements.

§ 34. **Location of known lodes within placers.** It often happens that land taken up as placer includes a lode. The possibility of lodes existing in placer ground was

---

(41)   U. S. R. S., § 2331.

(42)   McKinley Creek Min. Co. v. Alaska United Min. Co, 183 U. S. 563; Kern Oil Co. v. Crawford, 143 Cal. 298.

recognized in the act of 1872, and by it provision **was**
made whereby the patentee of the placer ground should
own all veins or lodes not known to exist at the time of
the application for patent, and might acquire at that time
if he saw fit those then known, and whereby other persons
might acquire known lodes which the patentee of the
placer did not make application to patent (43). All veins
known to be in placers are not "known veins" within the
meaning of this statute. To be "known veins" they
must have a certain value. A "known lode" is one
which at the time of the application for placer patent is
known to the applicant for placer patent, or to the community generally, to exist and to carry ore in quality
and quantity to justify its working, or which would have
been so known to the applicant if he had made a reasonable and fair inspection of the premises (44).

Known lodes within placers, not located as lodes by
the placer claimant, may probably be located by third
parties prior to the application for placer patent, and
clearly may be so located after an application for placer
patent in which the known lodes are not claimed by the
applicant for placer patent. But third parties who enter
upon an unpatented placer against the protest of the
placer owner to prospect for lodes cannot make a valid
location of the lodes discovered (45). A known lode in
a placer is located in the same way as any other lode (§ 17,

(43)   U. S. R. S., § 2333.
(44)   Mutchmor v. McCarty, 149 Cal. 603; McConaghy v. Doyle, 32
Colo. 92.
(45)   Clipper Min. Co. v. Eli Min. Co., 194 U. S. 220.

above) except that, if the placer location is valid, third parties cannot claim more of the placer ground than 1,500 feet in length along the vein and 25 feet on each side of the vein.

SECTION 3. MILL SITES, TUNNEL SITES, AND BLIND VEINS CUT BY TUNNELS.

§ 35. Location of mill sites. By Rev. St. U. S. § 2337 non-mineral unappropriated public land of the United States may be acquired as a mill site where either: (1) it is not contiguous to the vein or lode with which the claimant wants to use it (46), or, (2) the claimant has put a quartz mill or reduction works on the site without owning a mine in connection therewith. A mill site acquired in the second way is both technically and actually a mill site; but one acquired in the first way may be devoted to non-milling mining purposes, and so may be called a mill site only because that is the name given to it by the statute. To acquire a mill site in the first way, i. e., for use with a lode to which it is not contiguous, any mining use to which the land is bona fide put will justify the mill site (47), and its retention is dependent on reasonable use of the mill site in good faith for mining purposes in connection with the mining claim. To acquire a mill site in the second way, i. e., apart from lode ownership, nothing short of a mill or reduction works on the ground will serve. The federal statute prescribes no method of location of mill sites and the local rules and

---

(46) Now interpreted by the land department to mean not contiguous to the lode claim. Brick Pomeroy Mill Site, 34 Land Dec. 320.

(47) Silver Peak Mines v. Valcalda, 79 Fed. 886, 86 Fed. 90.

statutes must therefore be consulted. Where there are
none applicable to mill sites as such, the local requirements as to lode locations (§ 17, above) should be met,
except as regards discovery and discovery work.

§ 36. **Location of tunnel sites.** § 2323 Rev. St. U. S.
provides for the acquisition of tunnel sites for the discovery and location of veins not previously known to
exist, but found on the line of the tunnel within 3,000 feet
from its face. The veins so found are known as "blind
veins." While the statute does not prescribe the method
of locating tunnel sites for the discovery of such "blind
veins," the land department has a rule which prescribes
the posting and recording of notices and the marking of
boundary lines, and that rule should be complied with.
The rule provides that the tunnel locators, as soon as their
tunnel actually enters cover, shall "give proper notice of
their tunnel location by erecting a substantial post, board,
or monument at the face or point of commencement
thereof, upon which should be posted a good and sufficient
notice, giving the names of the parties or company claiming the tunnel right, the actual or proposed course or
direction of the tunnel, the height and width thereof, and
the course or distance from such face or point of commencement to some permanent well known objects in the
vicinity, by which to fix and determine the locus in manner heretofore set forth applicable to locations of veins
or lodes; and at the time of posting such notice they shall,
in order that miners or prospectors may be enabled to
determine whether or not they are within the lines of the
tunnel, establish the boundary lines thereof, by stakes **or**

monuments, placed along such lines at proper intervals, to the terminus of the three thousand feet from the face or point of commencement of the tunnel, and the lines so marked will define and govern as to specific boundaries within which prospecting for lodes not previously known to exist is prohibited while work on the tunnel is being prosecuted with reasonable diligence'' (48). The land office also requires that at the time of posting notice and marking lines, as above, ''a full and correct copy of such notice of location defining the tunnel claim must be filed for record with the mining recorder of the district, to which notice must be attached the sworn statement or declaration of the owners, claimants, or projectors of such tunnel, setting forth the facts in the case, stating the amount expended by themselves and their predecessors in interest in prosecuting work thereon, the extent of the work performed, and that it is bona fide their intention to prosecute work on the tunnel so located and described with reasonable diligence for the development of a vein or lode, or for the discovery of mines, or both as the case may be'' (49).

By the ''face'' of the tunnel is meant the first working face when the tunnel enters cover, and by the ''line'' of the tunnel seems to be meant the space bounded by 1,500 feet on each side of the bore of the tunnel, projected 3,000 feet in from the face of the tunnel—a 3,000 feet square space; but because the land department early defined the

---

(48)   Land Office Rules and Regulations on Mining, Rule 17.
(49)   Id., Rule 18.

''line'' of the tunnel to mean its bore (50), a prudent locator of a tunnel site will mark on the surface both the
projected bore of the tunnel and the larger area now
seemingly known as the line of the tunnel.

§ 37. **Nature of tunnel site. Appurtenant dumping
ground.** A tunnel site is not a mining claim and cannot
be patented (51). It is merely a means for the discovery
and location of blind veins, and an inchoate right to the
unlocated blind veins on the line of the tunnel belongs to
the tunnel site owner immediately upon the location of
the tunnel site. By the express provisions of the federal
statute a ''failure to prosecute work on the tunnel for six
months shall be considered as an abandonment of the
right to all undiscovered veins on the line of such
tunnel'' (52).

In the tunnel site location notice, the owner's right to
a reasonable amount of surface ground around the mouth
of the tunnel for dumping purposes is always asserted.
The notice should specify the number of feet claimed as
dumping ground, and the situation of the ground with
reference to the mouth of the tunnel. Wise precaution
would seem to dictate that the dumping ground be located
also as a mill site, as there is no express statutory author-
ization for claiming it otherwise.

§ 38. **Location of blind veins cut by tunnels.** The federal tunnel statute is really an incongruous part of the
act of 1872. It was based on the old notion that the lode

---

(50)   In re David Hunter, 5 Copp's L. O. 130. See also Corning
Tunnel Co. v. Pell, 4 Colo. 511.

(51)   Creede, etc., Co. v. Uinta Tunnel Co,. 196 U. S. 337, 357.

(52)   U. S. R. S., § 2323.

was everything and the surface only a necessary incident, and it clearly contemplated that, as the tunnel owner would not need any surface for his workings since he would mine through his tunnel, only the blind lodes dis-covered in the tunnel should be acquired, and that no rights outside the blind lodes themselves should be ac-quired, except the right of way in the country rock, along the dip or along the rise of the vein, needed to follow and work the vein where it was too small for the owner to stay within it. For many years it was supposed, and the case of Campbell v. Ellett, decided in 1897, fully sustained that supposition, that because the blind veins discovered in the tunnel were the only things intended to be given to the tunnel owner, and only 1,500 feet along the strike of such veins, surface locations need not be made by the tun-nel owner. "Indeed," the United States Supreme Court said in Campbell v. Ellett (53), "the conditions surround-ing a vein or lode discovered in a tunnel are such as to make against the idea or necessity of a surface location. We do not mean to say that there is any impropriety in such a location, the locator marking the point of discovery on the surface at the summit of a line drawn perpendicu-larly from the place of discovery in the tunnel and about that point locating the lines of his claim in accordance with other provisions of the statute. . . . But, with-out determining what would be the rights acquired under a surface location based upon a discovery in a tunnel, it is enough to hold, following the plain language of the

(53) 167 U. S. 116, 119-20.

statute, that the discovery of the vein in the tunnel,
worked according to the provisions of the statute, gives a
right to the possession of the vein to the same length as
if discovered from the surface, and that a location on the
surface is not essential to a continuance of that right. We
do not mean to hold that such right of possession can be
maintained without compliance with the provisions of the
local statutes in reference to the record of the claim, or
without posting in some suitable place, conveniently near
to the place of discovery, a proper notice of the extent of
the claim—in other words, without any practical location.''

§ 39. Same (continued). Campbell v. Ellet was a
clear recognition that a blind lode discovered in a tunnel
was given as such to the tunnel owner, if he appropriated
it and gave sufficient notice thereof, even though he did
not make a surface location. But in Creede, etc. Co. v.
Uinta Tunnel Co. the same judge who wrote the opinion
in Campbell v. Ellett, and without referring to that case,
gave utterance to the following dictum: ''The owner [of
the tunnel] has a right to run it in the hope of finding a
mineral vein. When one is found, he is called upon to
make a location of the ground containing that vein, and
thus create a mining claim, the protection of which may
require adverse proceedings'' (54). This dictum, so at
variance with the purpose of the tunnel act, and so in-
explicably overlooking the previous decision of the court,
cannot be regarded as law, if it means that a surface location must be made. The tunnel owner must locate the

---

(54)   Creede, etc., Co. v. Uinta Tunnel Co., 196 U. S. 337, 357-58.

vein, but not necessarily the ground containing the vein. The tunnel owner, who has discovered a blind vein, may be "called upon to make a location of the ground containing that vein, and thus create a mining claim," without being penalized by the loss of that vein if he does not do so, and the dictum is thus not necessarily in conflict with the earlier case. A surface location is requisite, however, if the locator wishes to patent.

§ 40. **Same: When surface location necessary.** A surface location is, of course, essential if one wishes to acquire title to veins discovered in tunnels not located and run in accordance with the provisions of the federal statute about tunnel sites; the discovery in the tunnel being as effectual as a discovery by shaft from the surface (55). A statutory tunnel owner who wishes to make a surface location should so lay out his surface claim as to have some part of it directly above the point of discovery, and should mark that point on the surface (56).

If a surface location of blind veins is not necessary, the tunnel site owner may claim in his notices and acquire 1,500 feet in length of the blind vein and may take that length on either side of the tunnel, or part on one side and part on the other, so long as a continuous length of vein is taken (57). If a surface location is necessary he

---

(55) Brewster v. Shoemaker, 28 Colo. 176.

(56) Campbell v. Ellet, 167 U. S. 116, 119. A discovery from the surface in addition to the discovery in the tunnel is, of course, not essential to the validity of the surface location, if in fact it includes the vein. Rico-Aspen Min. Co. v. Enterprise Min. Co., 53 Fed. 321; Ellet v. Campbell, 18 Colo. 510.

(57) Enterprise Mining Co. v. Rico-Aspen Min. Co., 167 U. S. 108, 113.

may claim only so much of the blind vein as apexes within the location made. Those veins that the tunnel owner does get he gets as a whole, both going down and going up on the vein, within the end line bounding planes. If a surface location is not necessary, the tunnel owner who seeks to acquire a blind vein cut in his tunnel need do no more than to post at the mouth of the tunnel and to record a notice sufficiently designating the extent and situs of the vein claimed, and to perform the requisite annual labor. If he wants to get a patent, however, he must make a surface location.

CHAPTER III.

PROCEEDINGS AFTER DISCOVERY AND LOCATION.

SECTION 1. ANNUAL LABOR OR IMPROVEMENTS.

§ 41. Statutory provision. By Rev. St. U. S. § 2324 it is provided: "On each claim located after the tenth day of May, 1872, and until a patent has been issued therefor, not less than $100 worth of labor shall be performed or improvements made during each year." This provision is found in the sections primarily applicable to lode claims, but it has been deemed applicable to placer claims, though separate work need not be performed on each 20 acres of a 160 acre placer (1). Annual labor must therefore be performed or annual improvements made on each unpatented placer as well as on each unpatented lode claim.

§ 42. What annual labor is. Annual labor, which is sometimes known as "assessment work" and sometimes as "representation work," is required in order that the unpatented public mineral domain shall not be monopolized by people who would let it lie idle for speculative purposes. Before there was any federal statute the mining district rules required periodical labor on claims. "It was soon discovered," said the Supreme Court of the United States, "that the same person would mark out

---

(1) Carney v. Arizona Co., 65 Cal. 40; McDonald v. Montana Wood Co., 14 Mont. 88.

many claims of discovery and then leave them for an indefinite length of time without further development and
without actual possession, and seek in this manner to exclude others from availing themselves of the abandoned
veins. To remedy this evil a mining regulation was
adopted that some work should be done on each claim in
every year or it would be treated as abandoned'' (2).
Annual labor or improvement expenditure is, therefore,
that expenditure required each year in order to test the
good faith of the locator and to keep prospectors from
monopolizing the public mineral domain. And to make the
requirement effective it is provided that upon a failure
to comply with it "the claim or mine upon which such
failure occurred shall be open to relocation in the same
manner as if no location of the same had ever been made,
provided that the original locators, their heirs, assigns,
or legal representatives, have not resumed work upon
the claim after failure and before such location'' (3).

§ 43. **Time for performing annual labor.** By the act
of Jan. 22, 1880, amending Rev. St. U. S. § 2324, the
annual labor periods begin on the first day of January
succeeding the date of the location of the claim. Since
the passage of that act no annual labor has been required
during the year in which a location is made, so far as the
federal statutes are concerned, and the locator has the
whole of the next year in which to do the annual labor
for that year. The discovery work required to perfect
the location is deemed sufficient labor to require for the

---

(2)   Chambers v. Harrington, 111 U. S. 350, 353.

(3)   U. S. R. S., § 2324.

year the location is made. While in the absence of local legislation to the contrary the locator has the whole of each year to do his $100 worth of work, or to put that amount of improvements on the claim, the fact that he does more work in any one year than is required for that year will not enable him to count it toward the next year's expenditure.

§ 44. **Place of** performance of annual labor. The work done as annual labor may be done: (1) within the boundaries of a single claim; (2) within the boundaries of one or more claims of a group held in common, or, (3) outside the boundaries of the claim or claims. While the federal statute speaks of the annual labor as done on each claim, meaning thereby on each piece of located mineral ground, it expressly provides that "where such claims are held in common, such expenditures may be made upon any one claim" (4), and by a statute passed in 1875 work done on a tunnel run to develop a lode or lodes owned by the person or company running the tunnel shall be considered as expended on said lode or lodes (5). The courts have gone beyond the statute and held that work done outside of a claim, or of a group of claims, and not in a tunnel, will count as annual labor if it is for the benefit of the claim.

Work done within the boundaries of a single location, whether upon the surface or below, if only so done as clearly to be intended to develop the claim, will satisfy the statute, and the court will not question the wisdom or

(4)   U. S. R. S., § 2324.
(5)   18 Stat., 315.

expediency of the method employed (6). With work **and**
with improvements the question is whether what has been
done is for the development of the claim. Where the work
has been done, or the improvement placed, upon the claim
itself, the good faith of the mining claimant entitles him
to every reasonable presumption. But where the work
has been done, or the improvement placed, outside of the
boundaries of the claim, there is no occasion to indulge
any presumption in favor of the mining claim owner and
unless what he has done actually does benefit the claim
by aiding in its development, it cannot count as the required annual expenditure for labor and improvement.

§ 45. **Same: Claims held in common.** It is quite
usual for the work to be done on one claim for a group,
but even in such case the work on the one claim cannot
count as work on any other of the group unless the work
really is of benefit to that other as one of the group (7),
and the work done on the group must aggregate as much
as if done on each claim separately. In a case where the
annual expenditure on one claim of a group of four
amounted only to $132, it was held that the claim upon
which the expenditure was made was safe from forfeiture,
but that the other three claims were subject to relocation (8). While the statute allowing work to be done on
one claim for a group refers to claims "held in common,"
that statute has been given a very liberal interpretation.
For instance, where three locations were made, each in
the name of a different locator, under an oral agreement

---

(6)   Mann v. Budlong, 129 Cal. 5'.

(7)   Little Dorritt Co. v. Arapahoe Co., 30 Colo. 431.

(8)   Fredericks v. Klauser (Ore.), 96 Pac. 679.

that they should be owned in common by all three locators, it was held that the equitable interest which each locator had in the other locations, together with the legal interest which he had in the location which he perfected, caused the locations to be owned in common within the meaning of the federal statute (9). So, too, it has been held that several different locators may combine to work together under this statute their separate locations. The work done, however, must be part of a general plan or scheme for the development of the several claims (10).

The statute says nothing about a necessity that the claims owned in common should be contiguous, i. e., have their boundaries touching, for work on one to count as work on all. While in several cases such contiguity is declared to be essential (11), the California case which holds contiguity not to be necessary would seem to be sound. As the court in that case said: "Mines may be conceived of as so situated that the same work may be, and appear to be, expended in opening or developing both mines, although they are not actually contiguous" (12).

§ 46. **What work will count as annual labor.** In considering where the annual labor may be performed and the presumptions indulged, we have incidentally discovered what work will count as annual labor. When the work is done within the claim's boundaries and is clearly

---

(9) Eberle v. Carmicheal, 8 N. M. 169.

(10) Jackson v. Roby, 109 U. S. 440; Hawgood v. Emery (So. Dak.), 119 N. W. 177.

(11) See Gird v. California Oil Co., 60 Fed. 531; Royston v. Miller, 76 Fed. 50.

(12) Altoona Min. Co. v. Integral Min. Co., 114 Cal. 100, 107.

intended for development work it counts. Even extract-
ing ore without doing development work has been held
to be sufficient (13), though to pick down from a vein
samples of rock and to assay them in an attempt to find
pay ore has been held not to be sufficient (14). A building will be an improvement, so as to count toward the
$100 expenditure, only if it is, and is intended to be, of
benefit to the claim (15). The cost of sharpening tools on
the premises may be a legitimate item of expenditure,
or may not, according to circumstances (16), and so may
the expense of unwatering a mine (17); but the expense
of taking tools, lumber, etc., to a mine, and then taking
them away after slight or no use, will not count (18).
So depositing waste on a claim from an adjoining claim
is not annual labor on the claim used as a dump, nor is
the building of a flume over such claim for the carriage
of such waste, for they clearly do not tend to develop
that claim (19). For the same reason bath houses and
appurtenances at salt springs are not mining improvements, nor is storing water on a placer to be used elsewhere (20). So work done by third parties for themselves and then purchased by the claimant, after suit has
been brought to recover possession from the claimant,

(13)   Wailes v. Davies, 158 Fed. 669.
(14)   Bishop v. Baisley, 28 Ore. 119.
(15)   Bryan v. McCaig, 10 Colo. 309.
(16)   Hirschler v. McKendricks, 16 Mont. 211.
(17)   See Emerson v. McWhirter, 133 Cal. 510.
(18)   Honaker v. Martin, 11 Mont. 91.
(19)   Jackson v. Roby, 109 U. S. 440.
(20)   Lovely Placer Claim, 35 Land Dec. 426; Robert S. Hale, 3
Land Dec. 536.

cannot inure to the benefit of the claim for annual labor purposes, though work performed by the claimant's grantor, of course, will (21); and so will work done by a corporation, the superintendent of which has a contract to purchase the claim, if the superintendent can be considered to hold the contract in trust for the company (22). While the value of powder, fuse, candles, etc., used in development work, the value of rails laid on ties in a tunnel on the claim, and the reasonable value of meals furnished the miners as part of their wages, will count as annual expenditure, it seems that the value of work-horses, tools, bedding, kitchen utensils, and cutlery will not, though the reasonable value of the use of such things may be counted (23). That payment to a watchman will serve as annual labor expenditure where the services of the watchman are reasonably necessary to guard ore and valuable improvements against theft and injury is held in an Arizona case (23a), but it would appear that only in exceptional cases will the employment of a watchman meet the annual labor expenditure requirement (23b).

The requirement of $100 worth of labor or improvements must be met by work or improvements reasonably worth that amount, and local rules or statutes to the

(21)   Little Gunnel Co. v. Kimber, 1 Morr. Min Rep. 536; Tam v. Story, 21 Land Dec. 440.

(22)   Godfrey v. Faust, 18 S. D. 567.

(23)   Fredricks v. Klauser (Ore.), 96 Pac. 679.

(23a)   Kinsley v. New Vulture Min. Co, (Ariz) 90 Pac 438.

(23b)   Hough v. Hunt, 138 Cal. 142. See note 23, above.

effect that so many days' labor shall be regarded as equivalent to $100 worth of labor must be disregarded (24).

§ 47. Same: Work done outside of claim. The kind of work which will count as annual labor when done outside of a claim or a group of claims is usually work in a tunnel run to develop the claim or claims, but other kinds have served. Constructing a flume to carry waste away from the claim, and building a road to the claim when that is necessary to its working (25), will serve as types. With reference to the road, however, it should be noted that the land department will not allow as part of the $500 worth of improvements for patent purposes (§ 57, below), a wagon road, lying partly within and partly without the claims and used for transporting supplies and machinery to and ores from the mines (26).

§ 48. Proof of annual labor. The doing of annual labor may be proved in the same way as other overt acts. Most of the mining law states and territories have enacted statutes providing for the filing for record of an affidavit of annual labor within a given time after the labor is done and making the affidavit prima facie evidence that the work has been performed. In such jurisdictions a failure to prepare and file the affidavit, or a mistake in the affidavit filed does not preclude other evidence of the fact of the performance of the labor (27),

---

(24) Wright v. Killian, 132 Cal. 56; Penn v. Oldhauber, 24 Mont. 287.

(25) Packer v. Heaton, 9 Cal. 568; Doherty v. Morris, 17 Colo. 105.

(26) Douglas Lode Claims, 34 Land Dec. 556; Fargo, etc. Claims, 37 Land Dec. 404.

(27) McCullough v. Murphy, 125 Fed. 147.

but in a few jurisdictions such failure is prima facie evidence that the labor has not been performed. In drawing and filing the affidavit, the statutes of the state where the claim is situated should be consulted and fully complied with.

§ 49. **Annual labor pending patent proceedings.** Considerable confusion of ideas has existed in regard to the effect of patent proceedings on the obligation to perform annual labor. The statute requires the work to be done each year on each claim "until a patent has been issued therefor" (28). After a patent actually issues no work need be done, of course; but will anything short of patent excuse? It seems perfectly clear that after entry in the land office—that is, after the patent proceedings have passed the point where the contract of purchase is complete by the payment of money for the land by the applicant—the applicant need perform no more actual labor if patent ultimately issues to him, or, more accurately, if the entry is not canceled by the land department (29). The reason is that in such case all proceedings in the land department after entry are immaterial, and the receiver's receipt makes the applicant the equitable, and for all practical purposes the actual, patentee. But the "if" above noted causes the trouble. If for any reason the receiver's receipt is canceled by the land department, the applicant finds himself governed by the general rule that until entry the annual labor must be kept up, and may therefore find himself without a claim because some

---

(28)   U. S. R. S., § 2324.
(29)   Benson Mining Co. v. Alta Mining Co., 145 U. S. 428.

third person relocates it on account of failure to keep up the annual labor (30). It seems needless to say that the doing of the $500 worth of work which enables one to apply for patent will not dispense with the necessity of annual labor thereafter.

§ 50. **Forfeiture to co-owner.** The failure of one of several co-owners of an unpatented mining claim to perform his share of the annual labor requisite to hold the claim throws the whole burden of performing that labor on his co-owners. Annual labor only partially performed gives no right, and since, therefore, a performance by one co-owner of his proportionate share of the annual labor will not save his interest, the delinquent co-owner really compels the diligent one to work for both. In the absence of statute, therefore, the delinquent co-owner would have his interest preserved by the diligent co-owner's labor (31). To overcome the injustice of that situation Congress enacted in 1872 the following provision: ''Upon the failure of any one of several co-owners to contribute his proportion of the expenditures required hereby, the co-owners who have performed the labor or made the improvements may, at the expiration of the year, give such delinquent co-owner personal notice in writing or notice by publication in the newspaper published nearest the claim, for at least once a week for ninety days, and if, at the expiration of ninety days after such notice in writing or by publication, such delinquent shall fail or

(30) South End Min. Co. v. Tinney, 22 Nev. 19, 221; Murray v. Polglase, 23 Mont. 401.

(31) Faubel v. McFarland, 144 Cal. 717.

refuse to contribute his proportion of the expenditure required by this section, his interest in the claim shall become the property of his co-owners who have made the required expenditures'' (32).

The foregoing statute relates, of course, only to the $100 of necessary annual labor or annual improvement. If any co-owner fails to contribute, and then his other co-owners expend more than $100, the delinquent co-owner may save his interest from forfeiture by paying his proportionate part of the $100. For anything beyond the $100 the co-owner who has made the expenditures must rely upon other legal rights, if any. The remedy given by the statute is extrajudicial, and is confined, therefore, to the exact situation legislated about. The statute is one of forfeiture, and should be strictly construed (33).

The statute gives the diligent co-owners the right to resort either to personal service or to publication at their option, and there is no saving of the rights of minor heirs (34). Moreover, the diligent co-owners may group in one notice the delinquencies of more than one year. If the delinquent co-owner has died, then, even though the estate has vested in minor heirs, it is not necessary to name them; but a notice addressed to the co-owner by name, ''his heirs, administrators, and to whom it may concern,'' is sufficient, if it contains the proper recitation of facts (34).

---

(32)   U. S. R. S., § 2324.
(33)   See Holbrooke v. Harrington (Cal.), 36 Pac. 365; Turner v. Sawyer, 150 U. S. 578.
(34)   Elder v. Horseshow Min. Co., 194 U. S. 248.

SECTION 2. RELOCATION OF MINING CLAIMS.

§ 51. Relocations by third persons. A relocation of a mining claim or a location covering part of a previous mining claim is effective, when made by third parties, only if the prior claimant has abandoned his claim or if he has failed to perform the condition of annual labor and hence his claim is forfeitable.

The first thing to notice about a relocation is that it does not require a new discovery. Noting and claiming a vein or lode discovered and disclosed to view by a previous prospector, who has abandoned or forfeited it, and adopting the discovery as one's own is making a discovery (35). But while a new discovery is not requisite to a relocation, the statutes make it necessary for the relocator to do the regular discovery work by sinking a new discovery shaft, or by sinking the old one 10 feet deeper (36). Then, too, under the statutes it is necessary to mark the location on the ground, so that its boundaries may readily be traced, and to comply with the state statutes in regard to staking the claim. A relocator, in "jumping" a claim, is required to do practically all that the original locator did except make a new discovery; but, under the state statutes, and by virtue of decisions in California, and Utah, he may adopt the old boundary markings of the first locator, so far as they still exist, and still comply with the state statutory requirements (37). The location stakes should, of course, be replaced,

---

(35)   Hayes v. Lavagnino, 17 Utah 185.

(36)   Carlin v. Freeman, 19 Colo. App. 334.

(37)   Conway v. Hart, 129 Cal. 480; Brockbank v. Albion Min. Co., **29 Utah 367.**

if lost, and the proper notice posted. The fact of the matter is, that while the statutes specifically relating to relocation are not as precise in their requirements as they might be, the relocator must locate and record in substantially the same manner as the original locator had to do, except that he may adopt the stakes and monuments of the original location, and may sink the old discovery shaft 10 feet deeper instead of sinking a new one (38). It seems to be assumed, although the relocation statutes do not always so specify, that the location requirements as to the time of posting notice, the time of staking the location, the size, placing, and marking of stakes and monuments, and the necessity of and time for record apply to relocations. The relocator of an abandoned or forfeited mining claim has the same length of time to perform each of the acts of location subsequent to discovery as an original locator would have (38). But it should always be remembered that in jurisdictions having relocation statutes, those statutes must be followed in all details.

§ 52. **Resumption of work: A**mount of work required. A relocation is often complicated by a claim of resumption of work by the prior locator. The federal statute about annual labor provides that ''upon a failure to comply with these conditions, the claim or mine upon which such failure occurred shall be open to relocation in the same manner as if no location of the same had ever been made, provided that the original locators, their heirs, and assigns, or legal representatives, have not re-

---

(38)   Armstrong v. Lower, 6 Colo. 393; Pelican Mln. Co. v. Snod-grass, 9 Colo. 339.

sumed work upon the claim after failure and before such location'' (39).

What, then, is a resumption of work within this section? Doing the full $100 worth of work in any year will be taken to be resumption in good faith, in the absence of any evidence to the contrary (40). This is the rule as against those who seek to relocate after the work is done; but as against a relocator, who comes in before the year is over and finds that the resumer has not proceeded with reasonable diligence to complete the $100 worth of work, but instead has acted as if resuming and doing some work permitted a postponement of the rest, no presumption of good faith should be indulged. As the Montana court said: ''The resumption of work by the original locator, whose rights are subject to forfeiture, without the expenditure, with reasonable diligence, during the year, of the sum of $100 for labor or improvements upon the mine, is an evasion of the statute'' (41). And that court very properly declared that the California case of Belcher Gold Min. Co. v. Defarrari (42), which decided that the expenditure of $24 on two claims in January was such a resumption of work as would defeat a relocation in August following, is unsound. The California court has since modified its views to the extent of declaring that ''to 'resume work,' within the meaning of said section 2324, is to actually begin work anew, with a bona fide intention of prosecuting it as required by said section''

---

(39)   U. S. R. S., § 2324.
(40)   Temescal Oil Co. v. Salcido, 137 Cal. 211.
(41)   Honaker v. Martin, 11 Mont. 91, 97.
(42)   62 Cal., 100.

(43). There is every reason to believe that it will yet hold that resuming work does not mean regaining a year's time to do the work of the year of resumption by making a slight expenditure, but instead means beginning in good faith and finishing with reasonable diligence $100 worth of work as a condition precedent to the rehabilitation of the claim. The prosecution of the work to a finish with reasonable diligence is an essential element of a bona fide resumption.

§ 53. Same: When resumption must take place. Having determined what a resumption of work is, the next thing to ascertain is when a resumption must take place to defeat a relocation. As between a relocator and one claiming to have resumed work under the statute, a very close question of fact may arise. The supreme court of Montana early decided and later reaffirmed the doctrine that the former owner may cut out a relocator by resuming work at any time before the relocator performs all the necessary acts of location, and California and New Mexico have held the same way (44). The Montana act of 1907 has recently changed the rule in that state. Opposed to the former Montana and to the California view is that of Judge Hallett, who in 1878 announced the doctrine that resumption could come only before another has taken possession of the property with intent to relocate it. "It is," said Judge Hallett, "the entry of the new claimant with intent to relocate the property, and not mere lapse of time, that determines the

---

(43) McCormich v. Baldwin, 104 Cal. 227.

(44) Gonu v. Russell, 3 Mont. 358; Pharis v. Muldoon, 75 Cal. 284; Lacey v. Woodward, 5 N. M. 583.

right of the original claimant'' (45). Wherever a mining code requires discovery work as an act of location, the correct rule to be followed is that adopted by the Montana act of 1907, namely: ''The right of a relocator of any abandoned or forfeited mining claim, hereafter relocated, shall date from the posting of his notice of location thereon, and while he is duly performing the acts required by law to perfect his location, his rights shall not be affected by any re-entry or resumption of work by the former locator or claimant'' (46).

While, as noticed above, a resumption must take place in good faith and be prosecuted to the completion of the work with reasonable diligence, it seems to be true wherever the question has come up that a resumption begun in good faith the last day of the year, when it is too late to complete the $100 required expenditure for that year, and continued in regular working hours the first and subsequent days of the new year till the expenditure be completed for that year, will give the resumer a title superior to that of one who attempts to relocate in the early morning hours of the first day of the new year and prior to any work by the resumer that morning (47). As an original question the correctness of that holding might be doubted, but as it furnishes a fair working rule it probably will be followed.

§ 54. **Premature relocation.** A word is necessary about premature relocations. A relocation is premature: (1)

---

(47)   Fee v. Denham, 121 Fed. 468; Willett v. Baker, 133 Fed. 937.

(45)   Little Gunnel Co. v. Kimber, 1 Morr. M. Rep. 536, 539.

(46)   Mont. Laws, 1907, p. 121.

if it is attempted before the required and perfected location is subject to forfeiture (48), and, (2) if it is attempted after a prior prospector has made discovery and
begun the acts of location, but before the time allowed
him to finish the acts of location has expired. In case (2)
the relocation is premature, even though after it is made
the original prospector does not do the discovery work,
or record, in time (49). Premature relocations remain
ineffective as against the original locator, but if they are
diligently looked after by the relocator should be given
priority over any subsequent relocation. The implication
of the latest decision of the United States Supreme Court
on the question is, however, contrary to any such
priority (50).

§ 55. **Complete relocation by** the forfeiting owner.
Relocations by the original locators or their grantors,
based on the relocators' own defaults, are justified by
the Utah supreme court (51); but where the same ground
is relocated by the forfeiting owners, the discovery work
will amount to less than the annual labor requirement,
and relocation is resorted to in order to escape doing the
annual labor, that doctrine seems unsound. Wherever
new discovery work will not equal or exceed the $100
annual expenditure for labor or improvements required
on each location by the federal statute, the true rule
would seem to be not to allow the delinquent locator to

(48) Belk v. Meagher, 3 Mont. 65; 104 U. S. 279.
(49) Sierra Blanca Co. v. Winchell, 35 Colo. 13.
(50) Farrell v. Lockhart, 210 U. S. 142. Compare Lavagnino v.
Uhlig, 198 U. S. 443.
(51) Warnock v. DeWitt, 11 Utah 324.

take advantage of his own delinquency. A method to redeem his delinquency is pointed out by the statute, namely, by resuming work and diligently prosecuting it until $100 worth of work is completed for the year in which the last part of the work of resumption has to be done. If he does not wish to redeem his delinquency in the way so pointed out by the statute, then since the expression of one thing in a statute is the exclusion of others, and since a penalty put upon a locator to be enforced against him by others cannot properly be regarded as a privilege of his, his claim should remain subject to relocation by others.

§ 56. **Relocation by amendment.** Since the boundaries of the claim may be changed whenever intervening rights of third persons are not injured, and the name of the claim may be varied so long as third persons are not misled, the claim owners may amend the location notices and the record to show such changes. With reference to relocation by amendment, just as with reference to relocation on forfeiture of the previous location, whatever is necessary to the success of the relocation must be done. If the location is moved, then the location notice and markings should be changed to conform thereto, and all posts and monuments, as well as discovery workings, etc., made to comply with the local statutory requirements. As the amendment takes effect by relation, the discovery shaft, if already the required depth, need not be deepened, and in general, so far as the original location conformed to the law and is not necessarily altered by the amendment, no change need be made. The new location certifi-

cate must, of course, be executed with the same particularity in every detail that was required in the original.
Relocations by amendment, of course, in no way avoid
the annual labor requirement.

SECTION 3. APPLICATIONS TO PATENT MINING CLAIMS.

§ 57. **In general.** Any qualified owner of a mining
claim upon which he and his grantors have expended
$500 worth of labor, or have made $500 worth of improvements of a kind that meets the requirements of annual
labor or annual improvements, may apply for a patent
for such claim. The $500 expenditure should be complete
before the application for patent; but a completion before the expiration of the period of publication of the
application for patent will do (52). The land office rule
provides: "The expenditures required may be made
from the surface or in running a tunnel, drifts, or cross
cuts for the development of the claim. Improvements of
any other character, such as buildings, machinery, or
roadways, must be excluded from the estimate unless it
is shown clearly that they are associated with actual
excavations, such as cuts, tunnels, shafts, etc., are essential to the practical development of, and actually facilitate the extraction of mineral from, the claim" (53).

As the applicant will act from the start on the advice
of the deputy mineral surveyor he selects to survey the
claim for patent, and after survey (and preferably from
the start) on that of his attorney, it will be necessary
to indicate only briefly here the steps in the patent pro-

(52)   Nielson v. Champagne Mining Co., 29 Land Dec. 491.
(53)   Land Office Rules and Regulations on Mining, Rule 157.

cess. The black letter headings in Chapters XVIII, XIX and XX, of Costigan's American Mining Law, are taken for that purpose.

§ 58. **Patenting lode claims.** The steps in the patenting of lode claims are: (a) The survey; (b) the filing of the application papers; (c) the filing of the final papers; (d) the issuance of patent.

§ 59. **Survey requirements.** The order of proceeding for survey consists of (1) the selection by the applicant of a deputy mineral surveyor, whose appointment to make the survey the applicant will request; (2) the application to the surveyor general for an order of survey; (3) the order of the surveyor general that a survey be made by the deputy mineral surveyor selected by the applicant; (4) the survey by the deputy, including the preparation by him of the field notes and of a preliminary plat of the property; and (5) the approval of the survey by the surveyor general, including the preparation and delivery to the deputy mineral surveyor for the applicant, or to the applicant himself, of the approved field notes and copies of the final plat.

§ 60. **First set of application papers.** The first set of papers filed by the applicant includes (6), three copies of the notice of application for patent posted on the claim, one copy having attached an affidavit showing that the notice and a copy of the final plat were posted in a conspicuous place on the claim; (7) a copy of the final plat; (8) a copy of the approved field notes; (9) the application for patent; (10) the proof of citizenship by affidavit of the applicant, and, if the applicant is a corporation, by a certified copy of the corporation's charter or certificate of incorporation; (11) the publisher's agreement, which is the contract of the proper newspaper publisher to publish the notice of application for patent and to hold the applicant alone responsible for the charges of publication; (12) a certified copy of each location notice; and (13) the abstract of title of each claim or equivalent evidence of title in the applicant.

The filing of these papers is at once followed by the posting of the notice and plat in the local land office and by the publication of the notice of application for patent. The notice of application for patent must remain posted on the claim and in the land office, and must be published for the full period of 60 days, and within that period adverse claims must be filed.

§ 61. **Adverse claims.** An adverse claim is one of title to part or all of the surface sought to be patented. It must be filed during the 60-day period of publication of the notice of application for patent, must show fully the nature, boundaries, and extent of the adverse claim, and must be followed, within 30 days after it is filed, by the commencement of the proper court proceedings.

§ 62. **Same: Court** proceedings. The court proceeding is, according as the situation calls for one or the other, an action in ejectment or a suit in equity. If it is an action in ejectment, there is a right to a jury trial. If it is a suit in equity, there is in most jurisdictions no such right. The adverse claimant is plaintiff in the proceeding, and the particularity of allegations required in the pleadings varies in the different jurisdictions. The trial is much like the ordinary trial where the ownership of real property is litigated; but the citizenship of the parties is involved, and judgment may be entered that neither party is entitled to the conflict area.

§ 63. Same: Relation of the land department to proceedings. Pending the determination of the court proceedings the land department stays all steps in the application for patent, except the completion of the posting and publication of notices, the posting of plats, and the filing of the necessary proofs of both. If the court proceedings are not begun, a certificate to that effect is obtained, and the patent application proceeds as in the case of no adverse claim. If the court proceedings are begun, and end by giving the whole conflict area to the applicant for patent, he simply files in the land office a certified copy of the judgment roll, and the patent application proceeds as if no adverse had been filed. If, however, part or all of the conflict area is awarded to the adverse claimant, that part is excluded from the application and will be patented to the adverse claimant without the necessity of posting and publication on his part, if he complies with the land department's rules. Where the court's judgment is that neither party is entitled, the filing of the certified copy of the judgment roll ends the application.

§ 64. Protests. A protest, unlike an adverse claim, is an objection made, not to acquire title for the objector, but to prevent the applicant for patent from getting title because of some fatal defect, and a protest will not lie where an adverse claim was proper. A protestant is in the nature of an amicus curiæ (friend or adviser of the court). The protest should set forth all material issuable facts with sufficient particularity to inform the applicant of the case against him.

§ 65. **Final set** of application papers. The second and final set of papers filed by the applicant for patent in an uncontested application includes: (14) Proof by affidavit that the plat and notice of application remained conspicuously posted during the publication period; (15) proof by the publisher's affidavit that the notice was duly published; (16) proof by affidavit of the items of the application expenses; and (17) the application to purchase the land, accompanied by the purchase money.

§ 66. **Entry and patent.** Upon the filing of the final application papers the register and receiver of the local land office at once forward a copy of (17), above, to the chiefs of field division of special agents, and the register makes (18) his certificate that the notice of application and the plat remained posted in the land office during the publication period. Upon a favorable report from the chiefs of field division, the register makes (19) his certificate of entry. The receiver of the local land office thereupon issues (20) his duplicate receiver's receipts.

The complete record is then forwarded to the commissioner of the general land office, and, if everything is regular, (21) a patent issues in due course.

§ 67. **Patenting mill sites.** Mill sites patented with lodes are included in the same survey and in the various lode application papers. The mill site must be carefully described in the papers, and a copy of the notice and one of the plats must be posted on the mill site, as well as upon the lode claim. Proof by affidavit must be furnished of the non-mineral character of the ground. Mill sites patented separately from lode claims are patented in exactly the same way as lode claims, except that proof by affidavit must be furnished of the non-mineral character of the ground and of the mill site use to which the ground is being put.

§ 68. **Patenting placer claims.** With the exception that no survey need be made for placers conforming to government survey subdivisions, and that a special kind of descriptive report by the deputy mineral surveyor is called for by the land department, the proceedings to obtain a patent for a placer claim are the same as those for a lode claim (§§ 58-66, above).

§ 69. **Known lodes within placers.** Known lodes in placers must be located as such by the applicant for placer patent if he intends to claim them in his placer application. Known lodes not claimed by the applicant for placer patent may be patented by third parties after a departmental inquiry establishes that they are known lodes.

§ 70. **Nature of a patent.** A patent is both a judgment in rem of the quasi-judicial land department and a conveyance of title by the United States to the patentee. If within the jurisdiction of the land department to issue and valid on its face, a patent is not subject to collateral attack. It is in the conclusiveness of title to the land conveyed that a patent excels a location.

CHAPTER IV.

EXTRALATERAL RIGHTS UNDER ACT OF 1872.

§ 71. Statutory provision. To explain extralateral rights properly would require more space than is allowed to this whole article, and as the topic is one primarily for the mining expert and the mining lawyer, it seems best to attempt here nothing but the bare general statement of what the extralateral right doctrine is under the act of 1872.

The extralateral right section of the act of 1872 is as follows: "The locators of all mining locations . . . shall have the exclusive right of possession and enjoyment of all the surface included within the lines of their locations, and of all veins, lodes, and ledges throughout their entire depth, the top or apex of which lies inside of such surface lines extended downward vertically, although such veins, lodes, or ledges, may so far depart from a perpendicular in their course downward as to extend outside the vertical side lines of such surface locations. But their right of possession to such outside parts of such veins or ledges shall be confined to such portions thereof as lie between vertical planes drawn downward as above described, through the end lines of their locations, so continued in their own direction that such planes will intersect such exterior parts of such veins or ledges. And nothing in this section shall authorize the locator or possessor of a vein or lode which extends in its downward

359

course beyond the vertical lines of his claim to enter upon the surface of a claim owned or possessed by another'' (54).

§ 72. Resulting doctrine. In the act of 1872 there is a requirement that the end lines of mining locations shall be parallel, though that provision is not found in the extra-lateral right section (55). But since there is no requirement that the side lines shall be parallel, and since the statute contemplates a location along the strike of the vein, it has been decided that the requirement of parallel end lines is for the purpose of bounding the underground extralateral rights which the owner of the location may exercise (56). The result is that, with the possible exception of cases where the end lines converge on the dip, parallelism of end lines is essential to the right of the locator or patentee to follow his vein outside of the common-law limits of his claim. The claim itself is valid if the end lines are not parallel; but in such case it has not the extralateral right feature (57).

Under these sections of the federal statute, the extralateral right doctrine is the doctrine that a lode claimant, who owns the apex of a vein which departs from the side lines of his claim in its descent into the earth, may pursue the vein into the laterally adjoining land within planes

---

(54)   U. S. R. S., § 2322

(55)   U. S. R. S., § 2320, § 2322.

(56)   Del Monte Mining Co. v. Last Chance Mining Co., 171 U. S. 55. To give extralateral rights, the end lines, in addition to being parallel, "must be straight lines, not broken or curved ones." Walrath v. Champion Min. Co., 171 U. S. 293, 311.

(57)   Iron Silver Min. Co. v. Elgin Mining Co., 118 U. S. 196; Montana Co. v. Clark, 42 Fed. 626.

drawn through the parallel end lines of the claim and extended in their own direction. For the detailed application of that doctrine, reference should be made to any of the standard treatises on mining law.

NOTE.

COAL, TIMBER AND STONE LAND ENTRIES AND PATENTS.

§ 73. **Departmental regulations.** A word should be said about coal land and timber and stone land entries. Very full regulations in regard to both are printed and distributed in separate pamphlets which may be had by anyone who will write to the General Land Office in Washington, D. C., and as they are subject to frequent changes it will not be desirable to give details here. For instance, by the circular of Nov. 30, 1908, very material changes were made in the method of obtaining timber and stone lands from the government.

§ 74. **Coal land entries.** Coal lands are entered by legal subdivisions by qualified individuals and associations. Any individual who is a citizen of the United States, or has declared himself to be such, and who is 21 years of age, may enter by legal subdivisions not to exceed 160 acres. Any association, which includes a corporation, composed of individuals qualified to make entry as individuals, may enter not to exceed 320 acres by private entry, and if the association consists of not less than four qualified persons, who shall have expended not less than $5,000 in working and improving a coal mine or mines, it may enter not to exceed 640 acres, including such mining improvements. The right to purchase coal lands can be exercised but once, whether the person exercising it did so alone or as a member of an association, and no entry can be allowed to an association which has in it a single person disqualified. The coal land laws recognize two kinds of entry: (a) Ordinary cash entry; and (b) cash entry under a preference right.

§ 75. **Ordinary cash entry.** Ordinary cash entry is without previous occupation or improvement of the land, and the steps in it are: (1) the filing of a sworn application; (2) the posting and publication of a notice of application; (3) the proofs of the completed posting and publication; (4) the determination in the land office of adverse claims and protests; (5) the report by the chiefs of field division of special agents of the land department; (6) the register's certificate for entry and the receiver's receipt; and (7) the patent.

§ 76. Cash entry under a preference right. The actual possession of coal lands and the bona fide opening thereon of a coal mine give a preference right in the lands, which must be exercised, if at all, within 60 days. The proceedings otherwise are substantially like those in the case of ordinary cash entry, except that entry claimed under a preference right cannot take place until a year after the expiration of the 60 day period allowed for filing the sworn application.

§ 77. Timber and stone land entries. Under the timber and stone act of June 3, 1878, as amended August 4, 1892, a somewhat different plan is now followed in the case of lands valuable chiefly for timber or stone and unfit for cultivation at the time of sale. Only 160 acres can be acquired by any one person, association, or corporation, but any qualified person may obtain title under the law if the following steps are satisfactorily taken, namely: (1) the examination of the land by the applicant not more than 30 days before the date of his application so that he may knowingly swear to the character and condition of the land; (2) the presentation of an application and sworn statement in a form prescribed by the regulations and accompanied by a filing fee of $10.00; (3) a report on the application by the chief of field division of special agents of the land department; (4) an appraisement, and, if required and the proper deposit of the cost thereof is made, a reappraisement of the land by an officer or employee of the government; (5) a deposit of the appraised price of the land with the receiver; (6) the posting and publication, for 60 days prior to the date of offering final proof, of a notice of the application and of the date of making proof; (7) the making of the final proof at the time and place mentioned in the notice; (8) the determination of contests and protests; and (9) final entry and patent.

IRRIGATION LAW

BY

ROSCOE POUND,

A. B., A. M., Ph. D. (University of Nebraska)
LL. M. (Northwestern University)

———

Story Professor of Law, Harvard University.

———

CHAPTER I.

SYSTEMS OF WATER LAW.

§ 1.   **Definitions.**   For legal purposes, water, whether above or below the surface, falls into two classes: (1) water in some definite body, including running water, whether in watercourses on the surface or subterranean, and standing water in definite bodies such as lakes or ponds; (2) diffused water or water not in any definite body or form, including surface water, that is, rain water, and water in swamps and marshes, and percolating water,

that is, diffused underground water. Systems of water
law have to do with the first class only. Accordingly the
law of irrigation comprises those legal rules and principles which govern the application of the water of natural
streams and watercourses to lands for the purpose of
raising agricultural crops and other products of the soil.

For a long time irrigation law only was important. Appropriations were made for domestic, agricultural or mining purposes, but those of chief importance to which,
therefore, legislation was chiefly directed were appropriations for irrigation. The present tendency is to think
of water law or the law of water rights rather than of the
law of irrigation and to provide for appropriation of
water for any and all beneficial purposes. In Kansas and
South Dakota, there is a special body of statute law dealing with irrigation from artesian wells and the use of
underground waters for that purpose. California, Kansas, Nebraska and New Mexico have statutes to prevent
waste from artesian wells. There are also statutes in
some states dealing with storage of surface water for
irrigating purposes. But the law of irrigation, in the
sense in which it has become a well-settled body of case-
law in the arid and semi-arid states and territories, has
to do only with the use of the water of natural streams
and watercourses.

SECTION 1. COMMON LAW DOCTRINE.

§ 2. Where in force. The common law with respect
to waters and riparian rights is in force in the great majority of the United States. It governs wholly or in part
in every jurisdiction except Arizona, Colorado, Idaho,

Nevada, New Mexico, Utah, and Wyoming. In a number
of states, however, as will be explained presently, it is
superseded over a considerable part of the state, or as to
the public domain, or may be superseded anywhere by
condemnation of pre-existing rights acquired thereunder.

§ 3. **Amount of use determined** by its character. The
fundamental principle of the common law with respect to
water is that running water, the water of natural streams
and watercourses, is not susceptible of ownership. It
may not be owned. It may only be used. The common
law determines who may use it and how he may use it.
Allowing no one to own the water and hence to claim an
exclusive right to appropriate, divert, or dispose of it,
the common law permits a reasonable use of the water
by all riparian owners, that is, by all owners along or
over whose lands the stream or watercourse flows. But
a distinction is made with respect to the character of the
use to which the water is put by the riparian owner. If
he uses the water for domestic purposes (see § 34, below),
there is no limit to the amount he may take. If he uses
it for purposes other than domestic, the use to which he
may put it is limited by the right of every other riparian
owner to make a like use and he is allowed only a reasonable use of the water.. Confusion has arisen in this connection from the unfortunate employment of the words
"natural" and "ordinary" to mark those uses which the
common law does not attempt to limit, and "artificial"
or "extraordinary" to mark those with respect to which
a limitation is imposed. It has been said that domestic
use is a use to satisfy a "natural" or an "ordinary"

want, while use in irrigation, in mining, for power, or to carry off waste is use to meet an "artificial" or "extraordinary" want. Misled by these words, men have indulged in no little argument in the semi-arid states to the effect that irrigation supplies a "natural" want and that use of water for that purpose is natural and ordinary in semi-arid regions, and the legislature has sometimes enacted that use for irrigation shall be so regarded. But this argument misses the real point of the common law doctrine. As one court has said: "The law does not regard the needs and desires of the person taking the water solely, to the exclusion of all other riparian proprietors, but looks rather to the natural effect of his use of the water upon the stream and the equal rights of others therein. The true distinction seems to lie between those modes of use which ordinarily involve the taking of small quantities and but little interference with the stream, such as drinking and other household purposes, and those which necessarily involve the taking or diversion of large quantities and a considerable interference with its ordinary course and flow, such as manufacturing purposes" (1). Manifestly irrigation is to be put in the latter category, and it is now conceded that, where the common law prevails, use of water for irrigation is not only confined to riparian owners, but is subject to the limitation that the use must be reasonable under the facts of the case in hand.

§ 4. **What is a reasonable use?** By "reasonable" use, the common law means a use consistent with a like right

----

(1) Meng v. Coffee, 67 Neb. 500, 513.

of use in all other riparian proprietors. The leading case upon this point is Embrey v. Owen (2). The plaintiff occupied a grist mill on the banks of a river. The defendant owned land on the river above the mill and was diverting part of the water to irrigate certain meadows. The working of the plaintiff's mill was in no way impeded by the amount of water diverted, there was no sensible diminution of the stream by reason of the diversion, and the loss of water was ascertainable only "by inference from scientific experiments on the absorption and evaporation of water poured out on the soil." The court held that the plaintiff had no case, since the use by the defendant was consistent with a like use by other riparian owners and hence reasonable. Baron Parke said (p. 368): "This right to the benefit and advantage of the water flowing past his land is not an absolute and exclusive right to the flow of all the water in its natural state. . . . but it is a right only to the flow of the water, and the enjoyment of it, subject to the similar rights of all the proprietors of the banks on each side to the reasonable enjoyment of the same gift of Providence." This case was recognized as having settled the law in the leading American case of Elliot v. Fitchburg R. Co. (3), and has been followed in the American cases on the common law of irrigation.

Obviously no fixed rules may be laid down with respect to what is a reasonable use. The common law, as courts have often said, "seeks to secure equality in the use of

(2)   6 Ex., 353.
(3)   10 Cush. (Mass.), 191.

the water among all those who are so situated that they may use it.'' But certain uses are so clearly unreasonable that the courts have settled that they will not be permitted. These are: (1) diversion to and use on non-riparian lands; (2) consumption of all the water; (3) waste of water; (4) needless diminution of the amount of water; and (5) failure to return the unused water to the stream, to the injury of other owners or so as to prevent reasonable use of the stream by them also. Subject to these propositions, the uses which a riparian owner may make of a stream for purposes of irrigation ''must be judged, in determining whether they are reasonable, with reference to the size, situation, and character of the stream, the uses to which its waters may be put by other riparian owners, the season of the year and the nature of the region. These circumstances differ in different cases, and what use is reasonable must be largely a question of fact in each case'' (4).

§ 5. **What are riparian lands?** The requirement that the use be upon riparian lands does not mean that use upon the whole tract owned by a riparian owner is necessarily permitted. If the tract is non-riparian, the use is obviously unreasonable. But the lands of a riparian owner may extend back a long way from the stream, and much ingenuity has been expended in the attempt to fix some absolute tests by which it may be determined to what extent he may claim a right of use upon his lands in such cases. Thus it has been said that lands beyond

---

(4)   Meng v. Coffee, 67 Neb. 500, 504, 515 (citing cases); Lux v. Haggin, 69 Cal. 255.

the divide or watershed, although part of the same tract with riparian lands, are not riparian; that contiguous land subsequently acquired by a riparian owner, which itself lies away from the stream, is not riparian; and that "the extent of riparian land cannot in any event exceed the area acquired by a single entry or purchase from the government." And it has even been suggested that riparian land "may not exceed the smallest legal subdivision of a section, that is, forty acres, or, in lieu thereof, if an irregular tract, a designated numbered lot, which is bordered by a natural stream or over which it flows" (5). Such attempts are futile and unnecessary. The requirement that the water be used on riparian lands is not a primary rule, but a corollary of the prime requirement that the use be reasonable. Hence it is not the number of acres in the tract nor the manner in which the tract was acquired, but the amount of water in the stream and the uses to which it may be put by others that should be looked to. If there is abundance of water and those who can possibly use it are few, use over large tracts may be in no way inconsistent with equality of use by others. If, on the other hand, there is little water and there are many to use it, use on all of the tract first acquired, or on the whole of the smallest government subdivision might prevent a like use by others.

SECTION 2. ROMAN AND CIVIL LAW DOCTRINES.

§ 6. Roman and civil irrigation law. The Roman law held that running water, along with light, air and the

---

(5) Crawford Company v. Hathaway, 67 Neb. 325. See Lux v. Haggin, 69 Cal. 425; Bathgate v. Irvine, 126 Cal. 135; Watkins Land Co. v. Clements, 98 Tex. 578. Contra: Jones v. Conn, 39 Ore. 30.

sea, was *res communis*, that is, that property in it was in
no one and the right to use it in every one. This proposition in one way or another has entered into all systems
of water law. Its real meaning is that streams and bodies
of water as natural resources are assets of society so that
the water in them is not and cannot be owned by individuals. There is a social interest, however, in the use as
well as in the conservation of such natural media. Consequently part of the water may be taken out and for the
time being, as it were, reduced to the possession of the
individual and while he is using it and to the extent of
his use he may have a property interest in such use. Accordingly every system of water law, starting with the
premise that running water may be used and not owned,
seeks to determine, first, who may use it, and, second,
how he may use it.

In Roman law a distinction seems to have been made
between public streams, those which flowed continually,
and private streams, those which were dry at certain
periods (6). According to the civil law, public streams are
natural watercourses, navigable by boats or rafts; all
others are private streams (6). Public streams are the
property of the state and the use of them belongs to the
state, which grants rights of using the water to individuals by way of concession (franchise), charging a toll
therefor (6). In the Roman law the owner of a private
stream had the same power with respect thereto that he
had over any other property (7). According to the civil

---

(6) Digest XLIII, 3, 1, § 3; Dernburg, Pandekten, J, § 73; French
Civil Code, § 538.

(7) Digest XLIII, 12, 1, § 4.

law (i. e., the modern law of continental Europe) a certain community of use in private streams is preserved; the upper owner cannot permanently withdraw the water that would naturally come down to the lower owner; he must restore the water to the bed of the stream after using it (8). Indeed this followed from the proposition of the Roman law that running water was *res communis*. It is important to remember that the civilians did not think of running water as owned by the state or by the public. They held that it was owned by no one, that it belonged to no one person any more than any other person, and that it could not be owned while in its natural condition. In considering the language of some of the statutes and decisions in our western states in recent years this is significant.

§ 7. **Not adapted to arid regions.** It is manifest that neither the common law nor the civil law systems were adapted to the necessities of the arid states and territories, nor even to all parts of the semi-arid jurisdictions. The difficulty with the common law rules was that where there was no more than water enough for one to use with advantage, the requirement of equality of use prevented anyone from using. The difficulty with the civil law rule was that at the time when the law upon this subject was evolving there was usually no organized government at hand on the public domain to license use of streams,

---

(8) Dernburg, Pandekten, I, § 73; French Civil Code, § 644. In Scotland, this doctrine seems to have been applied to all streams, so that the rules are about the same as those of the common law. Bell, Principles of the Law of Scotland, §§ 1100-1108. The Roman-Dutch Law on the subject may be found in Breda v. Silberbauer, L. R. 3 P. C. 94; the Spanish and Mexican law in Lux v. Haggin, 69 Cal. 255, 315-34.

there had been no survey of the water resources of the country, and the idea of such license or concession was foreign to the individualistic ideas of the pioneer. Hence a third system was evolved from the necessities of the situation by the pioneers of the Pacific slope, which has become the foundation of the American law of irrigation. This is based on what is known as the appropriation doctrine. Today after development along common law lines or along the lines of the appropriation doctrine has become substantially complete a collectivist tendency is moving many to urge the civil law idea or even to urge a new idea of ownership of running water by the state. Except so far as the latter means simply that the state as the guardian of social interests is to exercise a regulating power with respect to the use of a natural asset of society, to put these newer tendencies into action would require confiscation or else condemnation.

SECTION 3. APPROPRIATION DOCTRINE.

§ 8. **Origin in mining custom.** Whereas the fundamental notion of the common law is equality in use among riparian owners, the fundamental idea of the appropriation system is that priority of application to a beneficial use gives a right to use the water so appropriated, so long as the use is kept up, even though it be all the water of the stream, whether applied on riparian or non-riparian tracts, to the exclusion of those whose claims are subsequent in time. At one time there was a tendency in the common law toward such a doctrine. Thus in Williams v. Morland (9), Bayley, J., said: ''Flowing water is

(9) 2 B. & C. (Eng.), 910.

originally *publici juris.* So soon as it is appropriated by an individual, his right is co-extensive with the beneficial use to which he appropriates it. Subject to that right, all the rest of the water remains *publici juris.*" But the common law, as has been seen, eventually took another course. The idea of acquisition of a right by priority of appropriation to a beneficial use arose on the public domain at the time of the discovery of gold in California. Government and law had not been established, there was no agricultural population, there were no riparian owners, and streams could be put to no use except for mining. "From the necessities of the case, there being no law applicable, the miners held meetings in each district or locality and adopted regulations by which they agreed to be governed. As at that time streams could be put to no use except for mining, and as the use of large quantities of water was essential to mining operations, it became settled as one of the mining customs or regulations that the right to a definite quantity of water and to divert it from streams or lakes, could be acquired by prior appropriation. This custom acquired strength; rights were gained under it and investments made, and it was soon approved by the courts and by local legislation; and, though not originally available against the general government or its patentees, was made so available by act of Congress in 1866" (10).

§ 9. **Application to irrigation.** From mining this doctrine spread to irrigation. In California, where it originated, it was applied to the public domain only. Colo-

---

(10) See Atchison v. Peterson, 20 Wall. (U. S.), 507, 510.

rado applied it to private lands as well, and that state
has taken the lead in the development of the law upon
this subject. The common law doctrine and the appropriation doctrine are well contrasted by the supreme court
of Colorado in Oppenlander v. Left Hand Ditch Co. (11),
thus: "At common law the water of a natural stream
is an incident of the soil through which it flows; under
the constitution [of Colorado—i. e., the appropriation doc-
trine] the unappropriated water of every natural stream
is the property of the public. At common law their riparian owner is, for certain purposes, entitled to the exclusive use of the water as it flows through his land; under
the constitution the use of the water is dedicated to the
people of the state subject to appropriation. The riparian owner's right to the use of water does not depend
upon user and is not forfeited by non-user; the appropriator has no superior right or privilege in respect to
the use of water on the ground that he is a riparian
owner; his right of use depends solely upon appropriation and user; and he may forfeit such right by abandonment or by non-user for such length of time as that abandonment may be implied. A riparian proprietor owning
both sides of a running stream may divert the water
therefrom, provided he returns the same to the natural
stream before it leaves his own land, so that it may reach
the riparian proprietor below without material diminution in quantity, quality or force; the appropriator,
though he may not own the land on either bank of a running stream, may divert the water therefrom, and carry

(11)　18 Col. 142, 147.

the same withersoever necessity may require for beneficial use, without returning it or any of it to the natural
stream in any manner.''

The four distinctions between the common law and the
appropriation doctrine thus pointed out require some
comment. With respect to the first, it is not a sound
statement of the common law doctrine to say that the
water is an incident of the soil. It is the right to make
a reasonable use of the water which the common law
regards as appurtenant to riparian lands. The statement
that the unappropriated water of streams is the property
of the public is a bit of rhetoric of which western legislators and courts have been very fond. The truth is that
under the appropriation doctrine, as under any system
of water law, rights with respect to water are rights of
use only. Water in running streams is not owned by the
state in the sense in which public buildings or public
lands are owned. Possibly some legislators have intended to enact that the state should own the water as
it owns public buildings and that water rights should be
concessions or licenses from the state. But as to the
water on the public domain of the United States obviously
this could not be true and in localities where private water
rights under the common law or appropriation doctrine
had long been established such a legislative transfer of
property from the individual to the state without condemnation and compensation is inadmissible. Hence the
courts today are generally saying that running water
belongs to the state in trust for the people or in trust
for the public, meaning thereby simply that the state as
guardian of social interests and as an incident of its

sovereignty claims the right to regulate the use of this social asset. The third and fourth distinctions made in the opinion last quoted deserve careful attention since these are fundamental points of difference.

§ 10. **Where and to what extent in force.** The jurisdictions in which the appropriation system obtains may be divided into three classes: (1) those in which the system obtains exclusively over the entire domain; (2) those in which it is in force on the public domain, while the common law is in force on private lands, but appropriations made on the public domain are valid against subsequently acquired riparian rights; and (3) those in which the common law was originally in force but statutes have introduced the appropriation system for all or a part of the state, and it may be put in force by condemnation or acquisition of any previously acquired riparian rights. The water law in the first class is known as the Colorado system; that in the second class as the California system. To the first class belong Arizona, Colorado, Idaho, Nevada, New Mexico, Utah, and Wyoming. These are called the arid jurisdictions. The common law was not applicable to the conditions of these jurisdictions, hence, according to a settled principle, was not received therein as law, and in substance has been rejected from the beginning (12). Hence there never were any riparian rights in these jurisdictions. The jurisdictions in the second and third classes are called the semiarid states. In these jurisdictions the common law is

---

(12) The common law was held to be in force at first in Nevada in Van Sickle v. Haines, 7 Nev. 249. Afterwards this was overruled. Bliss v. Grayson, 24 Nev. 422.

entirely applicable to considerable portions of the state, and, as these were usually the parts first settled, was received and rights were acquired thereunder before the appropriation system was introduced or given sanction by legislation. The second class includes California, Montana, Oregon, and Washington. But a recent decision in Oregon holds that the federal Desert Land Act of 1877 abrogated riparian rights for the future as to all public land, so that patentees from the federal government get no riparian rights after 1877 except as to waters they are using and as to a so-called natural right to use the flow of the stream for domestic purposes. This construction of the federal statute is very doubtful (13). Moreover, recent statutes in California and in Washington have the effect of putting those jurisdictions in the third class.

§ 11. **Common law rule** changed by statute. The third class includes Kansas, Nebraska, North Dakota, Oklahoma, South Dakota, and Texas. In Kansas the appropriation system was introduced for the portion of the state west of the ninety-ninth meridian by statute from 1885 to 1891. In Nebraska, after the common law had been in force since 1855, the appropriation system was introduced potentially for the whole state by a series of statutes from 1889 to 1895. In North Dakota, the common law having been in force in the territory of Dakota at the time of the adoption of the state constitution, the state constitution provided that "all flowing streams and natural watercourses shall forever remain the property of the state for mining, irrigating, and agricultural purposes," and legislation has provided a system of appro-

_____
(13) Hough v. Porter, 51 Ore. 318.

priation. In Oklahoma, an act was passed in 1897, superseded by a new one in 1907. South Dakota has a brief statutory provision for appropriation of water. In Texas the appropriation doctrine was introduced for "the arid portion of the state" by legislation in 1895.

§ 12. **Same: Constitutional difficulties.** Serious questions have arisen upon this legislation in states of the third group. It is manifest that riparian rights existing prior to the new constitutional and statutory provisions could not be divested offhand without compensation. As has been seen, at common law, the riparian owner's rights do not depend upon use of them. They are annexed to the riparian land itself. Hence, confining the statutory provisions to unappropriated water does not obviate the difficulty. If such provisions operate to divest the pre-existing rights, they are unconstitutional (14). Appropriations under such legislation must be subject to previously acquired riparian rights except as the latter may be divested by condemnation. Here new difficulties arise. Granting that a public irrigation ditch which may be used by all who are accessible, on payment of reasonable rates, is a public use for which property rights may be condemned, is this true of a private ditch, for the use of the private owner only? This raises a question analogous to those arising under drainage acts, and would no doubt be decided in the same way (15). In Colorado, Montana, Washington, and Wyoming express constitutional provisions exist to obviate it.

----

(14) Lux v. Haggin, 69 Cal. 255; Clark v. Cambridge, etc., Irrigation Co., 45 Nev. 798; Bigelow v. Draper, 7 N. D. 152.

(15) Castle Rock, etc., Co. v. Jurisch, 67 Neb. 377, 382. See Clark v. Nash, 198 U. S. 361.

CHAPTER II

APPROPRIATION OF WATER FOR IRRIGATION.

§ **13.** **Basis of rights** of appropriation. At the present time the legal basis for rights of appropriation is to be found in legislation. With respect to the public domain of the United States, appropriations are founded primarily upon the act of Congress of 1866 and the act of 1870 amendatory thereof (1). The act of 1866 provides: "Whenever by priority of possession rights to the use of water for mining, agricultural, manufacturing, or other purposes have vested and accrued, and the same are recognized and acknowledged by the local customs, laws, and the decisions of the courts, the possessors and owners of such vested rights shall be maintained and protected in the same; and the right of way for the construction of ditches and canals for the purposes herein specified is acknowledged and confirmed." The act of 1870 provides: "All patents granted or preemptions or homesteads allowed, shall be subject to any vested and accrued water rights, or rights to ditches and reservoirs used in connection with such water rights, as may have been acquired under or recognized by the preceding section."

Secondarily they rest upon local customs, laws, and decisions of the courts in the jurisdiction where the land

---

(1) U. S. R. S., §§ 2339-40.

lies, to rights acquired whereunder Congress has given efficacy. Originally, appropriations were governed by custom just as mining claims were governed by miners' customs and district rules, and the courts have recognized and developed this body of customary law by judicial decision, taking judicial notice of it as a part of the local law (2). But legislation soon took the matter in hand, and in every jurisdiction the details are now regulated by statute. These statutes, however, follow the lines of the original customary law and a new common law of irrigation has grown up by judicial decision, applicable in all states wherein appropriation is permitted. Where appropriations are made on lands not part of the public domain, of course the local state or territorial law alone must be looked to.

§ 14. **Priorities between patentees and appropriators: Before act of 1866.** This question is important only in jurisdictions in classes two and three. As the Federal Constitution forbids the general government to deprive any person of property without due process of law, it follows that the act of 1866 could not cut off rights acquired by patentees of public lands prior thereto. In Union Mill & Mining Co. v. Ferris (3), the plaintiff sued to enjoin the defendant from diverting water from a river. The plaintiff held a patent to riparian lands from the federal government. Prior to its patent and prior to the acts that led up to it, the defendant made appropriations of water upon the public domain. He claimed

---

(2) Clough v. Wing, 2 Arizona 371; Crawford Co. v. Hathaway, 67 Neb. 325.

(3) 2 Sawy. (U. S.), 176.

priority by reason thereof and of the act of 1866. The court rejected the defense and held that an injunction should be allowed. It said: ''We consider it to be entirely clear that before the title to these lands was acquired from the government of the United States, no occupancy or appropriation of the water by either party, no state or territorial legislation, or rule of decision established by the state courts in controversies between occupants of the public land, without title from the government, can in any manner qualify, limit, restrict, or affect the operation of the government patent; . . . that a stream of running water is part and parcel of the land through which it flows, inseparably annexed to the soil; and the use of it as an incident of the soil passes to the patentee, who can be deprived of it only by grant, or by the existence of circumstances from which it is the policy of the law to presume a grant [i. e., adverse user for the period of the statute of limitations].'' In other words the act of 1866 was prospective, not retrospective in its operation. For the future, it sanctioned the right given to the appropriator by the local custom or statutes. But the custom, to be given effect under this statute, must have been general and recognized by the courts or else embodied in legislation(4).

§ 15. **Same: After act of 1866. Appropriation before patent.** In states of the second and third classes (§ 10, above), a patent carries with it the common-law rights of a riparian owner with respect to flowing streams upon the tract, except as rights may have been acquired

---

(4) Meng v. Coffee, 67 Neb. 500; Bascy v. Gallagher, 20 Wall. 670.

prior to those of the patentee by virtue of local custom or law since the statute of 1866.   But when such rights have accrued, the patentee takes subject thereto.   Thus in Kaler v. Campbell (5) plaintiff and defendant, each owning land upon a stream, each diverted water from a point above their lands which was upon the public domain. Subsequently by a patent from the United States, the plaintiff acquired title to the land upon which and from which the defendant was diverting the water.   The court held that the plaintiff, as patentee, could not claim riparian rights against defendant's appropriation and that the only question between the parties was as to the priority and extent of their appropriations.   It said: "The basis of the plaintiff's rights in the premises, and also of the defendant's, rests upon congressional legislation. With the doctrine of the common law as applied to riparian owners, we have nothing to do upon the facts made by this record.   It seems that when plaintiff settled [upon] his claim, there was no other person above him upon the stream running through his land, nor any appropriation of its water.   For the purpose of irrigating his soil and for domestic and stock uses, he went above his land and upon government land, and diverted the waters of Clover Creek.   This he had a right to do under the act of Congress; and to the extent he had actually appropriated and used, he had a vested right as to that amount or quantity of water, and whoever afterwards purchased above or below him took subject to such right of prior appropriation actually made by him.   When, afterwards,

(5)   13 Oregon, 596.

the defendant acquired the title to the adjoining land, his
right to appropriate the water of the creek to irrigate
his land was subject to the prior appropriation of the
plaintiff, and was necessarily limited to whatever surplus
remained. And when, subsequent to this, the plaintiff
bought of the government the land above his claim,
where both he and the defendant, by means of ditches,
had been diverting the waters of the creek to their own
lands, and appropriating the same, he took such land
from the government subject to the amount or quantity
actually appropriated by the defendant in such surplus.''
Under present holdings of the court in Oregon, however,
with respect to land patented since 1877 the proposition
that a patentee takes subject to riparian rights thereto-
fore acquired must be limited to uses of water which were
made at the time of the patent and to the right to use
water for domestic purposes (6).

§ 16. Same: Appropriation after patent. On the
other hand, after a patentee has acquired a portion of
the public domain, in jurisdictions where riparian rights
exist, no subsequent appropriation of the water which
flows over the land may be made to his injury (7). In
the case cited, the court said of the statute of 1866: ''The
practical construction of this statute has been that, as
long as land belonged to the United States, the water
flowing over the same was subject to appropriation for
any of the purposes named, when such appropriation was
recognized by the local customs, laws, or decisions of the
courts. But if the water was not so appropriated when

(6)   Hough v. Porter, 51 Ore. 318.
(7)   Cruse v. McCauley, 96 Fed. 369.

it flowed over the public domain, it was not subject to appropriation after the land over which it flowed became private property.'' The rights of the patentee in this respect date back to his first act toward the acquisition of title, and an appropriation after such act but before the patent, is no more efficacious against him than one made after the patent was issued .(8). This doctrine until recently was well settled in states of the second and third classes. A tendency away from it is manifest in recent legislation and in the decision of the Supreme Court of Oregon in Hough v. Porter (9).

§ 17. **Who may appropriate?** There are no limitations with respect to who may appropriate water. If an alien appropriates water on the public domain, that is a matter purely between him and the government of the United States. As to water not upon the public domain the state may, if it chooses, by legislation limit appropriations, for example, to citizens. Appropriations may be made by trespassers on private lands or by disseisors. But it has often been held that appropriation by a trespasser does not make the appropriation appurtenant to the property on which he uses the water, but that he acquires, as it were, an appropriation in gross which will fail unless by change of the use to other property he applies the water to a beneficial use in a reasonable time. Only the true owner can dispute use of water by a tres-passer or disseisor (10).

(8)   Sturr v. Beck, 133 U. S. 541.
(9)   51 Ore. 318.
(10)   Santa Paula Water Works v. Peralta, 113 Cal. 38; Hutchinson v. Watson Slough Ditch Co., 16 Idaho 484; Smith v. Logan, 18 Nev. 149; Hough v. Porter, 51 Ore. 318.

§ 18. What waters are subject to appropriation: **Watercourses (11)**. The constitutional and statutory provisions in the several states which authorize appro. priations of water use the words "natural streams and watercourses," "flowing streams," "running water in rivers or streams," or some equivalent expression. What, then, is a natural stream or watercourse, the water of which is subject to appropriation? In the first place the flow need not be continuous and uninterrupted at all times. Natural streams, well understood so to be, may be dry at times in periods of drought, or regularly in the dry season, either from failure of water or because they sink beneath the surface and become for a time subterranean. For example, in Barnes v. Sabron (12) the evidence showed that the stream in question was supplied partly at certain seasons of the year from springs along its banks, but was supplied chiefly from melting snow on the mountains. There was no regularity as to the quantity of water. The court held that there need not be a continual flow of water, but that the distinction was to be drawn between a regularly flowing stream of water which is dried up at certain seasons, and water flowing through hollows, gulches, or ravines only in times of rains or melting snow. As another court put the matter, "it must appear that the water usually flows therein in a certain direction and in a regular channel with banks and sides. It may not flow continuously and

(11) It should be observed that statutes governing the storage and appropriation of surface water are becoming common. They vary greatly and are not within the scope of this article.

(12) 10 Nev. 217.

it may at times be dry. It must have, however, a substantial existence" (13).

This requirement that there be a defined channel or bed was considered in Simmons v. Winters (14). In that case the question arose with reference to a draw caused by occasional bodies of surface water descending from the hills during times of melting snow and ice, into which the waters of a creek had been diverted. The court held it was not a watercourse, saying: "A watercourse is a stream of water usually flowing in a particular direction with well defined banks and channels. . . The term watercourse does not include water descending from the hills, down the hollows and ravines, without any definite channel, only in times of rain and melting snow, but . . . where water, owing to the hills or mountainous configuration of the country accumulates in large quantities from rain and melting snow, and at regular seasons descends through long, deep gullies or ravines upon the lands below, and in its onward flow carves out a distinct and well defined channel, which even to the casual glance bears the unmistakable impress of the frequent action of running water, and through which it has flowed from time immemorial—such a stream is to be considered a watercourse" (15).

The stream need not, however, have defined banks or channel throughout its whole course. Not infrequently, especially in arid or semi-arid regions, there will be shal-

---

(13) Geddis v. Parrish, 1 Wash. 587, 589.

(14) 21 Ore. 35.

(15) See an excellent discussion of cases of this sort in McClellan v. Hurdle, 3 Col. App. 430, 435.

low places along the course of a stream where it spreads
out into a marsh or is lost for the time being, to resume a
regular course farther down. Thus in Barnes v. Sabron
(note 12, above) it appeared that at a certain point in the
stream, which was held to be a watercourse, the water
flowing in the natural channel from above lost its force
and the bed of the stream rose, causing the water to
spread out and run in different channels or become lost.
Such conditions are discussed also in the leading case of
Lux v. Haggin (16), in which case the court, after declaring that "a channel is necessary to the constitution
of a watercourse," said: "It is not essential to a watercourse that the banks shall be unchangeable or that there
shall be everywhere a visible change in the angle of
ascent, marking the line between bed and banks. The
law cannot fix the limits of variation in these and other
like particulars. . . . We can conceive that along the
course of a stream there may be shallow places where
the water spreads and where there is no distinct ravine
or gully."

§ 19. **Same: Percolating and underground waters.**
Percolating waters are beneath the surface what surface
water is above the surface. Except in Kansas and South
Dakota and, as to waste of artesian water, in California,
Kansas, Nebraska, and New Mexico, it is governed by
the common law. Accordingly percolating waters are
not subject to appropriation. An interesting case involving this point is Willow Creek Irrigation Co. v. Mich-

(16)   69 Cal. 255, 418. See also Rait v. Furrow, 74 Kan. 1.

aelson (17). The plaintiff in that case had appropriated all the waters of a creek for irrigation. Afterwards the United States conveyed a tract of land to the defendant. There was no water on the tract at the time, but afterwards water appeared on the surface and formed a marsh. The water stood in a natural depression, gradually increasing in volume for some years, and finally broke through in a stream and flowed into the creek. The defendant diverted water from this marsh, preventing it from flowing into the creek, and claimed the right to use it on his land. The plaintiffs sought an injunction to prevent this. This was denied. The court said: "When the United States issued its patent to the respondent (defendant) neither the bog, nor marsh, nor the water in question was visible upon the land conveyed. Nor was there any known or defined subterranean stream thereon. At that time the water, if it existed at all, was . . . flowing in a subterranean stream having no defined or known channels, courses or banks. Water so percolating and flowing forms a part of the realty, and belongs to the owner of the soil. A conveyance or grant by the United States of any part of the public domain . . . carries with it the right of filtrating water, and to streams flowing through the soil beneath the surface, but in undefined and unknown channels, just the same as it carries with it the right to rocks and minerals in the ground."

§ 20. Same: Springs. So also a spring which is not

_____

(17) 21 Utah 249. See also Howard v. Perrin, 200 U. S. 71; Deadwood Cent. Ry. v. Barker, 14 S. D. 558.

supplied by a defined flowing stream and does not flow into a natural stream is not the subject of appropriation (18). On the other hand, where a spring is part of or flows into a natural stream, the water may be appropriated and diverted from the spring itself. In Cross v. Kitts (19) a tunnel in a mining claim intercepted and collected percolating water and formed a spring from which water flowed in a defined, running stream. The court held that it could be appropriated. But a tunnel into which water flows from the drainage of a mine is not a stream for this purpose (20).

§ 21. **Same: Defined underground streams.** Where underground water flows in a definite course, as where a portion of the course of a stream is below the surface, it is subject to the same rules as a watercourse upon the surface, and may be the subject of appropriation. In McClellan v. Hurdle (21) a plaintiff, who sought to recover from the defendant for diverting water by wells upon defendant's own lands, alleged that the water was part of the flow of a creek, the water of which he had appropriated, and that its course at the point in question was underground "as a subterranean current." The court held that a case was stated. For the same reasons the "underflow" of a natural stream, that is, that part of its waters which flow through the sand beneath the

(18)   Hudson v. McCue, 42 Cal. 303.

(19)   69 Cal. 217.

(20)   Cardelli v. Comstock Tunnel Co., 26 Nev. 284.

(21)   3 Col. App. 430. See also Whitmore v. Utah Fuel Co., 26 Utah 488.

surface, but with a defined course as a part of the stream, may be appropriated (22).

§ 22. Water used and returned. There may be an appropriation of water used and returned and the appropriator of such water may insist that the unused water be not diverted elsewhere, but be allowed to return to the stream to meet his appropriation (23).

§ 23. What constitutes appropriation? An appropriation of water is an actual diversion of the water of a natural stream, with the intent and purpose of applying it to a beneficial use, consummated in a reasonable time thereafter by actual application of the water to such a use. The requisites of an appropriation are: (1) by custom or statute a preliminary notice, posted and recorded, of the intention to divert the water, or in most states today application to state authority for permission to make the appropriation, and approval thereof; (2) actual diversion of water within a reasonable time thereafter; (3) intent to apply the water diverted to a beneficial use; (4) actual application of the water to such a use within a reasonable time after it is so diverted (24). In the main this analysis of the law as it stood until recently still holds. But a transition is in progress. The older doctrine has been called "a possessory system." This is gradually giving way as a result of judicial decision and of legislation to what may be called "a use

(22) Platte Valley Irrigation Co. v. Buckers Irrigation Co., 25 Col. 77; Buckers Irrigation Co. v. Farmers Ditch Co., 31 Col. 62.

(23) Anderson Land & Stock Co. v. McConnell, 188 Fed. 818.

(24) This analysis is substantially that in Long on Irrigation, § 36.

system.'' This change affects particularly the second and third requisites of appropriation noted above and tends so far as possible to make everything depend upon the fourth requisite, so that beneficial use shall be the sole measure of the right. This is a highly desirable change, but the fact that the law is in a process of transition from the one position to the other makes it very difficult at present on many points to state the exact law with precision.

§ 24. **Preliminary requirements: Notice. Statutory requirements.** Posting a notice was generally required by custom when the practice of appropriation grew up. But legislation soon took control of the matter and the preliminary step came to be governed by statute wherever required, except in Oregon. The usual statutory requirement was that one who intended to make an appropriation should post a written notice in a conspicuous place at the point where diversion is intended, setting out the quantity of water he claims, the purpose and place of use, and the means of diversion intended. A copy of this notice was then to be recorded, within a fixed time, in the county where the notice was posted. Statutory provisions of this sort obtain in Arizona, California, Kansas, and Montana. Colorado now requires two copies of a map showing the location of the head-gate and the route of the ditch or canal, to be filed with the state engineer within sixty days after construction has begun. Texas requires similar evidence of appropriation to be filed, and Montana requires both preliminary notice and subsequent evidence. A third type of preliminary requirement originated in Wyoming. The Wyoming method requires an application to the state engineer for a permit to appropriate, a determination by the latter whether there is unappropriated water and whether existing rights or public interests will be infringed, and approval by that officer. This method is rapidly superseding all others. It was adopted in Idaho, Nebraska, Nevada, New Mexico, North Dakota, Oklahoma, Oregon, South Dakota, and Utah. It is partly in force in Colorado. It has just been adopted in California and Washington.

§ 25. Same: Object of notice. The purpose of the preliminary requirement as to posting and recording notice is to preserve evidence as to priorities. If notice is posted and recorded, the appropriation, when complete, takes its date from the notice, whereas if such notice is not given, the appropriation, in determining priorities, takes its date from its completion. In general, when an act consists of successive stages, the law gives effect to it, when it is completed, from the date of the first step. But in appropriations of water in unsettled or sparsely settled regions, oral testimony as to the date of the first step, where it consists, perhaps, of labor upon a ditch by one man remote from all observers, leaves too much scope for fraud or dispute. Hence the preliminary notice was required by custom and sanctioned by legislation. As the notice serves the purpose of fixing priorities only, it is obvious that priority only should be affected by failure to give it or to give it properly. The appropriation, itself, when complete, should not fail for that cause. And the courts so hold. In De Necochea v. Curtis (25), plaintiff in 1880 constructed a ditch, diverted the waters of a creek, conducted them to his land and used them for domestic purposes and for irrigation. In 1885 the defendant constructed a ditch and diverted water from the creek to her land for irrigation. The plaintiff had not posted or recorded any notice. It was decided that the plaintiff was entitled to an injunction. The court said that the purpose of the statute "was merely to define with precision the conditions upon which the appropriator of water could have the advantage of the familiar doctrine of relation, upon which it had always been held before the statute that one who gave sufficient notice of his intention to appropriate, and followed up his notice by diligent prosecution of the work, was, upon its completion, to be deemed an appropriator from the date of his notice, and was, therefore, prior in time and stronger in right than an intervening appropriator, notwithstanding his diversion of the water might be first completed."

As the purpose of the statutes as to notice is to enable one who makes an appropriation to obtain priority over others who begin later but complete their work first, one who seeks the advantage of such a notice must pursue the statutory or customary requirement strictly. That is, he must do everything that the statute or custom prescribes and his notice must contain everything prescribed (26). But, while the requirements as to notice

---

(25)   80 Cal. 397.
(26)   Taylor v. Abbott, 103 Cal. 421.

and as to what the notice shall contain must be pursued strictly, the notice itself is to be construed liberally (27). Where the first step in appropriation is application to and a permit from a state officer, it would seem that such permission should be an absolute prerequisite and it has been so held (28). Several courts, however, take a contrary view, holding that an appropriation by actual diversion is still good under these statutes, but that in such case priority is reckoned from the time of diversion (29). This does not seem to be a fair construction of the statute and results from an attempt to adjust the statutory system to the older doctrines.

§ 26. **Diversion** of water: **Reasonable time.** In order that advantage may be taken of the preliminary step, water must be diverted actually (30) from the stream at the point designated in a reasonable time thereafter. Reasonable time in this connection means that the appropriator must proceed diligently and must not be guilty of any unnecessary delay. What is reasonable depends upon the circumstances of each case and, necessarily, is not capable of exact definition. The difficulties of the particular undertaking, the conditions of the region, the means at hand for prosecuting the work, and all the circumstances surrounding the enterprise must be taken into account. In Cruse v. McCauley (31) notice was posted in July, 1882. Another appropriator began his

---

(27)   Osgood v. El Dorado Mining Co., 50 Cal. 571.
(28)   Castle Rock, etc., Irrigation Co. v. Jurisch, 67 Neb. 377.
(29)   Morris v. Bean, 146 Fed. 423; Nielson v. Barker, 19 Idaho 727.
(30)   Gates v. Settlers' Milling, Canal & Reservoir Co., 19 Oklahoma 83.
(31)   96 Fed. 369.

appropriation early in the spring of 1883. Ten months after his notice, in April or May, the appropriator who had posted the first notice surveyed or located his ditch. The court held that he was not entitled to date his appropriation from the notice. It said: "It is perhaps true that in considering what would be reasonable diligence in marking out the line of a proposed ditch and commencing work on the same, a court would not be controlled by an arbitrary rule, but would consider the circumstances confronting an appropriator of water. A court should consider, however, that in a new country, subject to settlement, a proposed locator of water rights should not be guilty of any unnecessary delay in perfecting his appropriation. The rights of new comers should be considered. In this case the only excuse offered by the defendant for not marking out the line of his proposed ditch, and for not commencing the work on the same sooner than he did, after posting of his notice, is that at the time and place where the proposed ditch was to be dug it was difficult to procure men for the work. He does not show, however, that he made any serious endeavor to employ such men."

§ 27. **Same: Excuses for delay.** But the excuses for delay must be difficulties or obstacles inherent in the work itself under the circumstances surrounding its prosecution. Excuses purely personal to the appropriator, such as ill-health or lack of means, will not avail. Thus in Ophir Silver Mining Co. v. Carpenter (32), in which

(32) 4 Nev. 534; also, Keeny v. Carillo, 2 N. Mex. 480 (lack of means). The courts take the same view of a like question in mining law. Doe v. Waterloo M. Co., 70 Fed. 456, 460.

illness was advanced as an excuse, the court said: "We
are inclined to believe that his illness is not a circumstance which can be taken into consideration at all. Like
the pecuniary condition of a person, it is not one of those
matters incident to the enterprise, but rather to the person. The only matters in cases of this kind which can
be taken into consideration are such as would affect any
person who might be engaged in the same undertaking,
such as the state of the weather, the difficulty of obtaining laborers, or something of that character." While this
rule may seem harsh, it is necessary. Lack of diligence
does not prevent appropriation, but it results in postponement of priority to the date of completion of the
appropriation. One who is unfortunate because of illness
or poverty is not prevented thereby from appropriating
water, but his illness or poverty cannot be suffered to
keep out others. The water resources of the region cannot be suffered to go to waste while he is waiting for
better health or a longer purse (33). Under the present
tendency toward a "use system" as distinguished from
a "possessory system" of water law this consideration
should be controlling.

§ 28. **Mode of diversion.** Any mode of diversion
whereby the water is actually withdrawn from the stream
will suffice. In Thomas v. Guiraud (34) water was diverted by a dam by means of which the stream was
turned upon the land. The court said: "If a dam or con-
trivance of any kind will suffice to turn water from the

(33) But see Taughenbaugh v. Clark, 6 Col. App. 235, 244; Arnold
v. Passavant, 19 Mont. 575.
(34) 6 Col. 530.

stream and moisten the land sought to be cultivated, it is
sufficient, though no ditch is needed or constructed. Or
if land be rendered productive by the natural overflow
of the water thereon, without the aid of any appliances
whatever, the cultivation of such land by means of the
water so naturally moistening the same is a sufficient
appropriation of such water, or so much thereof as is
reasonably necessary for such use. The true test of
appropriation of water is the successful application
thereof to the beneficial use designed; and the method
of diverting or carrying the same, or making such application, is immaterial.'' Hence, while ditches or canals
or flumes or pipes are the ordinary means of diversion,
the appropriator may divert into or through a ravine;
or another stream, taking out what he put in, but no
more (35); or another's ditch by consent or by condemnation, where allowed (36); or an abandoned ditch upon
the public domain; or, if the stream is subterranean, a
well or a tunnel (37).

§ 29. **Diversion by sub-irrigation.** Under the appropriation doctrine merely settling on the banks of a stream
gives no right to use the water; being a riparian owner
is not an appropriator (38). With increased settlement
in the states where the appropriation doctrine obtains,
however, certain inherent advantages in the common-law
doctrine have become manifest. It is obvious that as be-

(35)   Paige v. Rocky Ford Co., 83 Cal. 84, 94; Hermann Irrigation Co.
v. Keel, 25 Utah 96.
(36)   Water Supply Co. v. Larimer & Weld Irrigation Co., 24 Col. 322.
(37)   Roberts v. Crafts, 141 Cal. 20.
(38)   Schodde v. Twin Falls Co., 224 U. S. 107.

tween riparian and non-riparian tracts the former are
in a better position to use the water beneficially and that
a riparian tract by its mere situation is enabled to use
water beneficially without any actual diversion.   Yet
under the strict doctrine of appropriation these natural
advantages may be entirely cut off by appropriation and
use of the water upon non-riparian tracts and the riparian owner who needs to make no diversion to acquire
the benefit of the flow of water past his land is in no position to protect himself.   This situation has been dealt
with in two ways, on the one hand by a judicial doctrine
of appropriation by sub-irrigation; on the other hand by
legislation.   The doctrine of sub-irrigation has a logical
foundation in the theory of appropriation measured by
actual use and amounts to holding that actual use without diversion is sufficient.   Thus in Cascade Town Co. v.
Empire Water & Power Co. (39), plaintiff built a hotel
and pleasure resort in a cañon in Colorado where a water-
fall made a natural garden.   There was no diversion but
the spray and seepage watered vegetation which made
the place attractive.   Defendant, a light and power company, appropriated water above the falls and was so diverting the stream as not to return the water.   Although
the plaintiff made no actual diversion the diversion by
the defendant was enjoined (40).   By statute, called the
Meadow Act, natural overflow or natural sub-irrigation
by which a tract of land is benefited may be given the
same effect as an appropriation by diversion and have

---

(39)   181 Fed. 1011.
(40)   See also Hill v. Standard Mining Co., 12 Idaho 223; Van Camp
v. Emery, 13 Idaho 202.

priority as to the time of first cultivation of the land. Colorado Revised Statutes, 1908, § 3176.

§ 30. **Change in mode of diversion.** One who has made an appropriation is not bound to continue the point or mode of diversion made use of at the outset. Provided he does not injure others whose rights have accrued in the meantime, he may change the point of diversion, the mode of diversion, or the course of his ditch or canal to suit his convenience (41). But he cannot add to the quantity of water to which he is entitled in this way. If he takes more under the new plan than under the old, his right to the additional quantity must rest on a new appropriation (41). At present this subject is usually governed by statute.

§ 31. **Intent to apply the water to a beneficial use.** Diversion merely to forestall others, in the expectation that an opportunity for use will develop or as a matter of speculation, will confer no right. In order to be the basis of an appropriation, the diversion, when made, must be made as a means to a beneficial use, which the appropriator has in mind at the time, and must be in furtherance of that purpose. Thus, in Thomas v. Guiraud (note 34, above), the court said that a claimant of water rights could not divert water ''for the purpose of irrigating lands which he did not cultivate or own, or hold by possessory right or title, to the exclusion of a subsequent bona fide appropriator,'' and that ''removal of water for drainage simply, without applying the same to any beneficial use, is not such an appropriation as

(41)   Smith v. Corbitt, 116 Cal. 587.

gives a prior right thereto." This is a very enlightened opinion for one which stands so early in the development of the law. Indeed it represents the beginning of the newer view called the "use system." As to the first proposition, the decisions generally have been to the contrary because of the logical requirements of the old "possessory" conception (42). But there are recent holdings in accord (43). This does not preclude appropriation by a company to supply water to all users in a designated area, capable of using it, at a reasonable price (44). In the latter case, the company is exercising a public calling, and its rates are subject to regulation by statute, and, no doubt, to judicial investigation at common law (45). The purpose may be changed after the diversion or after the appropriation is complete, without destroying the right (46). But recent legislation is strictly limiting such changes.

§ 32. **Application of water to beneficial use. Reasonable time.** Finally, to take advantage of the preceding steps for the purpose of claiming priority from the date of the notice or other first step, there must be actual use of the water for a beneficial purpose within a reasonable time (47). Such actual use completes the appropriation.

---

(42) Calkins v. Sorosis Fruit Co., 150 Cal. 426; Davis v. Randall, 44 Colo. 488; Nevada Ditch Co. v. Bennett, 30 Ore. 59.

(43) Avery v. Johnson, 59 Wash. 332.

(44) See a discussion of the difference between this and an attempt to impound all the water as a speculation, in Combs v. Agricultural Ditch Co., 17 Col. 146.

(45) Castle Rock Irrigation Co. v. Jurisch, 67 Neb. 377, 382.

(46) Ramelli v. Irish, 96 Cal. 214; Strickler v. City, 16 Col. 61.

(47) Gates v. Settlers Milling Co., 19 Okla. 83.

If it follows the other steps without unreasonable delay, the appropriation will be regarded as dating from its inception. If not, it dates from this final step. As has been seen, the purpose need not be the one first entertained. One may start with the intention of irrigating one tract, for example, and ultimately find it more to his advantage to irrigate another. So, also, what we have seen in another connection as to reasonable time applies here also, with, perhaps, one qualification. The application of the quantity of water contemplated at the inception of the appropriation must often be gradual, extending over a number of years as it becomes possible to put all the land for which the water was appropriated under cultivation. Of course, in order to claim priority from the inception of the enterprise, the amount finally used must not exceed that originally contemplated. But, within this limit, the appropriator may begin what part of his tract is ready for cultivation and increase the amount year by year until the whole is cultivated, provided he proceeds with reasonable diligence (48). If he is not diligent and delays the increase unreasonably, he will be confined, so far as priority is concerned, to what had been applied prior to the delay (49). Even as long a period as ten years has been held reasonable, where additional water was applied as the appropriator was able to prepare the land for cultivation (50). It seems also that in this connection the means of the appropriator are

---

(48)   Senior v. Anderson, 115 Cal. 496; Elliott v. Whitmore, 23 Utah 342.

(49)   Low v. Rizor, 25 Ore. 551.

(50)   Arnold v. Passavant, 19 Mont. 575.

to be taken into consideration. Thus in Taughenbaugh v. Clark (note 33, above), the court said: "Men of limited means, pioneers in a new territory, who have not only to grub and clear land, but erect houses and provide a means of living while making a home, should not be held to the same rule with those more favored and having abundant capital. As long as the settler in the desert does not abandon but continues in good faith to prosecute his construction of a ditch and the application of water to his land as rapidly as his means and circumstances will permit, he should be held to be within the limit of a reasonable time; nor should his incipient construction and application of water be held as the extent of the application" (51). Subject to the foregoing explanations, application to a beneficial use is the final and decisive criterion of an appropriation, determining its creation, its existence, and its duration. With the qualification that the use may be changed, the matter is put tersely in Thomas v. Guiraud (note 34, above): "The true test of appropriation of water is the successful application thereof to the beneficial use designed."

---

(51) But this is by no means certain. In U. S. v. Whitney, 176 Fed. 593, difficulty of financing a large project was held no excuse. See § 27 *ante.*

CHAPTER III.

PRIORITIES, TRANSFER, AND EXTINGUISHMENT OF WATER RIGHTS.

SECTION 1. PRIORITIES.

§ 33. **General principles.** Three general principles may be laid down with respect to the conflicting claims of appropriators from the same stream or its sources or tributaries:

(a) Priority of appropriation gives priority of right to the extent of the appropriation. Only unappropriated waters are subject to appropriation. Hence a subsequent appropriator must show that there is water left to be appropriated after the needs of the prior appropriator to the extent of his appropriation are satisfied, and, whenever there is a failure of water, must yield to the right of the prior appropriator to be satisfied. And where there is an appropriation senior to both, the last in time must yield to the first. Thus, in Water Storage Co. v. Larimer & Weld Reservoir Co. (1), the storage company diverted from the main stream, the reservoir company from a tributary. There were appropriations senior to both below the point where the tributary joined. The storage company's appropriation was prior to that of the reservoir

(1)   25 Col. 87.

company's. The court said: "In times of scarcity of water in the main stream, there is insufficient flowing to the headgate of the storage company to supply it and the senior appropriations below, and, therefore, when these conditions exist, the storage company has the right to demand that the reservoir company shall first surrender the water which it claims the right to divert from Dry Creek [the tributary] in favor of the senior appropriations below the mouth thereof in the main stream, thereby to this extent augmenting the flow which shall reach such senior appropriations and correspondingly decreasing the volume which must pass by the headgate of the storage company for the use of such appropriations."

(b) Every appropriation is limited, both as to its extent and its continuance, by the beneficial use to which the water is put; water cannot be claimed unless it is used, except as the appropriator is proceeding with reasonable diligence to use it, nor can it be claimed for any purpose but use (see §§ 35-38, below).

(c) Appropriation of the water of a stream includes the water of its tributaries and sources of supply, such as lakes or springs, so far as necessary to enable the appropriator to obtain therefrom, for diversion from the stream, the amount to which he is entitled (2).

§ 34. **Priority as determined by character of use. Domestic use.** By constitutional provision in Colorado and Idaho and by statute in Nebraska, domestic uses are entitled to priority. The term domestic use here has the same meaning as at common law. In Crawford v. Hatha-

---

(2)   Baxter v. Gilbert, 125 Cal. 580; Strickler v. City, 16 Col. 61.

way (3) the plaintiff was under contract to furnish water to a village for general municipal purposes, including sprinkling streets and power for lighting plant, and also to furnish water to the general government to flush the sewers at a military post. It claimed priority for these as domestic purposes. The court said: "The term 'domestic purposes,' as used in the statute, has reference to the use of water for domestic purposes as known and recognized at common law. . . . The common law distinguishes between those modes of use which ordinarily involve the taking of small quantities of water and but little interference with the stream, and those which necessarily involve a taking or diversion of large quantities and a considerable interference with its ordinary flow. The use of a stream in the ordinary way by riparian owner for drinking and cooking purposes and for watering his stock is a domestic use. It involves no considerable diversion of water and no appreciable interference with the stream." Diversion of water by ditches or pipes does not come within these provisions (4).

§ 35. **Limitations upon the quantity that may be claimed as against subsequent appropriators: Needs of land irrigated.** Application of the water to a beneficial use is the measure of the appropriator's right. Hence

(3) 67 Neb. 325, 371.
(4) See Town of Sterling v. Pawnee Ditch Extension Co., 42 Colo. 421; Montpelier Mining Co. v. City of Montpelier, 19 Idaho 212, where appropriations for municipal water works are spoken of as domestic appropriations and so it is said a subsequent domestic appropriation in order to prevail over prior agricultural or manufacturing appropriations must condemn and compensate. The same result could have been reached through the power of the municipality to condemn for a public use without any such straining of the term domestic use.

his right, as against other appropriators, must be limited
by the needs of the land for which the water is appropriated. He has no claim to more than is reasonably needed
for the irrigation of that land, though to the extent of
such need he may, if properly appropriated, use all the
water of the stream(5). Hence the surplus not used
must be returned to the stream for use by subsequent
appropriators; he cannot sell it or dispose of it to others.
In Creek v. Bozeman Water Works Co. (6), there being
several other appropriations, the first appropriator after
his individual needs had been supplied, which was the
purpose of his original appropriation, sold the surplus
to the inhabitants of a city. On suit to prevent this,
brought by the subsequent appropriators, the court held
that he should be enjoined. It said: "The right acquired
by an appropriator in and to the waters of a natural
stream is not ownership of a running volume of the dimensions claimed, like the individual ownership of a chattel, so that it may be transferred corporally and carried
away, but the right acquired by the appropriator is a
right to use a certain quantity for necessary and beneficial purposes, such as supplying household needs and
the carrying on of some useful industry; and when such
want is supplied, or the use is subserved, all the rest of
the creek, and all that returns thereto after such use, is
subject to appropriation and use by another for some
beneficial purpose. The same volume of water, therefore, in its flow down the creek, may supply many per-

---

(5)   Hammond v. Rose, 11 Col. 524; Meng v. Coffee, 67 Neb. 500, 511.
(6)   15 Mont. 121.

sons, even though the first appropriator claims the whole
volume and can, at times, or even constantly, use the
same for some industrial purpose, because such use does
not usually swallow it, but leaves it available to others.
But by such an appropriation the first appropriator does
not acquire a preemption of the whole creek, so that he
. . . may, after enjoying the use of it for some beneficial purpose, convey the creek away and cut off subsequent appropriators. Therefore a subsequent right to
use the same water, or so much of it as returns to the
creek, and to use the waters of the creek when the first
is not using the same, may be acquired.''

§ 36. **Same: Capacity** of ditch. A second limitation is
the capacity of the appropriator's ditch at its point of
least capacity; though if its capacity is greater than the
reasonable needs of the land supplied, of course the latter
will fix the limit. The rule was stated thus in Barnes v.
Sabron (7): "If the capacity of his ditches is greater
than is necessary to irrigate his farming land, he must
be restricted to the quantity needed for the purposes of
irrigation, for watering his stock and for domestic purposes. If, however, the capacity of his ditches is not
more than sufficient for those purposes, then . . .
he must be restricted to the capacity of his ditches at
their smallest point, that is, at the point where the least
water can be carried through them.''

§ 37. **Same: Economical use. Ordinary means of
use.** A third limitation is that his manner of using and

(7) 10 Nev. 217. See also Stenger v. Tharp, 17 S. D. 13.

applying the water must be reasonable; he can claim no
right to take water which he wastes in using it. In
Shotwell v. Dodge the defendant dug a single ditch for
a long distance through his farm, diverted the water of
a creek into it, and allowed the water to flow through it
until it became lost at the end of the ditch. The soil
was porous and the water percolated sidewise through
the banks and enabled him to grow fruit trees and vege-
tables, but large quantities of water were lost and no
means were taken to prevent waste. The court said:
"This was not irrigation at all; much less, reasonable
irrigation. Where water is an important feature in the
success of farming operations, it becomes the irrigator
to use proper means to bring water to points where it is
needed, to use it only at such times and in such quantities as are necessary for the purpose, and then, if others
situated like himself require the water, to stop its flow
until it shall again become necessary. The constant
flow of water in the ditch all the summer through to the
extent to which the defendant caused the water of the
Mima Creek to flow would be inexcusable under any circumstances, when others had equal need of the water for
irrigation" (8). Hence the court may require an appropriator to improve his means of diversion so as to avoid
unnecessary waste. Thus in Natoma Water & Mining
Co. v. Hancock (9) the question, as stated by the court,
was whether the defendants, who were appropriators of
the surplus waters above plaintiff's dam, "must be en-

(8) 7 Wash. 217. See also Sterling v. Pawnee Ditch Co., 42 Col. 421;
Irrigation Co. v. Willard, 75 Neb. 408.
(9) 101 Cal. 42, 48.

joined from diverting the surplus merely because such diversion would compel the plaintiff to perform its annual task of raising its dam earlier in the year, and of making it tight and efficient oftener than it has been accustomed to do." The question was answered in the negative. But appropriators are entitled to use the ordinary and usual means of diverting and applying water, and cannot be compelled to use other and more expensive ones because thereby more would be saved for others. In Barrows v. Fox the court said: "Ditches and flumes are the usual and ordinary means of diverting water in this state, and parties who have made their appropriations by such means cannot be compelled to substitute iron pipes, though they may be compelled to keep their flumes and ditches in good repair so as to prevent any unnecessary waste" (10).

§ 38. **Same: Periods of use.** Finally, the appropriator can claim a prior right to receive and use the water only for the times or periods when it is needed for the use to which he puts it, and in consequence of this limitation, a court has the power to apportion the use of the water in point of time, allowing the first appropriator to use at stated periods or intervals, as his needs require, and then allowing use of what remains by subsequent appropriators until the time arrives when the first in right is again entitled because of recurring need of the water (11).

§ 39. **Judicial determination of priorities.** The ordi-

---

(10) 98 Cal. 63; also, Rodgers v. Pitt, 129 Fed. 932.

(11) Wiggins v. Muscupiabe Water Co., 113 Cal. 182; Stowell v. Johnson, 7 Utah 215.

nary mode of trying questions of priority is by an action
at law for damages caused by diversion of water to the
injury of the plaintiff's right or by a suit in equity to
enjoin such diversion. In such cases, however, the judgment or decree is only conclusive between the parties to
the litigation. It happens often that there are a large
number of claimants along a stream whose appropriations conflict and that it is desirable, if not actually necessary, to include all of them in one suit and adjudicate the
rights and priorities of all of them in the one litigation.
Although as an original question of equity jurisdiction
the question is a difficult one, the courts in the states
where irrigation is practised have agreed that it may
be done. Such suits are expressly authorized by statute
in Montana, Oregon, and Oklahoma. But such proceedings have proved cumbersome, expensive, and dilatory,
and in consequence in 1879 and in 1881 Colorado provided an improved special procedure for judicial determination of the extent and priority of water rights.
Utah has similar legislation.

§ 40. Administrative determination. In 1890, Wyoming took the radical step of providing for administrative determination by a state board in advance of controversy, with provisions for appeal to the courts. This legislation has been followed in Nebraska, Idaho, Oklahoma,
and Washington. When legislation of this sort was first
attempted, the courts held it invalid on the ground that
it attempted to confer judicial power upon executive
officers (12); but it is now upheld on the theory that the

_____

(12)   Thorp v. Woolman, 1 Mont. 168.

provisions of the statute are "in the nature of police regulations to secure the orderly distribution of water for irrigation purposes" (13).

Section 2. Transfer of Water Rights.

§ 41. Water rights are appurtenances of land upon which water is used. Construction of deeds. Because water rights may be severed from the land, for which the appropriation was made or on which the water was applied, and annexed to other land or conveyed separately from the land, there is some language in the books to the effect that such rights are not appurtenances of land. But these rights exist only for the benefit of land, must be used to apply water on land, and are measured by the needs of the land for which they are used. They are not rights in gross, belonging to the owner personally; they belong to him as owner of the land, though, like any other thing so owned, they may be severed from the land. Hence the courts have now repudiated the language above referred to and have established that such rights are to be regarded as appurtenances (14). It follows that conveyance of the land upon which the water is applied will carry with it the water right and the ditch or other means of diversion, unless excepted in the deed (15). In Colorado, however, there is an anomalous doctrine. Instead of the water right passing where the contrary intention is not shown, it will pass, if at all, be-

---

(13) Farm Investment Co. v. Carpenter, 9 Wyo. 110; Boise Irrigation Co. v. Stewart, 10 Idaho 38.

(14) Gelwicks v. Todd, 24 Col. 494; Smith v. Deniff, 23 Mont. 65.

(15) Cave v. Crafts, 53 Cal. 135; Toyaho Creek Irrigation Co. v. Hutchins, 21 Tex. Civ. App. 274; Snyder v. Murdock, 20 Utah 419.

cause the parties intended it to do so, and hence it is a question of construction of each conveyance of land whether the water rights are included. Where no mention is made of them, the circumstances surrounding the conveyance are considered, especially the necessity of the right to beneficial use of the land conveyed (16). Where a ditch is conveyed without reservation, it will carry with it the water right for which it is used (17).

§ 42. **Conveyance of water rights.** As the place of application may be changed without loss of the appropriation, it follows that a water right, for that matter like other appurtenances, may be severed. Recent legislation is attacking this rule and providing that use of water inheres in the land and cannot be separated or at least cannot be separated without permission from the state engineer. Such statutes exist in Idaho, Nebraska, Nevada, New Mexico, Oklahoma, Oregon, and Utah. Such severance may take place through condemnation or through adverse user of the right by another for the benefit of other lands, or it may take place by grant of the right to another, retaining the land, or by conveyance of the land, retaining the right, or by grant of the right to one and conveyance of the land to another. We have seen also that the means and mode of diversion may be changed. Hence it may well happen that the ditch is owned by one, the land over which the ditch runs by another, and the water rights which make use of the ditch by others (18). If the water right or the ditch is con-

---

(16)   Arnett v. Linhart, 21 Col. 188.
(17)   Williams v. Harper, 121 Cal. 47.
(18)   McLear v. Hapgood, 85 Cal. 555.

veyed separately, it must be by deed. It is held, however, that a water right may be conveyed by a parol sale if the grantee takes possession. This is a remnant of the old possessory idea (19).

SECTION 3. EXTINGUISHMENT OF WATER RIGHTS.

§ 43. **Loss of water rights by abandonment.** Any property or right may be lost by abandonment. For instance, one may throw a chattel upon the garbage pile, intending to give up all rights to it. Here, it will be seen, there are two elements: (a) the giving up of possession; (b) the intention to relinquish all right. So it is with abandonment of a water right. To show loss of a water right in this way, both an act of abandonment and an intent to abandon must be established (20). Obviously no particular time is required; a clear abandonment might be made in a very short time. But as the act relied on is generally non-user of the right, the actual cases are not so simple, because there may be many other reasons for the non-user, and intent to relinquish as well as non-user must be shown (21). Still, long non-user may be evidence of such intent (22).

§ 44. **Loss and acquisition** through adverse user. Exactly the same principles apply here as in the loss and acquisition of easements and profits by adverse user and prescription. Open, notorious, continuous, exclusive, ad-

---

(19) Griseza v. Terwilliger, 144 Cal. 456.
(20) Gassert v. Noyes, 18 Mont. 216; Edgmont Improvement Co. v. Tubbs Sheep Co., (S. D. 1908), 115 N. W. 1130.
(21) Utt v. Frey, 106 Cal. 392.
(22) Davis v. Gale, 32 Cal. 27; Sieber v. Fink, 7 Col. 148.

verse use for the statutory period of limitation is a mode
of original acquisition of water rights, the same as of
any other rights of the sort.   See the article on Title to
Real Estate, §§ 144-71, elsewhere in this volume.

§ 45.   **Forfeiture for non-user.**   The distinctions between acquisition by appropriation, on the one hand, and
by adverse use on the other, and between loss through
adverse use by another, by abandonment, and by failure
to apply the water to beneficial use, are well put by the
supreme court of California in Smith v. Hawkins (23),
thus: "The differences are twofold.   A prescriptive
right could not be acquired against the United States,
and can be acquired only by one claimant against another
private individual.   Again, such an appropriation, to
perfect the rights of the appropriator, does not necessi-
tate use for any given length of time, while time and
adverse use are essential elements to the perfection of a
prescriptive right.   One who claims a right of prescription must use the water continuously, uninterruptedly
and adversely for a period of at least five years (24).
. . . Section 1411 of the Civil Code declares that the
appropriation must be for some useful or beneficial purpose, and when the appropriator or his successor in interest ceases to use it for such a purpose, the right ceases
(25).   This section deals with the forfeiture of a right
by non-user alone.   We say non-user as distinguished

---

(23)   110 Cal. 122, 125.

(24)   In California.   At common law the period is twenty years.   In
many states it is ten.   The matter is governed by statute in all jurisdictions at present.

(25)   There are similar statutes in Nebraska and Oregon, Utah and
Wyoming.

from abandonment. If an appropriator has, in fact, abandoned his right, it would not matter for how long a time he had ceased to use the water, for the moment that the abandonment itself was complete his rights would cease and determine. Upon the other hand, he may have leased his property, and paid taxes thereon, thus negativing the idea of abandonment, as in this case, and yet may have failed for many years to make any beneficial use of the water he has appropriated. The question presented, therefore, is not one of abandonment, but one of non-user merely, and as such involves a construction of section 1411 of the Civil Code. That section, as has been said, makes a cessation of use by the appropriator work a forfeiture of his right, and the question for determination is: How long may this non-user continue before the right lapses? Upon this point the legislature has made no specific declaration; but, by analogy, we hold that a continuous non-user for five years will forfeit the right. The right to use the water ceasing at that time, the rights of way for ditches and the like, which are incidental to the primary right of use, would fall also. . . . In this state five years is the period fixed by law for the ripening of an adverse possession into a prescriptive title. Five years is also the period declared by law after which a prescriptive right depending upon enjoyment is lost for non-user; and for analogous reasons we consider it to be a just and proper measure of time for the forfeiture of an appropriator's rights for failure to use the water for a beneficial purpose'' (26).

---

(26) See also accordingly Smith v. Logan, 18 Nev. 149; People v. Farmers' Reservoir Co., 25 Col. 202; Farmers Co. v. Frank, 72 Neb. 136.

In Utah the statute expressly fixes the period of forfeiture for non-user at seven years. Wyoming, by statute, makes the period two years. The Kansas statute provides that any failure to apply the water continuously without reasonable cause shall be taken as an abandonment. Montana, by statute, makes non-user a mere matter of abandonment and provides that its effect shall be a question of fact. The courts hold that all statutes of this nature apply only to voluntary non-user (27). The foregoing doctrines flow from the doctrines of the possessory system. If in accord with the present tendency in water law actual use at the time of controversy is made the sole measure of the rights of the parties, it would seem that an appropriation ought to be lost wholly or partially by non-user for an unreasonable time. In such a view the statutes above referred to should be construed as simply fixing a maximum period of non-use and, if no period is fixed, instead of the court fixing an arbitrary period by the statute of limitation, it would seem that it ought to adopt the common-law view that where no time is fixed, a reasonable time is meant. It is likely that the development of the law in the future on this subject will be in this direction.

---

(27)   Morris v. Bean, 146 Fed. 423.

APPENDIX A

HISTORY OF REAL PROPERTY LAW.

§ 2. How freely could land be sold or left by will under the early Anglo-Saxon law?

§ 4. What effect did the Norman Conquest have upon the general system of land tenure in England?

§ 8. What were the chief incidents of knight service tenure and what was the extent of these various incidents?

§ 10. When and how were military tenures abolished in England?

§ 12. Are there any feudal tenures in the United States?

§ 14. John Dale holding land in fee simple under his overlord conveyed it in fee simple to William Doe. What would be the difference in Doe's tenure according as this conveyance was made before or after the statute of Quia Emptores (1290)?

§ 15. What was the original effect of a grant of land to "John Doe and his heirs" as regards the rights of the heirs?

§ 16. How was this grant later construed by the courts?

§§ 17 to 20. What was the effect of the Statute De Donis (1285) upon the common law estate known as a fee simple conditional?

§ 21. Describe the means that were finally sanctioned by the courts to enable a tenant who held an entailed estate to bar the entail and convey a fee simple.

§ 23. Abbott owned a piece of land and conveyed it to Jones in fee simple but with a condition that if Jones ever attempted to convey it away the land should revert to Abbott. Is this condition valid?

§ 27. For how many years is it possible to limit the alienation of lands by the creation of future contingent or conditional estates?

§ 28. Explain the feudal conception of the difference between an estate of freehold and an estate less than freehold?

§ 29. Hale leased a farm to Doe for 30 years. Hale then sold the land to Dale and Dale wrongfully ejected Doe. Before the year 1225 what remedies, if any, had Doe?

417

After that date what remedy did he have?

§ 30. What remedy did he have before 1370 if ejected by Yoe, a stranger?

What remedy did he have after 1371?

When did it first become possible for the wrongfully ejected tenant to recover his land?

How did the courts come to give him this right?

§ 31. How was the position of the tenant further strengthened in the 16th century?

§ 33. Describe the method of conveying land by livery of seisin?

§ 35. Give the reasons for the origin and growth of the doctrine of uses in lands.

§ 36. What were the advantages of holding the use of land instead of the actual legal title thereto?

§ 37. State the substance of the Statute of Uses (1535).

§ 39. What effect did this statute have upon conveyancing?

§ 40. Describe the method of conveying land by each of the following conveyances:

1. A bargain and sale.

2. A covenant to stand seized.

3. A lease and release.

APPENDIX B

TRANSFER OF TITLE TO REAL ESTATE.

§ 3. Hare leased a house to Dix for five years. When the lease had still two years to run Hare and Dix had a quarrel and Dix went to Hare and gave him the keys of the house and said he was going to quit. Hare took the keys and said he was glad to get through with any business with a man like Dix. Dix thereupon moved out. Later Hare attempted to hold him for the rent for the balance of the lease. A statute in the state provides that no surrender of a lease shall be valid unless in writing. Has Dix a defense?

§ 4. What, if any, interests in land may be created without a written instrument?

§ 7. Is it necessary, in order to pass title in fee simple, that the transfer should be by an instrument under seal?

§§ 8, 9. John Doe died and by his will left two pieces of land as follows: He left the first piece to James Fox for life and on his death to Will Todd in fee simple; he left the second piece to Fox for life and if he died without any sons to Todd in fee simple. Todd conveyed to Hale all his interest under Doe's will. Assuming that Fox dies leaving no sons, what are Hale's rights in the two tracts?

§ 10. What is the difference between a "warranty deed", a "special warranty deed", and a "quit claim deed"?

§ 10a. What are the essential parts of a deed?

§ 11a. Luce owned a farm. He executed a deed of part of it to Roe. The land was described thus: Beginning at the north-east corner of my dwelling house, and thence running in a northeasterly direction 500 feet to the corner of the stone wall; thence West 1000 feet to the southeast corner of John Guy's land; thence due South to the point of beginning containing 12 acres." The distance from the corner of the stone wall to the Southeast corner of Guy's land was 1700 feet; and from that point to the point of beginning was not due South but East-South-East, and the total area embraced by a line extending to the Southeast corner of Guy's farm, then back to the point of beginning was 18 acres. Luce claimed that all Roe was entitled to was to measure off from the corner of the stone wall 1000 feet in the direction of the Southeast corner of the Guy land and then go about

419

South to the point of the beginning which would give about **11 acres.** Roe claimed that he was entitled to the larger tract. Which was right?

§ 12. Vale gave a deed of land to Ball; part of the description was as follows: "Northwest to the Clear creek; thence along the shore of the creek in a Southerly direction 1000 feet; thence East 500 feet." Suppose that Vale had owned to the center of the creek and that later on it entirely dried up. Who would own the strip between the former shore line and the centre of the creek, Vale or Ball?

§ 13. A conveys to B "that portion of my land in section 20 described as follows: Beginning at the Northeast corner of said section, thence East 87 rods to a large wild-cherry tree, thence South, etc." The only wild-cherry tree in the section is 97 rods East of the corner. Who owns the ten rods immediately West of the wild-cherry tree?

§ 16. Into what classes and subclassses are estates in real property commonly divided?

Is an estate for 999 years an estate of freehold?

§§ 17, 18. What is the difference between a fee simple and a fee tail?

§ 20. What is the difference between a fee tail general and a fee tail special?

§ 22. John Doe had the following clause in his will: "I devise the home farm from and after the death of my son Albert to all my heirs at law who shall then be alive." There was no other clause in the will affecting the home farm. Who was entitled to it during the life of Albert?

§ 25. Nale gave a deed of land to Nill that contained the following language: "I hereby convey the above described premises to Nill, his heirs and assigns——to have and to hold to the said Nill for his life." Did Nill have a fee simple or a life estate?

§ 26. A conveyance of land was made to Gay, Roe and Dane, as joint tenants. Dane sold his interest to Dix. Roe and Dix then both died, Roe devising all his property to Hare, and Dix devising all his property to Vale. Who were the owners of the land and in what proportion.

§§ 27, 28. Todd owned a wood lot and back of it a farm lot. There was a well defined and frequently used lane running from the farm lot over the wood lot to the highway. Todd sold the farm lot to Fox "together with all the appurtenances thereunto belonging," but not giving Fox in express language a right of way over the wood lot. May Fox continue to use the way if Todd objects? Would it make any difference if there was no other access to the farm lot?

§§ 29, 30. If in the last question Todd had kept the farm lot and conveyed the wood lot to Fox, could Todd have exercised the right of way over the wood lot, assuming that it was not a way of necessity?

Suppose Todd in the deed of the wood lot to Fox had expressly reserved a right of way for the farm lot over the wood lot, but the deed had been executed only by Todd, would Todd be entitled to the way?

§ 32. Which of the following estates are vested and which contingent?

A grant to Luce for life, then to the oldest living son of Hale in fee, Hale at the time having no son.

To Luce for life, then to Hale for life, then to Ball in fee.

To Luce for life, and if Dix shall during Luce's life pay him $1000, then on the termination of Luce's estate, to Dix in fee?

§ 37. What were the feudal objections to the creation of future estates in land?

§ 41. What effect did the statute of uses have upon the creation of future interests in land?

§ 45. Dole by his will left a farm "to John Todd for life, remainder to his heirs"; he left another farm "to James Luce for life, remainder to his children." What is the difference in the legal estates of Todd and Luce?

§ 46. Doe left his real estate to Hull for his life, and upon his death to such of Hull's children as should be 21 or over. Hull died two days before his oldest child became 21. What rights if any, has the child in the property?

§ 51. Dye conveyed a lot of city land to Dane, the deed containing the following clause: "Subject to the conditions that no flat building shall be erected on the land". Later Dane erected a flat building. Dye claimed that he had a right to regain the land because of breach of conditiion. Dane claimed that Dye's only right was to sue him for breach of contract. Which was correct?

§ 53. Dole devised land to "Nill for life and if Nill shall die without issue then to Todd in fee". What are the various possible interpretations of this clause?

§ 54. What interpretation has been affixed to it by statute?

§§ 55, 56. William Hare devised land "to my son, John Hare, for his life and on his death to all my grandchildren". At the time of William Hare's death John Hare had two children, James and Jane. John Hare's brother Fred was married but had no children. At John Hare's death he left three children, Jane, Arthur and Maud, James

APPENDIX B

having died. Fred Hare had at John's death a son Robert, and a year after John's death Fred had a daughter Lucy born. Who are entitled to share in the property left to John by William?

§ 60. What is the substance of the rule against perpetuities?

§ 61. Gray devised land as follows: "To my son Arthur for his life, on his death to his wife, if he should marry and if she should survive him, and on the death of the survivors to their children in fee. Is this devise in violation of the rule against perpetuities?

§ 65. Dye conveyed land to Hale. The deed contained this clause: "Subject to the condition that if the land shall be used as a race track that the title of the said Hale shall be forfeited". Is this condition in violation of the rule against perpetuities?

§ 66. Hill granted land to Doe in fee simple with a condition that if Doe attempted to convey it his estate should be forfeited. Is this clause valid?

§ 67. Would the result be otherwise if the conveyance to Doe had been for his life?

§§ 71, 72. Mill by his will left all his property to Dix as trustee for the benefit of Mill's three children, the share of each child to be paid him when he attained 25. May a child on reaching 21 compel the trustee to pay him his share of the estate?

§ 74. What is the difference in the principles of construction applicable to contracts and those applicable to wills?

§ 95. What are the various modern convenants of title and what is the general scope of each?

Is it always necessary today to incorporate them at length in a deed?

§ 96. What is meant by the doctrine that "convenants of title run with the land"?

§ 97. Abbott conveyed a piece of land to Bates and convenanted that it was free from incumbrances. In fact Dane held a mortgage on the land. Bates conveyed to Luce, who conveyed to Hill. Dane then foreclosed the mortgage. Who is entitled to bring action on the covenant against Abbott?

§ 98. Gray conveyed a piece of land to Dodd and covenanted that he should enjoy quiet possession of the land. In fact Gray had no title at all to the land. Dodd sold to Cox who was put out by Luce, the rightful owner. May Cox enforce the covenant against Gray?

§ 99. Suppose in the last case that Gray had died before Luce had retaken the land. Who, if anyone, would be liable on the covenant when broken?

§§ 100, 101. Dill executed to Hall a deed of a certain piece of land, the deed containing the usual covenants of title. In fact the land was at that time owned by Yoe. After the conveyance by Dill to Hall, Dill bought Yoe's title to the land. Hall then attempted to take possession of the land and found it occupied by Fox. He brought ejectment against Fox. Should the judgment be given in his favor?

§ 104. John Doe was going to make a gift of one of his farms to his son Richard. He drew up, signed, sealed and acknowledged the deed and then gave it to his son Richard and said "take this down to the office of Hill, my lawyer, and ask him to keep it for me." Richard did so and Hill took and kept the deed. Six months later John Doe died insolvent and his creditors sought to sell the farm in question as being his property. Can Richard successfully assert a title to it under the deed?

§ 106. Mill agreed to sell Hare his house and lot. Mill executed a deed to Hare and delivered it to Dane with instructions to turn it over to Hare when the latter paid the purchase price. Dane in violation of his instructions delivered it to Hare before the latter paid. Hare recorded the deed and then sold the premises to Gray, who paid full value and bought in good faith. Hare absconded without paying Mill. Mill seeks to recover the land from Gray. May he do so?

§ 108. What would have been the result in the last case if Mill had delivered the deed directly to Hare, but with the understanding between them that it was not to become effective until Hare had paid the purchase price, and Hare had then sold to Gray as before?

§ 109. What are the more important differences between the various kinds of recording acts?

§ 110. Dale agreed to sell a tract of land to Hill, who recorded his contract. Dale then sold the land to Chase and gave him a deed to it, which Chase recorded. Chase paid full value and did not know of Hill's prior contract. Dale then gave a deed to Hill. Which one is entitled to the land?

§ 117. Fox sold his farm to Dill for $7000 and gave him a deed for it. Dill did not record his deed. Roe knew of Dill's deed and that it was not recorded, and went to Fox and offered him $1000 for a deed of his farm, which Fox gave him. Roe at once recorded his deed. Dill having found out what Roe had done, then had his deed recorded. A week subsequent to Dill's record, Roe gave a deed of the farm to Luce for $5000, Luce being in ignorance of Dill's deed. As between Luce and Dill, who is entitled to the farm?

§§ 120, 121. What are the weaknesses of the ordinary system of recording titles to land?

§§ 124, 125. What are the results sought by the Torrens system of Registration, and what are the steps taken to bring about these results?

§ 128. Is the likelihood of the rightful owner of land being wrongly deprived of his title thereto greater under the Torrens system of registration than under the older system?

§§ 129, 132. Mention the more important general advantages of the Torrens system of registration.

§ 133. May the title to land of a criminal be forfeited as a punishment for his crime?

§ 137. What were the conditions under which, at common law, the right to dower or curtesy arose?

§ 139. What are the rights of husband and wife in "community property"?

§ 145. Allen was the owner of a tract of land. In 1880, Dale took possession of the land and held it as his own for over 20 years, which was the term of the statute of limitations. In 1903, Allen peaceably regained possession of the land, and Dale then brought ejectment against him. For whom should judgment be given?

§ 147. Hill leased a piece of land to Dix. After Dix had been in possession for a while he wrote Hill that he (Dix) did not believe that Hill had any title to the land and that he intended to claim it and hold it as his own. Hill took no steps to forfeit Dix's lease. This state of affairs went on for 20 years (the statutory period) and shortly after the 20 years were up, Hill brought action against Dix to have his lease forfeited and to regain the land to which he had originally a clear title. May Dix successfully set up the Statute of Limitations as a defense?

§ 153. Hill got a deed from Dye to a tract of 500 acres, about 100 acres farm land, 200 acres pasture, 100 acres woodland and the rest useless swamp land. There was a farm house and barn on it, but most of it was unfenced. Hill occupied the farm and used about 25 acres of farm land and 50 of pasture land for more than the statutory period. If then sued in ejectment by Roe, the rightful owner, how much may he successfully claim by adverse possession?

§ 154. Would it make any difference in the last case if the 500 acres had been divided by a creek, with the farm and pasture land on one side, and the wood and marsh land on the other?

§ § 158, 160. What would be the result, if, after Hill had kept the property 15 years, he had given a deed of the whole property to Gray, who had kept it for the balance of the statutory period and had then been sued?

§ 161. What is the difference in the nature of the rights that may be acquired by adverse possession and those that may be acquired by prescription?

§ 166. Gray and Dane had adjoining farms. Dane began to drive down a lane over Gray's farm and told Gray that he was going to keep on doing it. Gray said: "All right, go ahead, it won't do any harm." Is this enough to prevent Dane's user from being adverse?

§ 169. May one land owner acquire by prescription a right to free and uninterrupted light and air from his neighbor's lot?

APPENDIX C

MORTGAGES.

§1. Under the old common law what were the rights of a mortgagor who failed to repay the mortgage debt on the day it was due?

§2. In what way were the common law conceptions of the rights of the mortgagor and the mortgagee modified in equity:

(1) With regard to the right of the mortgagor to redeem the land from the mortgage debt?

(2) With regard to the right to the possession of the land during the period when the debt was unpaid?

(3) With regard to the right to the rents and profits of the land during the period when the debt was unpaid?

§3. What are the differences in legal theory between the view that a mortgagee has title to the land and the view that he has only a lien thereon?

What are the differences, if any, between the two views in practical results?

§4. Vale executed a mortgage of his land to Mill; the mortgage in addition to the usual clauses had this proviso: "The said mortgagor hereby waives any right of redemption beyond the period given by this mortgage deed." A statute allowed the mortgagor to redeem within 6 months after the debt fell due. Vale failed to pay the mortgage in the time fixed in the deed, but within three months thereafter tendered Mill the amount of the debt with interest. Mill contended that the tender was too late because of the proviso in the deed. Is his contention sound?

§5. Assume on the facts of the last case that three weeks after the execution of the mortgage Vale agreed with Mill in consideration of $25 cash to convey to Mill his equity of redemption at any time that Mill should offer him $500 therefor. Could this contract be enforced against Vale?

Would it make any difference that $500 was a fair price for the equity of redemption?

426

Would it make any difference if Vale, instead of agreeing to sell the equity to Mill, had made a present sale of it to him for $500?

§ 6. Mention some of the more common interests in land that may be mortgaged.

§ 77. Todd executed to Dane a mortgage of a certain piece of land. At the time of the mortgage Todd owned only half of the land. He later bought the other half and also erected a barn on the part he had owned at the time of the execution of the mortgage. He then sold the whole farm with all improvements to Hill, who paid value, but knew of the Dane mortgage. May Dane enforce his mortgage, (1) as against the part of the farm bought subsequent to the execution of the mortgage; (2) as against the barn?

Would it effect the result if Hill had bought without knowing of the mortgage?

§ 10. Fox executed a deed of his house and lot to Luce for $1200. The place was worth about $2000. At the same time and as part of the transaction Luce wrote Fox a letter whereby he gave Fox a legally binding option to buy the place back at any time in the next 18 months for $1500. Fox did not buy back in the next 18 months, but two years after the deed he brought proceedings to have the deed declared a mortgage and to be given the right to redeem on paying $1200 with interest and costs. The evidence given by Fox and Luce was just evenly balanced as to whether the transaction was really a sale with an 18 months' option or a mortgage. Should the Court decree in favor of Fox or Luce?

§ 13. Hare loaned Doe $3000 and took a mortgage on Doe's farm. Ball later loaned Doe $2000 more and took a second mortgage on the farm. Hare then loaned Doe $1000 more. The farm was then sold by agreement of Hare and Ball to satisfy the mortgages, and brought $4500. What are the respective rights of Hare and Ball in the money?

§§ 19, 21. Guy executed to Hale a three year mortgage of his land in a state in which the title theory of a mortgage prevails. Guy then gave a lease of the land to Dix at $20 a month. Six months later Hale served notice on Dix that he held a mortgage on the land and ordered Dix to pay the rent to him (Hale). As between Guy and Hale who is entitled to the rents, (a) already accrued; (b) to accrue?

Would it make any difference if Guy was insolvent and the land not worth the amount of the mortgage debt?

§ 20. Suppose that on the facts of the last case Hale had taken possession, letting Dix stay in as his tenant and had collected the rents, but Guy later paid off the mortgage debt. Could Guy have compelled Hale to account to him for the rents received from Dix?

§§ 23, 24. Hull mortgaged his house and lot for $2000 to Dye, who took possession. While in possession Dye expended the following sums:

$1000 to pay off an earlier mortgage to Luce,
$150 for painting the house,
$100 for setting out new shrubbery around the house,
$775 for a special assessment for a sewer.

Which, if any, of these sums must Hull repay to Dye in addition to the amount of the mortgage before he is entitled to have the mortgage discharged?

§ 26. If the mortgagor remains in the possession of the premises and attempts to cut down and sell a large forest of trees, forming the most valuable part of the premises, what relief has the mortgagee?

What are the rights of the mortgagee as to trees already cut (1) in a "lien theory" state, (2) in a "title theory" state?

§§ 30, 31. Gale mortgaged a tract of 1000 acres to Dale to secure a debt of $3000. Gale then sold 300 acres of the tract to Foss; he later sold 400 acres more to Hill; after that he sold the balance to Roe. What are the respective rights of Dale against Foss, Hill, Roe and Gale, and what are their respective rights against each other?

How would it affect the case if Hill had agreed with Gale to assume the mortgage debt?

§ 34. Todd held a $6000 mortgage on Hare's land, the debt being in the shape of four promissory notes of $1500 each. Todd endorsed one of the notes to Roe and another to Dix. Hare then paid the two held by Todd, and Todd released the mortgage. What are the rights of Roe and Dix against Hare?

§ 39. Guy had a mortgage for $2000 on Mill's land. Mill did not pay the mortgage when due, but three months later paid Guy in full. Is it necessary that Guy should give Mill a deed back of the land to make his title clear?

Suppose that Guy refused to perform the necessary steps to release the mortgage, what redress has Mill?

§ 45. Doe owned two tracts of land, one tract worth $5000, the other $2000. He owed Vale $4000 and to secure him gave him a mortgage on both pieces. Later, to secure a debt which he owed Roe, he gave him a $1500 mortgage on the first piece. Vale then foreclosed his mortgage on the first piece, which was sold for $4500. Roe's claim being due and unpaid, what are his rights against Vale?

§ 49. Ball executed to Todd his note for $1000 June 1, 1900, and secured by a mortgage on Ball's house and lot. The note was not paid. Todd did nothing until 1910, when he attempted to foreclose the mortgage. The statute of limitations in the state was five years for actions on promissory notes and fifteen years for actions for the recovery of land. May Todd maintain his action to foreclose?

§ 56. Suppose in the last case, that in 1902 Todd had transferred Ball's note to Cox, but no mention had been made of the mortgage. If the note was still unpaid in 1910, who would have a right to foreclose the mortgage?

§ 62. What is the difference between a pledge and a chattel mortgage?

§§ 65, 66. Bates owned a tract of land on which was a sawmill. He bought from Gill a boiler and engine, gave him a chattel mortgage back for the purchase price and then built them into the sawmill. Some time before this, Bates had given Gray a mortgage on the land and mill. Two years later Bates became insolvent, both Gray and Gill being unpaid; and each claiming the boiler and engine under his mortgage. Which had the better right thereto?

Who would have had the better right thereto if the real mortgage to Gray had been executed after the boiler and the engine had been annexed to the sawmill?

§§ 72, 73. Dale mortgaged to Hill his horse and buggy, but Dale still kept possession of them. The mortgage was not recorded, although there was the usual chattel mortgage act in the state. Later Hill found that Roe, a creditor of Dale, was about to attach the horse and buggy as Dale's property, and compelled Dale to give him (Hill) possession. Is this enough to make the mortgage good as against Roe?

APPENDIX D

MINING LAW.

§ 2. State the origin of mining law in the United States.

§§ 4, 5. Suppose a claim is made and a mine opened in a mining district in which there are mining rules, and these rules are disregarded, is the claim thereby forfeited?

§ 8. Into what classes are mining claims divided and what is the difference between them?

§ 10. Abbott took up a claim on mineral-bearing land belonging to the United States. On working the vein it was discovered to contain lead, but in such slight quantity that it was not worth while to work the mine. He then began to use the land for agricultural purposes. Did he thereby forfeit his claim?

§ 12. Jones discovered a lode, claimed it and worked it for a while, and finally gave it up. Stone then located the same lode in the place where Jones had uncovered it by his workings, and claimed it. Jones then reappeared and contested Stone's claim on the ground that it was not a discovery on ''unappropriated land,'' as required by statute. Who is entitled to the claim, Jones or Stone?

§ 13. Brown was in possession of a piece of land and searching for a lode, but had not yet discovered one. Jones forcibly ejected him from the land and found thereon the lode, which he then claimed. Brown then also put in a claim for the same lode. Which is entitled thereto?

§ 15. John Schmidt, not a citizen of the United States, located a vein and filed his claim thereto in due form; Gray, a citizen, then filed his claim for the same vein and brought suit to obtain possession, on the ground that Schmidt being an alien, his claim was invalid. For whom should judgment be given?

Would the result be different if the action were brought by the United States government?

§ 17. What are the acts more commonly required to be done to perfect a lode mining location?

§ 18. If the location is to be marked by the sinking of a discovery shaft, what are the requirements as to the size and location thereof?

§ 22. Where the location is to be marked by posts, what are the requirements as to the location and number thereof?

§ 24. What should be stated in the notice posted on the claim?

§ 27. Is it sufficient to justify the location of a placer claim that the locator has discovered traces of mineral-bearing soil?

§§ 28, 33. What are the requirements for the legal location of a placer claim?

§ 34. Walker filed an application for a placer claim which had been duly located by him. At that time there was within the limits of the placer claim (1) a vein of valuable silver-bearing ore, which was not known to Walker, but which he could have discovered by a reasonably careful inspection of the land; (2) another vein of silver ore of which he knew and which he claimed in his placer claim; (3) a hidden vein which was subsequently disclosed by one Abbott, who was on the land by Walker's permission; (4) a hidden vein which pending the issuance of the patent to Walker was discovered by one Hill, who came on the land against Walker's objection, to prospect. Walker got his patent and claimed all 4 veins. Abbott filed claims for 1, 2 and 3, and Hill filed a claim for 4. What judgment in each case?

§ 35. May land acquired under Rev. Stat. U. S. Sec. 2337 for a mill site for use with a lode to which it is not contiguous be used for any other than mill purposes?

§ 36. What are the requirements that must be complied with to properly locate a tunnel site?

§§ 38, 39. Brown ran a tunnel and met a blind vien which he proceeded to work. He did not make a surface location nor seek a patent as a mining claim. Does his failure to do this forfeit his right to the blind vein?

§ 43. Field located a claim on April 15th, 1890. He did no more work on the claim until August, 1891, when he did $150 worth of work. He did no more work until December, 1892, when he did $60 worth of work ending December 31, 1892. What is the earliest date at which his claim could be relocated by another on the ground of failure to perform assessment work?

§ 44. Mahon had a mining claim on an exposed vein in which he had sunk a shaft. He then decided to run a tunnel, and during the year the only work he did was $125 worth on the tunnel. This did not even reach the vein. Is this enough work to keep his claim alive?

Would it make any difference that the tunnel was so poorly located that it would be practically useless even if it reached the lode?

§§ 46, 47. Which of the following items will be allowed to be counted in making up $100 of annual labor and expenses to be performed on a claim in order to preserve it?

(1) The meals furnished the miners doing the work.

(2) Labor in getting out pieces of ore for assaying in the hope of finding pay ore.

(3) Building a wagon road to the claim.

(4) Building a flume over the claim to another claim.

(5) The value of the blankets furnished the miners.

(6) The value of the drills and powder used in drilling and blasting.

(7) Ten days' labor on claim under a district rule that labor to preserve a claim should be valued a. $10 a day.

(8) Work done during the year by the person from whom the present owner purchased.

§ 49. Nolan located a claim and took the proper steps to justify him in applying for a patent, which he then did on Jan. 1, 1903. In August, 1903, he received word that his claim had been allowed and that the patent would be issued. He did no work on his claim in 1903. In February, 1904, he was notified that his entry had been cancelled. The next day Rowe relocated the claim on the ground that Nolan had lost it by failure to perform $100 worth of labor in 1903. Who is entitled to the claim?

§ 50. Brown, Todd and Davis staked a claim as co-owners. In 1901 Brown did $150 worth of work; Todd did $35 worth of work and Davis none. What are the rights of Brown and Todd against Davis; of Brown against Todd?

§ 52. Lane had a claim, but during the year 1905 he did no work on it. In March, 1906, hearing that Gould was about to relocate it, Lane did $10 or $15 worth of work on the claim and notified Gould that he would do enough during the year to hold it. In September, Lane having done no more work, Gould went on the claim, relocated it, and did $150 worth of permanent work. Who is entitled to the claim?

§ 53. Suppose in the last case that after Gould had relocated the claim and done his $150 worth of work, Lane had also in good faith done $200 worth of work, who would be entitled to the claim?

§ 56. Jones having a claim properly located and worked, changed the boundaries and the name of the claim so as to embrace somewhat more ground. Is it necessary for him to sink a new discovery shaft or deepen the old one in order to hold the altered claim?

§§ 58, 60. What are the steps that must be taken in order to receive a patent to a lode claim after the necessary amount of work has been done?

§ 74. What are the requirements for making an entry on coal lands of the U. S.?

§ 77. What are the requirements for making an entry on timber lands?

APPENDIX E

IRRIGATION LAW.

§ 3. Allen and Bates own land abutting on a small stream in a state governed by the common law, Allen living higher up the stream. In getting water for his house and his horse and cow, he practically exhausts the stream so that Bates does not have enough for his house. Has Bates a cause of action against Allen?

Within the common law meaning of the term, is a user of water for irrigation purposes a "natural" or an "artificial" user?

§ 6. In what respect do the Roman law and the modern civil law differ as to the right of the owner of a private stream with respect to the water thereof?

§ 8. What is the origin of the modern law of irrigation?

§ 9. What is the essential difference in the view of the common law and irrigation law as to individual rights in flowing water?

§§ 10, 11. Into what three groups may the states in which irrigation law is in force to a greater or smaller degree be divided?

§ 15. Olsen and Todd were living in a state in which the common law of water is in force on private lands, but the theory of appropriation of water prevails on public lands. Olsen and Todd were using water from a creek on the public land, Todd having begun to use first. Olsen obtained a patent for a tract of land on the creek, including the part where Todd has his irrigation ditch. Olsen then put in a new ditch higher up, on his own land, and withdrew so much water that Todd could not get his former amount. Has Todd a right of action against Olsen?

§ 16. How would it affect the result of the last case if Olsen had obtained his patent first and then Todd had tried to appropriate the water for irrigation?

434

§ **18.** Dale had a patent to land bordering on a stream. Hatch claimed the right to withdraw water from the stream for irrigation purposes because of a prior appropriation thereof. Dale denied his right on the grounds (1) that the creek flowed only during certain portions of the year; (2) that at parts of its course it lost its defined channel and spread out into a mere marsh. Is Dale's claim sound on either ground?

§ **19.** Suppose the water mentioned in the last case had been nothing but a marsh of standing water, could Hatch have legally claimed it by virtue of a prior appropriation?

§§ **24. 25.** Fales desired to appropriate water from a creek. On March 1, 1896, he duly recorded a notice, stating the location of his ditch and the amount of water he proposed to use; on March 10, 1896, Gould who had no actual knowledge of Fales' notice, started a ditch which he completed and began to use by April 1, of the same year. He did not record his notice. On April 5th, of the same year, Hale who also had no actual knowledge of Fales' notice, began a ditch which he finished and began to use by April 25th. On the 15th of the same month Fales began his ditch and started to use it on May 15th. There was not sufficient water to supply all three ditches. In what order should the rights be fixed?

§ **26.** Suppose in the above case that after Fales had filed his notice as stated, he did not begin work on his ditch until May, 1897, being delayed because of ill-health and lack of money. How would this affect his rights?

§ **30.** Rolfe first appropriated water from a stream; later Smith appropriated the rest of the stream, his ditch being below Rolfe's. Later, Rolfe decided it would be easier to put in his ditch lower down the stream, so he closed the old intake and opened a new one below Smith. Smith now being above, increased his intake so that Rolfe could not get the former amount. Has he a cause of action against Smith?

§ **32.** Would it make any difference in the last case if Rolfe at the time of changing the intake and ditch had taken and used the water to irrigate land other than that which he originally irrigated?

§ **33.** White and Young had both appropriated water from a creek, White having done so first. Generally the stream supplied enough for both, but in dry seasons the supply was inadequate. White claimed that he was still entitled to take out his full amount and that Young could have only the residue. Young claimed they ought to divide the limited amount in proportion to the amount each took from the full stream. Who was right?

§ 35. Fox was the first appropriator of water and Gould the second. Fox found that he had claimed and was drawing off more than he needed, so he sold his surplus to Smith. Gould claimed he ought to return it to the stream. Which was right?

§ 37. Suppose in the above case that Fox's ditch was improperly made and that a large amount of water escaped. Could Gould compel him to repair it?

§ 41. Kline owned a tract of land, irrigated by water from a distant stream. He sold the tract to Hill, but the deed did not mention the ditch or water rights. Who is entitled to them, Kline or Hill?

APPENDIX F

Warranty Deed, with Full Covenants (Common Law Form).

THIS INDENTURE, Made this .... day of ...., in the year One Thousand Nine Hundred and ...., between A. B., of ...., in the County of ...., and State of ...., [and C. B., his wife], party of the first part, and Y. Z., of the same place, party of the second part,

WITNESSETH: That the said party [or, parties] of the first part, for and in consideration of the sum of .... dollars, lawful money of the United States, to him [or, them] paid by the said party of the second part, at or before the ensealing and delivery of these presents, the receipt whereof is hereby acknowledged, and the said party of the second part, his heirs, executors, and administrators forever released and discharged from the same by these presents, has [or, have] granted, bargained, sold, aliened, remised, released, conveyed, and confirmed, and, by these presents, does [or, do] grant, bargain, sell, alien, remise, release, convey, and confirm unto the said party of the second part, and to his heirs and assigns forever, all [here insert description]; together with all and singular the tenements, hereditaments, and appurtenances thereunto belonging, or in anywise appertaining, and the reversion and reversions, remainder and remainders, rents, issues, and profits thereof; and also all of the estate, right, title, interest [dower and right of dower], property, possession, claim, and demand whatsoever, both in law and equity, of the said party [or, parties] of the first part, of, in, and to the above-granted premises, and every part and parcel thereof, with the appurtenances:

TO HAVE AND TO HOLD all and singular the above-granted premises, together with the appurtenances and every part thereof, unto the said party of the second part, his heirs and assigns forever. [If there is any incumbrance state it thus: subject, however, to a certain indenture of mortgage for .... dollars, dated ...., 19..., and recorded in the office of ...., in liber .... of Mortgages, at page ...., and also subject, etc.]

AND THE SAID A. B. [*not naming the wife*], for himself, his heirs, executors, and administrators, does hereby covenant, promise, and agree to and with the said party of the second part, his heirs and assigns, that the said A. B., at the time of the sealing and delivery of these presents, is lawfully seized in his own right [*or otherwise, as the case may be*], of a good, absolute, and indefeasible estate of inheritance, in fee simple, of and in all and singular the above-granted and described premises, with the appurtenances [*if conveyed subject to incumbrance, say*, subject as aforesaid]; and has good right, full power, and lawful authority to grant, bargain, sell, and convey the same, in manner aforesaid. And that the said party of the second part, his heirs and assigns, shall and may at all times hereafter peaceably and quietly have, hold, use, occupy, possess, and enjoy the above-granted premises, and every part and parcel thereof, with the appurtenances, without any let, suit, trouble, molestation, eviction, or disturbance of the said party [*or,* parties] of the first part, his [*or,* their] heirs or assigns, or of any other person or persons lawfully claiming or to claim the same; and that the same now are free, clear, discharged, and unincumbered of and from all former and other grants, title, charges, estates, judgments, taxes, assessments, and incumbrances, of what nature or kind soever [*if conveyed, subject to an incumbrance, say*, except as aforesaid].

AND ALSO That the said party [*or,* parties] of the first part, and his [*or,* their] heirs, and all and every other person or persons whomsoever, lawfully or equitably deriving any estate, right, title, or interest, of, in, or to the above-granted premises, by, from, under, or in trust for him [*or,* them], shall and will at any time or times hereafter, upon the reasonable request, and at the proper costs and charges in the law, of the said party of the second part, his heirs and assigns, make, do, and execute, or cause or procure to be made, done, and executed, all and every such further and other lawful and reasonable acts, conveyances, and assurances in the law, for the better and more effectually vesting and confirming the premises hereby granted or intended so to be in and to the said party of the second part, his heirs and assigns forever, as by the said party of the second part, his heirs, or assigns, or his or their counsel learned in the law, shall be reasonably devised, advised, or required. And the said A. B. [*not naming wife*] and his heirs, the above-described and hereby granted and released premises, and every part and parcel thereof, with the appurtenances, unto the said party of the second part, his heirs and assigns, against the said party [*or,* parties] of the first part and his [*or,* their] heirs, and

against all and every person and persons whomsoever, lawfully claiming or to claim the same, shall and will warrant, and, by these presents,
forever defend.

IN WITNESS WHEREOF, the said party [or, parties] of the first part
has [or have] hereunto set his hand and seal [or, their hands and
seals], the day and year first above written. [*Signatures and seals.*]

Signed, sealed, and delivered in presence of [*Signature of witness.*]

Quitclaim Deed (Common Law Form).

KNOW ALL MEN BY THESE PRESENTS, that I, A. B., of the city of
.........., in the county of ...., and state of ....,
farmer [*or, we A. B., of, etc., as above,* and C. B., his wife], in consideration of .... dollars to me [*or, us*] paid by Y. Z., of
.........., the receipt whereof is hereby acknowledged, have remised,
released, and forever quit-claimed, and by these presents do, for my-
self, my [*or ourselves, our*] heirs, executors, and administrators, remise, release, and forever quit-claim unto the said Y. Z., his heirs and
assigns forever, all such right, title, interest [dower and right of
dower], property, possession, claim or demand, as I [*or, as we, or
either of us*] have or ought to have, in or to all [*here insert description
of premises*], together with all and singular the tenements, hereditaments, and appurtenances thereto belonging, or in anywise appertaining, and the reversion and reversions, remainder and remainders, rents,
issues, and profits thereof, and also all of the estate, right, title,
interest, claim, and demand whatsoever, as well in law as in equity of
the said party [*or, parties*] of the first part, of, in and to the above
granted premises, and every part and parcel thereof.

TO HAVE AND TO HOLD the said premises unto the said Y. Z., his
heirs and assigns, to his and their only proper use and behoof forever; so that neither I, the said A. B., nor any other person in my
name and behalf [*or, we, the said A. B. and C. B., or either of us, or
any other person in our or either of our names and behalf*] shall or
will hereafter claim or demand any right or title to the premises, or
any part thereof; but they, and every of them, shall by these presents
be excluded and forever barred.

IN WITNESS WHEREOF, I [*or, we*] have hereunto set my hand and
seal [*or, our hands and seals*], this .... day of ...., in
the year one thousand nine hundred and .... [*Signatures and
seals of grantors.*]

Signed, sealed, and delivered in the presence of
[*Signature of witness.*]

Statutory Warranty Deed with Covenant (Illinois Form).

The grantor, A. B., of ...., and state of ...., for and in consideration of .... dollars, in hand paid, conveys and warrants to Y. Z., the following described real estate [*description*]; situated in the county of ...., in the state of Illinois.

Dated the .... day of ...., 19....

A. B. [*Seal.*]

Statutory Quitclaim Deed (Illinois Form).

The grantor, A. B., of ...., in the county of ...., and state of ...., for and in consideration of .... dollars, conveys and quit-claims to Y. Z., of ...., in the county of ...., and state of ...., all interest in the following described real estate [*here insert description*], situated in the county of ...., in the state of Illinois.

Dated this .... day of ...., 19....

A. B. [*Seal.*]

APPENDIX G

Real Estate Mortgage.

THIS INDENTURE, Made this second day of October, in the year of our Lord One Thousand Nine Hundred and Nine, between Henry Holland, of the City of Chicago, in the County of Cook, and State of Illinois, party of the first part, and John Ellis, of the City of Chicago, in the County of Cook, and State of Illinois, party of the second part:

WHEREAS, The said party of the first part is justly indebted to the said party of the second part in the sum of Twelve Thousand ($12,000.00) Dollars, secured to be paid by two certain promissory notes, bearing even date herewith, for the sum of Six Thousand ($6,000.00) Dollars each, with interest at five (5) per cent per annum, payable to the order of the said party of the second part five years after date:

Now, THEREFORE, THIS INDENTURE WITNESSETH, That the said party of the first part, for the better securing the payment of the money aforesaid, with interest thereon according to the tenor and effect of the said promissory notes above mentioned, and also in consideration of the further sum of One Dollar to him in hand paid by the said party of the second part, at the delivery of these Presents, the receipt whereof is hereby acknowledged, has granted, bargained, sold, remised, released, conveyed, aliened and confirmed, and by these Presents does grant, bargain, sell, remise, release, convey, alien and confirm, unto the said party of the second part, and to his heirs and assigns forever, all the following described lot, piece, or parcel, of land, situate in the County of Cook, and State of Illinois, and known and described as follows, to-wit: Lot twenty-one (21) of Block two (2) of Watkins' Subdivision of Section twenty-eight (28), Township thirty-nine (39), Range fourteen (14), east of the Third Principal Meridian:

To HAVE AND TO HOLD THE SAME, Together with all and singular the tenements, hereditaments, privileges, and appurtenances thereunto belonging, or in any wise appertaining; and also, all the estate, interest, and claim whatsoever, in law as well as in equity, which the said party of the first part has in and to the premises hereby conveyed, unto the said party of the second part, his heirs and assigns, and to their only proper use, benefit, and behoof, forever;

PROVIDED ALWAYS, And these Presents are upon this express condition, that if the said party of the first part, his heirs, executors, or administrators, shall well and truly pay, or cause to be paid, to the said party of the second part, his heirs, executors, administrators, or assigns, the aforesaid sum of money, with interest thereon, at the time and in the manner specified in the above mentioned promissory notes, according to the true intent and meaning thereof, then and in that case these Presents, and everything herein expressed, shall be absolutely null and void.

AND The said party of the first part, for himself and his heirs, executors, and administrators, does hereby covenant and agree with the said party of the second part, that at the time of the delivery hereof, the said party of the first part, is the lawful owner of the premises above granted, and seized thereof, in fee simple absolute; that he will warrant and defend the above granted premises in the quiet and peaceable possession of the said party of the second part, his heirs and assigns forever, that they are free from all incumbrances whatsoever, and that the said party of the first part will, in due season, pay all taxes and assessments on said premises, until said indebtedness aforesaid shall be fully paid.

AND The said party of the first part does hereby expressly release and waive all rights, under and by virtue of the Homestead Exemption Laws of the State of Illinois, in and to said premises.

IN WITNESS WHEREOF, The said party of the first part has hereunto set his hand and seal the day and year first above written.

                        HENRY HOLLAND.   [Seal]

Signed, Sealed and Delivered
    in the presence of
            RALPH HENRY.

APPENDIX H

Trust Deed.

THIS INDENTURE WITNESSETH, That the Grantor, John Dale, of the City of Chicago, in the County of Cook, and State of Illinois, for and in consideration of the sum of Eight Thousand ($8,000.00) Dollars, in hand paid, conveys and warrants to Harry Jones, of the City of Chicago, County of Cook, and State of Illinois, the following described real estate, to-wit: Lot two (2) in Block twenty-one (21) in Charles H. Watkins' Subdivision of the City of Chicago, Section twenty-eight (28), Township thirty-nine (39), Range fourteen (14), east of the Third Principal Meridian, situated in the County of Cook, in the State of Illinois, hereby releasing and waiving all rights under and by virtue of the Homestead Exemption Laws of the State of Illinois and all right to retain possession of said premises after any default in payment or a breach of any of the covenants or agreements herein contained, in trust, nevertheless, for the following purposes:

WHEREAS, The said John Dale is justly indebted unto the legal holder of the principal promissory note hereinafter described, in the principal sum of Eight Thousand ($8,000.00) Dollars, being for a loan thereof, on the day of the date hereof, made to said John Dale, and secured to be paid by a certain principal promissory note of the said John Dale, bearing even date herewith, made to the order of Henry Cook for the principal sum aforesaid, payable four years after the date thereof, with interest thereon at the rate of Five (5) Per Cent per annum, payable semi-annually, to-wit: On the first day of January and of July in each year, and both principal and interest payable at the First National Bank in Chicago, aforesaid, which said several installments of interest for said period of four years are further evidenced by eight interest notes or coupons, of even date herewith, for the sum of Twenty ($20.00) Dollars each, the identity of said principal note being evidenced by the certificate thereon of said Trustee.

Now, If default be made in the payment of the said Promissory Notes, or of any part thereof, or the interest thereon, or any part thereof, at the time and in the manner above speci-

fied for the payment thereof, or in case of waste, or non-payment of taxes or assessments on said premises, or of a breach of
any of the covenants or agreements herein contained, then in such
case the whole of said principal sum and interest, secured by the
said Promissory Notes, shall thereupon, at the option of the legal
holder or holders thereof, become immediately due and payable;
and, on the application of the legal holder of said Promissory
Notes, or either of them, it shall be lawful for the said grantee,
or his successor in trust, to enter into and upon and take possession of the premises hereby granted, or any part thereof, and
to collect and receive all rents, issues and profits thereof; and, in
his own name or otherwise, to file a bill or bills in any court
having jurisdiction thereof against the said party of the first part,
his heirs, executors, administrators and assigns, to obtain a decree for the sale and conveyance of the whole or any part of said
premises for the purposes herein specified, by said party of the
second part, as such trustee or as special commissioner, or otherwise, under order of court, and out of the proceeds of any such
sale to first pay the costs of such suit, all costs of advertising,
sale and conveyance, including the reasonable fees and commissions
of said party of the second part, or person who may be appointed
to execute this trust, and Two Hundred ($200.00) Dollars attor-
neys' and solicitors' fees, and also all other expenses of this trust,
including all moneys advanced for insurance, taxes and other liens
or assessments, with interest thereon at seven per cent per annum, then to pay the principal of said notes, whether due and
payable by the terms thereof or the option of the legal holder
thereof, and interest due on said notes up to the time of such sale,
rendering the overplus, if any, unto the said party of the first
part, his legal representatives or assigns, on reasonable request,
and to pay any rents that may be collected after such sale and before the time of redemption expires, to the purchaser or purchasers of said premises at such sale or sales, and it shall not be the
duty of the purchaser to see to the application of the purchase
money.

AND the said Grantor does covenant and agree to keep all buildings and improvements that may at any time be upon said premises insured against fire, until all indebtedness of said Grantor arising hereunder is fully paid, for their full insurable value in such
insurance companies as the legal holder of said notes shall ap-
prove, and make the loss, if any, payable to, and assign and deliver all policies or renewal certificates therefor to said legal holder

as additional security for the aforesaid indebtedness; and in case of the failure of said Grantor to so insure, then said party of the second part or said legal holder is hereby empowered to have said buildings and improvements so insured for the benefit of said legal holder or owner of said notes, in which event the said Grantor hereby agrees to repay to said second party, or said legal holder, the amount expended for such insurance, with interest thereon at seven per cent, at the time of maturity of the then next ensuing coupon or interest note above described. Said Grantor hereby further covenants and agrees to repay to said second party or said legal holder at the time of maturity of the coupon or interest note then next ensuing, with interest thereon at seven per cent, all monies paid out for taxes or assessments upon said premises by said second party or said legal holder.

WHEN The said notes and all indebtedness arising hereunder shall be fully paid, including costs, taxes, insurance commissions and attorney's fees, the said Grantee or his successor or legal representatives shall reconvey all of said premises remaining unsold to the said Grantor or his heirs or assigns, upon receiving his reasonable charges therefor. In case of the death, resignation, removal from said Cook County, or other inability to act of said Grantee Harry Jones, then John C. Ellis of Chicago is hereby appointed and made successor in trust herein, with like power and authority as is hereby vested in said Grantee. It is agreed that said Grantor shall pay all costs and attorney's fees incurred or paid by said Grantee or the holder or holders of said notes in any suit in which either of them may be plaintiff or defendant, by reason of being a party to this Trust Deed, or a holder of said notes, and that the same shall be a lien on said premises, and may be included in any decree ordering the sale of said premises and taken out of the proceeds of any sale thereof.

WITNESS, The hand and seal of the said Grantor this second day of October, A. D. 1909.

JOHN DALE. [Seal]

APPENDIX I

Chattel Mortgage.

THIS INDENTURE, Made this fifth day of October, in the year of our Lord, One Thousand Nine Hundred and Nine, between William Stone, of the City of Chicago. in the County of Cook, and State of Illinois, party of the first part, and John C. Davis, of the City of Chicago, in the County of Cook, and State of Illinois, party of the second part:

WITNESSETH, That the said party of the first part, for and in consideration of the sum of One Thousand ($1,000.00) Dollars, in hand paid, the receipt whereof is hereby acknowledged, does hereby grant, sell, convey and confirm unto the said party of the second part, his heirs and assigns, all and singular the following described goods and chattels, to-wit: Two bay horses, weight about fifteen hundred pounds each; one gray horse, weight about one thousand pounds; one wagon; three sets of harness.

TOGETHER with all and singular the appurtenances thereunto belonging, or in any wise appertaining: To have and to hold the same unto the said John C. Davis, his heirs, executors, administrators and assigns, to his and their sole use forever. And the said William Stone, for himself and his heirs, executors and administrators, does covenant and agree with the said John C. Davis, his heirs, executors, administrators and assigns, that he is lawfully possessed of the said goods and chattels as of his own property; that the same are free from all incumbrances; that he will, and his heirs, executors and administrators shall warrant and defend the same unto the said party of the second part, his heirs, executors, administrators and assigns, against the lawful claims and demands of all persons, and that he will keep the said goods and chattels insured against loss by fire for the full insurable value thereof, in such companies as the holder of the note hereinafter mentioned may direct, and make the loss, if any, payable to, and deposit the policies with, the holder of said note, as further security for the indebtedness hereinafter mentioned.

PROVIDED, NEVERTHELESS, That if the said William Stone, his heirs, executors, administrators or assigns, shall well and truly pay,